The Puggrie Wallahs

The Puggrie Wallahs

The 14th (King's) Light Dragoons in India
During the Second Sikh War and in the
Indian Mutiny, 1841-59

Henry Blackburne Hamilton

LEONAUR

The Puggrie Wallahs
The 14th (King's) Light Dragoons in India During the Second Sikh War and in the Indian Mutiny, 1841-59
by Henry Blackburne Hamilton

FIRST EDITION

Leonaur is an imprint of Oakpast Ltd

Copyright in this form © 2013 Oakpast Ltd

ISBN: 978-1-78282-211-0 (hardcover)
ISBN: 978-1-78282-212-7 (softcover)

http://www.leonaur.com

Publisher's Notes

The Puggrie Wallahs

The 14th (King's) Light Dragoons in India
During the Second Sikh War and in the
Indian Mutiny, 1841-59

Henry Blackburne Hamilton

LEONAUR

The Puggrie Wallahs
The 14th (King's) Light Dragoons in India During the Second Sikh War and in the
Indian Mutiny, 1841-59
by Henry Blackburne Hamilton

FIRST EDITION

Leonaur is an imprint of Oakpast Ltd

Copyright in this form © 2013 Oakpast Ltd

ISBN: 978-1-78282-211-0 (hardcover)
ISBN: 978-1-78282-212-7 (softcover)

http://www.leonaur.com

Publisher's Notes

Contents

Historical Record of the 14th (King's) Light Dragoons in India 1841-1859

1841

In January a recruiting party was sent to Worcester. On 3rd January the Fourteenth were placed under orders for India to relieve the 4th Light Dragoons in Bombay, and the establishment was augmented to 9 troops, 55 sergeants, 12 trumpeters, 8 farriers, 40 corporals, 627 privates, and 701 troop-horses. The recruiters at Worcester and at headquarters were actively engaged enlisting men to complete the strength.

On the 30th March the Fourteenth proceeded to Canterbury, and arrived there on the 10th April preparatory to embarkation for India. Major-General J. W. Sleigh, C.B., Inspector-General of Cavalry, made a farewell inspection of the regiment at Canterbury on the 20th April, and afterwards wrote a very complimentary letter to Lieutenant-Colonel J. Townsend, commanding the regiment, of which the following is a copy:—

> My Dear Townsend,—It gives me much pleasure to be able to beg of you to express to the officers and men of the 14th (King's) Light Dragoons the gratification I have had in making my inspections of the regiment since I have held the appointment of Inspector-General of Cavalry. I am aware I can add nothing to establish the character of a corps which has ever borne so distinguished a place for gallantry in the field, and good conduct in quarters; yet it is a pleasing task for me to bear record on your departure for India that the same good conduct still exists which has heretofore gained you the high opinion

of all those officers under whom your regiment has served.—
Believe me, my dear Colonel, faithfully yours,   J. W. Sleigh.

After this inspection on the 20th April the Fourteenth Regiment
were dismounted, and the horses were drafted to several other cavalry
regiments during the four following days.

On the 30th April, Major William Havelock, K.H., eldest brother
of the renowned Major-General Sir Henry Havelock, K.C.B., was
appointed second Lieutenant-Colonel from the 4th Light Dragoons
on augmentation.

Captain C. Harvey was promoted Major on augmentation, and
Lieutenant C. W. Thompson[1] (afterwards General) joined the 14th
Light Dragoons from the 81st Regiment.

On the 15th May, Lieutenant-General Sir Edward Kerrison, Bart.,
G.C.B., G.C.H., full Colonel of the 14th Light Dragoons, inspect-
ed them at Canterbury, and afterwards issued a very gratifying and
most highly complimentary farewell order to Lieutenant-Colonel
Townsend, the officers, non-commissioned officers, and men. The
13th Light Dragoons being at this time quartered at Canterbury, the
Fourteenth renewed their old friendship with them, and as related by
Cannon in his *Record of the 13th Light Dragoons:*—

> The friendship of the Ragged Brigade, which had begun with
> and had continued throughout the eventful careers of the two
> regiments in the Peninsula, was cemented afresh, and on this
> occasion the Fourteenth presented to the Thirteenth their
> handsome mess-tables to perpetuate in the latter corps a kindly
> remembrance of their old companions in arms. *Sic, viret in æter-
> num.*

The Fourteenth marched from Canterbury to Herne Bay on the
24th May. The 1st division under Lieutenant-Colonel J. Townsend
embarked on the same day at Gravesend in the *Repulse* freight steamship of the East India Company, and arriving at Bombay on the 7th
September, disembarked there on the 8th in boats, and marched to
Kirkee, arriving on the 19th September.

The 2nd division under Major Barton embarked at Gravesend on
the 14th June in the East India steamship *Reliance*, landing at Bombay
on the 5th October, and marched to Kirkee, where it arrived on the
13th October, and the whole regiment was concentrated there under
command of Lieutenant-Colonel Townsend.

1. General C. W. Thompson was Colonel of the 14th (King's) Hussars, 1882-96.

8

On the 1st October, 150 volunteers from the 4th Light Dragoons were transferred to the Fourteenth.

It was about this period that moustaches were generally worn in the cavalry, and it is commonly said that H.R.H. Prince Albert (the late Prince Consort) introduced them into our service. [2] On the 12th November the regiment was inspected at Kirkee by His Excellency Lieutenant-General Sir Thomas McMahon, Bart., K.C.B., Commander-in-Chief in Bombay. On the 23rd November, Lieutenant-Colonel J. Townsend was appointed A.D.C. to Her Majesty the Queen, with the rank of Colonel in the army.

1842

The regiment was inspected at Kirkee by Major-General Sir Charles J. Napier, K.C.B., commanding the Poona Division of the Bombay Army, on the 7th January, and again on the 13th June by the same general officer. The commander-in-chief at Bombay (Sir Thomas McMahon, Bart.) also inspected the regiment at Kirkee on June 23rd, and gave the highest credit to all ranks. On the 18th August, His Excellency Lieutenant-General Sir T. McMahon, Bart., K.C.B., again inspected at Kirkee in the presence of the Honourable the Governor of Bombay (Sir George Arthur, Bart.), and they both made the most complimentary remarks as to the high state of efficiency in which they found the regiment.

A draft arrived from England on the 9th November, consisting of 1 sergeant and 99 men, under Cornet Brown, per steamship *Coromandel*.

Cornet William McMahon, son of Lieutenant-General Sir Thomas McMahon, Bart., K.C.B., joined the Fourteenth on the 25th November; and Captain F. H. Stephens became Major on the same date *vice* Barton, who retired. On 20th December, Major-General Macneil inspected at Kirkee, and reported that he found everything in the highest state of efficiency.

This year a hospital-sergeant was added to the establishment of the regiment, and one private was reduced. A hospital-sergeant had previously been appointed to the regiment in 1824.

1843

On the 3rd February, Major C. P. Ainslie joined the Fourteenth as Major *vice* Stephens, and Lieutenant R. P. Apthorp became Adjutant in

---

2. As far back as 1812 Hussars wore moustaches, and other cavalry (Dragoons and 'Heavies') shaved the upper lip.

succession to Captain William Clarke, promoted. On 5th June, Major-General Macneil made his half-yearly inspection at Kirkee, and expressed himself very much pleased with all he saw, and His Excellency Lieutenant-General Sir Thomas McMahon, Bart, again inspected on the 7th November. In October 2 squadrons left Kirkee and proceeded on field-service to Kolapore under Major Harvey. They took part in the southern Mahratta campaign during this and the following year, when the forts of Monshin and Munsomtosh were taken. The 2 squadrons on field-service numbered 15 officers, 289 non-commissioned officers and men, with 289 troop-horses.

1844

On 20th January, Major-General Macneil made his first half-yearly inspection, and his second on the 29th of June, both at Kirkee. His Excellency the Commander-in-Chief of the Bombay army (Lieutenant-General Sir Thomas McMahon, Bart.) also made an inspection on the 27th June.

1845

The Fourteenth were inspected by Major-General Macneil at Kirkee on 21st January in light marching-order, for outpost and picquet duty, and in review-order on the following day; and Lieutenant-Colonel Havelock was directed to convey to the regiment the major-general's entire approbation of the results of both days' work.

Colonel J. Townsend, *A.D.C.*, had gone home on leave in the spring, and he died at Castle Townsend, County Cork, Ireland, on 22nd April, after nearly forty years' service in the Fourteenth and sixteen years in command.

Lieutenant-Colonel William Havelock, K.H., succeeded to the command of the Fourteenth, and Lieutenant-Colonel E. Harvey became second Lieutenant-Colonel on 23rd April.

On 16th May, Captain W. H. Archer became Major.

The 2 squadrons from Kolapore rejoined headquarters on 19th March, having been present at the investment and capture of the fortresses of Panulla and Powrghur.

On 10th June, His Excellency Lieutenant-General Sir Thomas McMahon, Bart., K.C.B., Commander-in-Chief at Bombay, made an inspection of the regiment in 'watering-order,' and was very pleased.

On 20th June, Major-General Macneil made his half-yearly inspection, and the Honourable the Governor General of Bombay, together with His Excellency the Commander-in-Chief, made an inspection a few days later and expressed their entire satisfaction.

On 27th November, His Excellency General Sir Thomas Mc-Mahon, Bart., G.C.B., inspected the Fourteenth for the last time, in marching-order, previous to its departure from Kirkee, which station it left on 15th December to march to the upper provinces of Bengal.

After the inspection Sir Thomas McMahon made a most flattering report of the state of the Fourteenth, and he said he should convey the same to the Governor of Bombay, the Commander -in-Chief of the forces in India, and to the authorities in England. He said he considered the 14th (King's) Light Dragoons in as high a state of efficiency as any regiment in Her Majesty's service.

On 14th December the major-general commanding the division promulgated a very complimentary farewell order. He particularly remarked on what an excellent school he considered the 14th (King's) Light Dragoons must be to produce good officers, when such as Lieutenant-Colonel Talbot, Colonel Sir Felton Bathurst Hervey, Colonel T. W. Brotherton, and the late lamented and gallant Colonel Townsend had been brought up in it.

On 15th December the regiment left Kirkee, marching towards Agra.

1846

The Fourteenth had now to undergo a long monotonous march of nearly three months, during which time the cholera was raging in the Malwa Jungle. [3] Lieutenant F. D. Gray, 1 sergeant, 1 corporal, and 15 privates died in passing through the jungles between Ahmednuggur and Mhow. Lieutenant Herbert Gall had a most wonderful recovery. At some halting-place *en route* he was left behind for dead, to be interred, but it is said that some champagne brought him round. He was actually being placed in a coffin, when he uttered some ejaculation, and the hospital apothecary gave him champagne, having been told by the surgeon to let him have anything he asked for!

A very remarkable circumstance occurred during the four days' halt of the Fourteenth at Indore. Owing to some display of fireworks by the native prince, 250 of the troop-horses broke loose in a stampede, and were not recovered for some days, and then with the greatest difficulty. The terrified animals broke away from their picquet-ropes in a

---

3. Malleson relates that Lord Elphinstone (Governor of Madras, 1837-42), who was revisiting India in 1845-46, marched in company with the 14th Light Dragoons under Lieut.-Colonel Havelock, his former Military Secretary, from Bombay through Central India to the headquarters of the British Army before Lahore.

dark night, and scampered far and wide over the surrounding country. In about 5 days, however, all were brought back, excepting 6 or 7, and these were afterwards discovered at Kirkee, over 400 miles away.

On 22nd and 27th February the Fourteenth entered Agra; on 4th March they proceeded to Meerut, and reached that station on 16th March.

In April the march was continued towards Umballa, which was reached about the 17th. On 2nd May, at Umballa, Major-General Gilbert, Commanding Sirhind Division, made a minute inspection of the Fourteenth in marching-order, and expressed complete satisfaction at their turn-out and general state.

On 8th September, Major J. W. King, previously in the 5th (Princess Charlotte of Wales's) Dragoon Guards, joined the Fourteenth as Major *vice* Archer.

The Resident of Indore, Mr. R. N. C. Hamilton, wrote a very complimentary letter, dated Camp Cheetawond, 7th March 1846, in which he expressed his gratification at the excellent conduct of all ranks of the regiment when passing through that district.

On 1st December, Major-General Sir W. R. Gilbert, K.C.B., Commanding Sirhind Division, made his second half-yearly inspection, and was very much pleased.

1847

On 7th January, at Umballa, Lieutenant-General Lord Gough, Commander-in-Chief in India, inspected the Fourteenth, and on the 19th he visited the Cavalry Brigade, to which the 14th Light Dragoons belonged, and was pleased to express his entire approbation of their appearance in the lines and in barracks. On the 7th May, Major-General Sir W. Gilbert inspected the regiment in watering-order, which, he said, was a most satisfactory turn-out, and he inspected again on the 16th December in complete marching-order.

On 30th March, Lieutenant Arthur Need was appointed to the Fourteenth, and joined at Umballa, and on 23rd November Captain H. E. Doherty became Major.

1848

The Fourteenth left Umballa on the 15th February for Ferozepore, where they arrived on the 29th February, and remained there till about 13th August; but the left wing, consisting of the 3rd and 4th squadrons, had been previously detached to Anarkullee (Lahore) on the 8th May, and arrived there on the 12th May. Strength—10 officers, 213 men and 213 troop-horses.

The regiment was inspected at Ferozepore on 24th April by Major-General Sir Walter Raleigh Gilbert, K.C.B., who gave it great credit and was much pleased with its appearance.

On the 1st June the 3rd squadron, 4 officers, 91 men and horses, left Lahore under Major King on field-service, and proceeded across the River Ravee to operate against Bahre Maharajah and his adherents. The squadron returned to Lahore on the 7th June. Lieutenant-Colonel Patrick Grant, [4] Adjutant-General of the Army in India, by direction of the commander-in-chief, wrote a very complimentary letter from Simla as to the success achieved by this detachment in the expedition across the Ravee, in which he spoke very highly of the zealous exertions of both officers and men engaged.

The headquarters arrived in Lahore on the 19th August, having left Ferozepore on the 14th.

The second Sikh campaign, which ended in the fall of the Sikh power and the annexation of the Punjaub, shortly after this broke out, and during the time the regiment was on field-service with the army of the Punjaub (3rd November 1848 to 1st May 1849) a depot was formed at Anarkullee (Lahore) for the baggage, regimental stores, and the women and children of the regiment left behind.

The establishment of the Fourteenth at this period was 9 troops, 56 sergeants, 12 trumpeters, 8 farriers, 40 corporals, 627 privates, and 701 troop-horses. There were 2 lieutenant-colonels and 2 majors, *viz.* Lieutenant Colonels William Havelock, K.H., and J. W. King (who had succeeded Lieutenant Colonel Harvey recently), and Majors H. C. Doherty and Charles Steuart, the latter having been appointed to succeed Lieutenant-Colonel J.W. King, promoted to the second Lieutenant-Colonelcy.

The 14th Light Dragoons now took the field with Lord Gough's Army of the Punjaub. They numbered 442 sabres besides officers, and their first engagement with the enemy took place at Ramnuggur, on the banks of the Chenab, on the 22nd November 1848. Here the regiment, led by their gallant colonel, William Havelock, made those brilliant charges, against overwhelming numbers of the enemy, which have since become matters of history. The memory of that glorious day has ever since been held sacred by the Fourteenth, and as year by year comes round the anniversary is celebrated, especially in the sergeants' mess, where a ball or other entertainment takes place.

---

4. Afterwards Field-Marshal Sir Patrick Grant, G.C.B., G.C.M.G.

THEATRE OF THE
PUNJAUB CAMPAIGN
1848-1849.
Scale of English Miles.

British
Sibhs

GOOJERAT
WAZIRABAD
Kalra. Barra Kalra.
Feb. 21
Sultan.
Shadiwal
Kunjah
Tubca
Feb. 20

R. CHENAB
Ravaki.
Churwki.
Saddulapore
Dec. 3.

Lassoorie
Dinghi
Noor Jmal
Knoree
Chillianwallah
Jan. 13.
Lulliance
Moong
Beylah
Ramnuggur
Nov. 22
Nov. 22
Nov. 22

Shelum Road
R. JHELUM
R. CHENAB

Past and present officers with friends and guests are invited, and on these occasions it is the time-honoured custom to revive old memories and stirring scenes long past, by toasts and libations freely taken from the celebrated 'Ramnuggur Cup,' a handsome silver bowl presented to the sergeants' mess, many years ago, by the gallant 5th Light Cavalry who shared in the glories of that day, and charged along with the Fourteenth as brave and trusty comrades. The cup is emblematic of the occasion and has a suitable inscription engraved upon it, with a glorious list of the actions in which the regiment has been engaged with the enemy, in their campaigns in the Peninsula, Punjaub, Persia, and Central India, numbering no less than 28, as follows:

Douro.	Chillianwallah.	Betwa.
Talavera.	Goojerat.	Jhansi.
Fuentes d'Onor.	Persia.	Koonch.
Salamanca.	Dhar.	Golowlee.
Vittoria.	Mundesor.	Calpee.
Orthes.	Rathgur.	Morar.
Peninsula.	Barodia.	Gwalior.
Kolapore.	Muddenpore Pass.	Jowra-Alipore.
Punjaub.	Chanderi.	Ranode.
Ramnuggur.		

Ramnuggur was essentially a cavalry affair, and was brought about by a reconnaissance in force under the Commander-in-Chief in India, General Lord Gough, G.C.B., who intended merely to reconnoitre the enemy and explore the fords of the river in that locality. It was probably between the hours of 1 and 2 p.m. in the afternoon, or perhaps earlier, when Lieutenant-Colonel Havelock received his orders from a staff officer sent by General Lord Gough, who was not far off, to charge the Sikh cavalry that had crossed the river in large masses and were clearly visible to our front. Havelock was thirsting for glory, and to use his own expression, he felt the opportunity had come to 'win his golden spurs.' He led off with 2 squadrons of the Fourteenth in column of troops across the plain, and for half a mile at least these squadrons were exposed during their advance to an incessant fire from the Sikh guns posted on the banks of the river.

They then approached a steep bank leading down to the *nullah*, a partially dry channel of the river, beyond which lay the Sikh forces who had crossed the river from the right bank and were posted on a sort of island formed by the main channel of the river and a small stream. Here they undoubtedly had guns in position and infantry entrenched, hitherto unseen and quite unknown to us. As the Fourteenth came up to this steep bank, each squadron in turn paused, thus causing some temporary confusion in the ranks, but they soon plunged down, following their gallant colonel, forming squadrons and line on the move as best they could, and galloped rapidly across the *nullah*, charging the Sikhs, horse and foot.

They were now exposed to the close matchlock fire of the enemy, and as the ground near the island was of a boggy nature, ill suited to cavalry, water having recently subsided, many horses floundered about and frequently got into difficulties, but the men rode gallantly forward against the opposing Sikhs, sabring hundreds of them and driving the 'Gorchurras' (Sikh irregular cavalry) back helter-skelter into the river and numerous channels which ran up the creeks and banks on all sides.

It was now that Havelock perceived for the first time the large bodies of infantry concealed in these dry channels running along the bed of the river, and although his first attack had been eminently successful in driving back the Gorchurras as desired by Lord Gough, his characteristic dash and headlong pluck seem to have overswayed his prudence and better judgment, for without hesitation, brave leader that he was, he determined, notwithstanding the overwhelming odds against him and the adverse circumstances in which he was placed, to make another charge, and assail the heart of the Sikh position. Accordingly, he retired his men a little and re-formed the squadrons, which by this time had been reinforced by another squadron of the Fourteenth, as well as by a considerable body of the 5th Light Cavalry under Brevet Lieutenant-Colonel Alexander, and placing himself in front of the line, Havelock once more boldly advanced to meet the foe.

The squadrons were exposed to a murderous fire from the batteries on the right bank of the river, as well as from the guns posted on the island, yet nothing daunted they charged right into the centre of the Sikhs, driving them back towards the river, and sabring right and left in a desperate *mêlée* which ensued. They were also confronted with the fire of the matchlock men, both horse and foot, who slowly retired disputing every inch of the ground. Both regiments behaved splendidly, and it was not to be wondered at that both lost heavily, the total number of casualties in each regiment being about equal in proportion to the numbers of each engaged. The gallant but too daring chief of the Fourteenth fell in this attack, and not less than 74

men, including officers, with 96 horses, were placed *hors de combat*. Of these numbers the 14th Light Dragoons had 44 men (including 6 officers) and 56 horses either killed, wounded, or missing, whilst no less than 30 men (including 3 officers) and 40 horses belonging to the 5th Light Cavalry bit the dust.

The numbers of the Fourteenth engaged were about 350 sabres. It was a short but very sanguinary business. Colonel Havelock's body was found and fully identified, though headless, about twelve days after the engagement. It was lying with the bodies of 9 troopers of the Fourteenth heaped on it, showing that his men had rallied round and fought for their chief. His left arm and leg were nearly severed, as well as the thumb of his right hand.

Captain Fitzgerald of the Fourteenth was mortally wounded in the *mêlée* and died subsequently: one of his sword-cuts penetrated the brain and another the spine. Major Doherty brought the charging squadrons out of action, and Lieutenant-Colonel King, who had been ordered to command the support when the Fourteenth advanced, came up just at the right moment with a squadron which formed a welcome nucleus for the other squadrons to form on. Alas! the brave Havelock was not amongst them. He was last heard of wounded and hacked at by several Sikhs in the *mêlée*.

As Ramnuggur was considered merely an affair of outposts and a purely cavalry fight, no honorary distinction was conferred for it, but none the less most will concede that these charges of the 14th Light Dragoons and 5th Light Cavalry deserve a high place amongst cavalry charges delivered under unfavourable circumstances. The Sikhs were immensely superior in cavalry, besides being assembled in great force with infantry and artillery posted and partially entrenched beyond a *nullah*, having the further advantage of a sandy river-bed and boggy ground between them and the attacking squadrons. Hence it is that the memory of Ramnuggur has always been held very dear by all in the Fourteenth, and both Havelock and his brave companions-in-arms have ever been reckoned heroes by succeeding generations of those serving in the regiment.

The casualties of the regiment in this affair were as follows:

Killed:—1 officer (Lieutenant-Colonel William Havelock, K.H.).[5]
      1 sergeant (John Harwood).
      1 corporal.

---

5. Lieutenant-Colonel Havelock was officially reported 'Missing.'

12 privates.

37 horses.

Wounded:—5 officers—Captain J. F. Fitzgerald, [6] very severely.

Captain R. H. Gall, severely.

Captain A. Scudamore, slightly.

Lieutenant William McMahon, severely.

Cornet the Hon. R. W. Chetwynd,

slightly.

4 sergeants.

18 privates.

15 horses.

Missing:—2 rank and file.

4 horses.

The 5th Light Cavalry had:

1 non-commissioned officer and 12 privates killed.

2 officers and 15 privates wounded.

40 horses killed and wounded.

Brevet Lieutenant-Colonel Alexander lost his arm by a round-shot which killed the quartermaster-sergeant and wounded Lieutenant Reilly in the foot. The 3rd Light Dragoons and 8th Light Cavalry, who had made some charges against the Sikh Gorchurras at an earlier part of the day, but had not crossed the *nullah*, suffered very slight casualties. The 3rd Light Dragoons had 5 privates wounded and 3 or 4 horses struck by round-shot; the 8th Light Cavalry lost a *subadar-major* killed; and the 12th Irregular Cavalry had Captain Holmes wounded. The troop of Horse Artillery, under Lieutenant-Colonel Lane, which lost a gun and a couple of wagons about the time of the advance of the 3rd Light Dragoons and 8th Light Cavalry, only had 1 private wounded and 4 horses killed. Amongst the staff, Brigadier-General C. R. Cureton, C.B., commanding the Cavalry Division, who was a very distinguished cavalry leader with brilliant war services, was shot in the chest and killed, and Lieutenant Hardinge, *aide-de-camp*, was wounded.

It will be seen by the above list of casualties that the losses of the Fourteenth were much heavier than those of any other regiment engaged, and there is no doubt that they and the 5th Light Cavalry had the brunt of the affair all to themselves. It is true the 3rd Light Dragoons and 8th Light Cavalry charged across the plain several hours before the charges of the Fourteenth took place, and the Sikh Irregu-

---

6. Captain Fitzgerald died of his wounds a few days afterwards.

lar Cavalry (Gorchurras) retreated before them, but neither regiment penetrated into the position of the Sikh forces posted beyond the *nullah*, as it is believed Brigadier White did not consider the ground suitable for cavalry, and was induced to retire his brigade from the ground subsequently crossed by Havelock, in the exercise, as was afterwards proved, of a very wise and soldierly judgment. This would naturally account for their lighter list of casualties.

The lamented loss of Brigadier Charles Robert Cureton, C.B., *A.D.C.*, which occurred about the time of Colonel Havelock's second attack, deserves more than a passing notice, not only on account of his great reputation as a brilliant cavalry officer, already distinguished in former campaigns, but also because of his old connection with the 14th Light Dragoons in which he enlisted when a youth under the name of 'Charles Roberts,' serving with them in the Peninsula. The probably true and authentic account of Cureton's death is as follows:— He was riding at the time along with the commander-in-chief (Lord Gough) and the rest of his staff, among whom were Lieut.-Colonel J. B. Gough,[7] officiating quartermaster-general, (in India) and Major F. P. Haines,[8] Military Secretary. Following closely was the chief's personal escort, a troop of the 5th Light Cavalry. Cureton, perceiving that Havelock was forming up his squadrons with the evident intention of making another charge, and not approving of this under the circumstances, rode off hurriedly to stop him, but was almost immediately shot dead by a bullet which struck him in the chest.

This version of Cureton's death is strongly corroborated by an original letter in the handwriting of the late General Sir J. B. Gough, G.C.B. (then Lieutenant-Colonel J. B. Gough), who says in the letter, dated 23rd November 1848, 'Poor Cureton was shot dead within five yards of me and close to Lord Gough.' This is certainly at variance somewhat with the statement in Brigadier-General C. Campbell's despatch quoted in Appendix A, but it agrees with the well-known water-colour picture by Henry Martens of the 'Charge of the 14th Light Dragoons at Ramnuggur,' and the engravings of that picture by Harris, published by Rudolph Ackermann of 191 Regent Street, in 1851,[9] where Cureton is depicted as shot in the throat and chest as he was galloping over the

7. Afterwards General Sir John B. Gough, G.C.B.

8. Now Field-Marshal Sir Frederick P. Haines, G.C.B., G.C.S.I., C.I.E.

9. At the foot of these coloured engravings a quotation from the *Illustrated London News* of 27th January 1849 is usually printed, giving some account of the supposed third charge of the Fourteenth at Ramnuggur, which is clearly proved never took place. See page 21.

plain towards the charging squadrons, apparently in the endeavour to deliver some message or order. We can only conclude therefore that the allusion in Brigadier Campbell's despatch was written under some slight misapprehension or confusion of details.

General Brotherton gives the following account of Brigadier Cureton as he knew him in the Peninsula, amongst his interesting episodes. The general writes as follows:—

I went out to the Peninsula in command of a troop, and that troop produced besides numerous brave and good soldiers an extraordinary man, notorious throughout the service for bravery and intelligence. He afterwards became Brigadier-General Cureton, so highly extolled in Major-General Sir Harry Smith's despatch on the Battle of Aliwal. He served all through the Peninsular War in the 14th Light Dragoons, and there learned the rudiments of outpost duty, for his consummate knowledge of which he is so highly praised by Sir Harry Smith.[10] Baron Osten perfectly recollects a dialogue that passed between Corporal Cureton and me, in Portugal, he under the name of "Roberts," in which he had enlisted.

Cureton, the son of most respectable parents, trades-people in Lancashire, became first a corporal in my troop, and then a sergeant. He distinguished himself daily in the field, but being, moreover, a well-educated young man, and a particularly good penman, Lord Fitzroy Somerset asked for him to go to headquarters, to write in his office. I reluctantly parted with him, and even tried to dissuade him from going, representing to him that as we were then daily engaged with the enemy, he would have such frequent opportunities of distinguishing himself as would infallibly lead to promotion, and bring him conspicuously into notice.

His better star, however, prevailed, and he did go to headquarters, where he was not only employed in writing, but acted as mounted orderly to Lord Fitzroy Somerset in all the sub-

---

10. 'The manner in which this famous officer handles his cavalry, under the hottest and most galling fire, ranks him amongst the first cavalry officers of his age.'—(Sir Harry Smith's despatches. Battles of Aliwal and Sobraon, 28th January and 10th February 1846.) *The Hero of Aliwal* (The campaigns of Sir Harry Smith in India, 1843-1846, during the Gwalior War & the First Sikh War with a short history of the Gwalior War & First Sikh War by Hugh Murray) by James Humphries is also published by Leonaur.

sequent battles. His merit being very conspicuous, he soon got a commission, ultimately became Adjutant-General in the East Indies, witnessing all the late operations in that part of the world, was in the unfortunate Cabul expedition, shared, most conspicuously, in many glorious fights against the Sikhs, and fell at last on the battlefield of Ramnuggur, when in the act of distinguishing himself. It was by a most extraordinary chance he fell gloriously with his old corps, the 14th Light Dragoons, which he had left many years before.

His modesty was equal to his bravery, for though he had become a most distinguished person, and had been mainly instrumental by his daring and judicious management of the cavalry in gaining the critical and glorious Battle of Aliwal under Sir Harry Smith, yet his modesty, and I may say humility, were remarkable.

On his return once to England, Lord Fitzroy Somerset invited him to meet me at dinner at his house, and though he had perfectly the manners of a gentleman, though risen from the ranks, he never presumed, and showed me the same deference and respect as when he was a corporal in my troop. When the clasps for the battles in the Peninsula were issued, instead of sending in his application for his share of them (which was *every battle* that had been fought, as he had been present at all of them) through the regular channel, and direct to Horse Guards, by way of paying me a compliment he sent it through me, saying that "I knew his services better than anyone."

The affair of Ramnuggur is very graphically described in the *Illustrated London News* of 27th January 1849, where two letters from correspondents are published, one from 'Eyewitness,' dated 25th November 1848, and one from 'An Officer of Bengal Horse Artillery,' dated 1st December 1848. In Appendix A, extracts from these are published, as they appear reliable and are in accordance with the recollections of officers now living who were present and took part in the events of the day. They also coincide in most respects with the narrative of Ramnuggur given in *The Sikhs and the Sikh Wars*, by General Sir Charles Gough, V.C., G.C.B., and A. D. Innes, M.A. (published in 1897), with one obvious discrepancy, and this demands some mention here.

In 'Eyewitness's' letter in the *Illustrated London News* there is a detailed account given of a supposed third attack and charge made by the 14th Light Dragoons and led by Lieutenant-Colonel King after Havelock fell. There appears to be no corroboration whatever of this charge, and absolutely no other authority for it. The incident has therefore been altogether omitted in the extracts published in the Appendix. If such a charge had taken place, surely some of the survivors with whom the author has had the advantage of both personal conversation and correspondence would know of it. Again, the 'Regimental Digest of Services' kept in the orderly-room of the regiment states distinctly 'the regiment made two charges;' and in *The Sikhs and the Sikh Wars* there is no allusion to such an event, for it is, after mentioning Cureton's death:—

> Before any fresh order could be despatched, Havelock had made the second fatal charge, and the horses began to flounder in the sandy river-bed. The Sikhs swarmed down on them; and though the brigade succeeded in cutting its way back, Havelock was slain.'

Now, Sir Charles Gough, one of the authors of this work, was one of the officers who on that day charged with the 8th Light Cavalry at Ramnuggur, and was also an eyewitness of the charge of the Fourteenth. The official account given in the Regimental Records above alluded to is as follows:—

> *22nd November* 1848. Ramnuggur.—The regiment made two successive charges, in the latter against an overwhelming force of cavalry and infantry, and exposed to the fire of three batteries.

Surely the above is sufficient to prove that there never was a third charge as described in the letter in the *Illustrated London News*, which was probably written hastily and without full and reliable information of the actual facts, so misleading on a field of battle to observers from different points of view,—indeed an *advance* of cavalry at a rapid pace might easily be mistaken for a *charge* by anyone witnessing it from a distance.[11]

In the *Illustrated London News* account there is one other point, but

---

11. Even Captain Apthorp in his remarks (published in Appendix A, etc.) speaks of three charges, but he explains that he calls the advance of Havelock before his first change of front a charge. As Captain Apthorp was Adjutant of the 14th Light Dragoons at the time, he would be the person to make the entry in the 'Digest of Services,' under the orders of the commanding officer of the regiment, and the entry is, 'The regiment made *two* successive charges.'

of less importance, which appears at variance with facts. It is the statement in the 'Bengal Horse Artillery Officer's' letter, which seems to connect closely the loss of the gun and wagons of Lieutenant-Colonel Lane's troop of Horse Artillery with the charges of the 14th Light Dragoons. The real version of this incident appears to be that the gun stuck in the sand, and had to be abandoned at an earlier part of the day than that at which the Fourteenth made their two charges, in the second of which they were supported by the 5th Light Cavalry. The *contretemps* of the gun sticking in the sand probably happened at the time the charge under Brigadier-General Michael White of the 3rd Light Dragoons took place, and when the latter regiment with the 8th Light Cavalry advanced across the plain, driving back the Sikh cavalry to the bank of the *nullah*, but thence retired in good order, not deeming a further advance advisable.

On 23rd November, Lieutenant-Colonel J. W. King succeeded to the command of the Fourteenth; on the 28th November, Major H. E. Doherty became second Lieutenant-Colonel, and Captain William Clarke, who had risen from the ranks, became Major. Subsequently Lieutenant-Colonels King and Doherty were each awarded a Companionship of the Order of the Bath.

After the affair of Ramnuggur the whole army remained there watching the enemy till the 30th November, when a body of troops was despatched at midnight, under Major-General Sir Joseph Thackwell (a Waterloo veteran), to Wazirabad ford, 22 miles up the river, and effected a passage of the Chenab at that point. There were two safe fords nearer than Wazirabad, namely Ghurriki, 7 miles from Ramnuggur, but 4000 Sikhs held this; another higher up at Runniki was also guarded. There was yet another, higher up still, at Ali-Shor-Ke-Chuk, but it was dangerous, the stream being too rapid. The division that was sent under Sir Joseph Thackwell consisted of White's Cavalry Brigade, 3rd Light Dragoons, 5th and 8th Light Cavalry, and 2 Irregular Native Cavalry Regiments, in place of the Fourteenth, with Colin Campbell's Infantry Brigade, consisting of Her Majesty's 24th and 61st Foot, and 5 Regiments of Native Infantry; also 30 field-guns and 2 heavy guns.

The whole force crossed over from the left bank safely on the 1st and 2nd December, and commenced to march down the right bank in the direction of Ramnuggur, with a view to driving out the Sikhs from their position opposite our camp, for our evacuation of Ramnuggur was out of the question whilst they remained there, as such

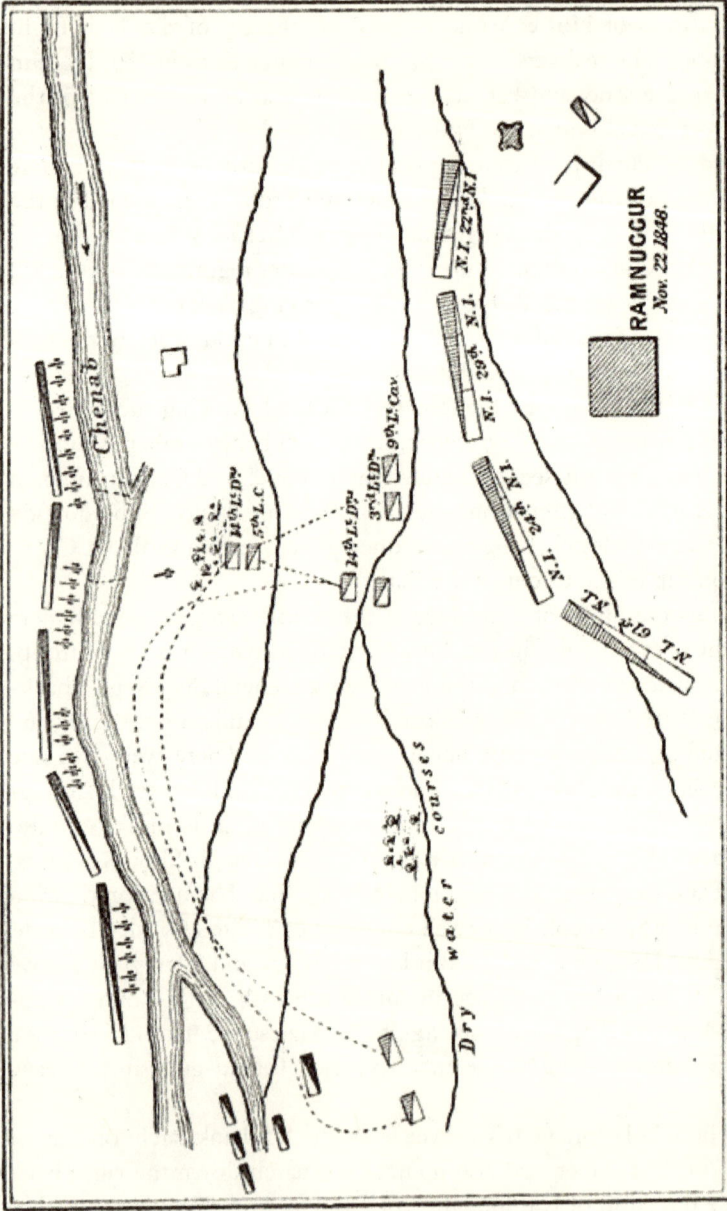

Troops of Horse Artillery accompanied the cavalry. The remainder of the artillery was massed in front of the Second Brigade from the right. The position of the abandoned guns is marked in front of the grove.

N.B. —For "22nd" read "2nd Europeans."

a step would leave the way to Lahore unguarded. By the evening of the 2nd December, Major-General Sir Joseph Thackwell had reached within 9 miles of the Sikh position on the right bank, and having driven off the outposts from the fords at Ghurriki and elsewhere, had established communication with Lord Gough at Ramnuggur. On the 3rd December, Thackwell moved to Sadulapore, sending a sufficient force to guard the Ghurriki ford, whence reinforcements were expected under Brigadier Godby.

Shere Singh, at this juncture, late in the afternoon of the 3rd December, came forward with his troops, occupying a strong position, covered by sugar-cane fields lying in front of him, and the British accordingly fell back somewhat to gain better ground, but the Sikhs did not come on. A cannonade on both sides was maintained till evening, and when darkness set in Shere Singh retired from his entrenchments, carrying with him his artillery, setting fire to his magazine, and withdrawing his whole army northwards.

He afterwards took up a strong position covered by jungle near the banks of the Jhelum. The losses incurred at Sadulapore by our force were slight, being about 80 men killed and wounded. The Sikhs suffered heavily: it is believed their losses were ten times as great as ours, owing to the greater precision of our artillery fire. On hearing of the retreat of the Sikh army, Lord Gough at once pushed forward across the Chenab as a pursuing force the 9th Lancers and 14th Light Dragoons, and these troops joined Sir Joseph Thackwell's main body. The Sikhs, it appears, retreated in the greatest disorder, leaving in the villages numerous wounded men. They subsequently divided into three divisions, which became more a rout than a retreat.

The 14th Light Dragoons arrived at Camp Heylah on 4th December, and were at once sent by orders of Major-General Sir Joseph Thackwell along the road to Dinghi. The 9th Lancers took another route, to try and come up with the fugitive Sikhs, but they were reported to have gone over the Jhelum, so the cavalry returned to Heylah without having effected anything decisive.

1849

The beginning of the new year found the regiment in camp at Heylah, the depot troop being at Maidstone with a strength of 103 men.

On 12th January, Lord Gough's army advanced on Chillianwallah, and next day was fought that sanguinary battle in which, after several hours' desperate fighting, the British forces held their ground, having gained a somewhat indecisive victory, and bivouacked on the battlefield. Our losses were 2357 men and 176 horses, of whom 1000 were Europeans, including 89 officers. The killed alone were about 700 of all ranks. On the other hand the Sikhs, whose men and guns considerably outnumbered ours, lost heavily in killed and wounded— 1000 killed, 2000 wounded. Of the latter many died subsequently. The enemy was not absolutely driven off the field, but remained in an entrenched position about 2 miles from the British camp, having his centre at Russool village and his right flank resting on the Jhelum.

Lord Gough's army at the Battle of Chillianwallah was composed as follows:—

Cavalry Division.—Major-General Sir Joseph Thackwell, K.C.B., commanding.

    1st Brigade. Brigadier M. White:
        3rd Light Dragoons,
        5th and 8th Light Cavalry.
    2nd Brigade. Brigadier Pope:
        9th Lancers,
        14th Light Dragoons,
        1st and 6th Regiments Light Cavalry.

The European cavalry regiments numbered about 400 men each, the Native cavalry 300, effective in the field.

Infantry (2nd Division) [12] under Major-General Sir Walter Gilbert, K.C.B.

    1st Brigade. Brigadier Mountain:
        Her Majesty's 29th Regiment,
        The 30th and 56th Regiments Native Infantry.
    2nd Brigade. Brigadier Godby:
        2nd European Regiment,
        The 31st and 70th Regiments Native Infantry.

3rd Division.—Brigadier General Colin Campbell, commanding.

    1st Brigade. Brigadier Pennycuick:
        Her Majesty's 24th Regiment,
        The 25th and 45th Regiments Native Infantry.
    2nd Brigade. Brigadier Hoggan:
        Her Majesty's 61st Regiment,
        The 36th and 46th Regiments Native Infantry.

12. The 1st Division of the army of the Punjaub was employed in the siege of Mooltan.

BATTLE OF
CHILLIANWALLA
Jan. 13th 1849.

Sikh Infantry — 1 Christie
  „ Cavalry — 2 Dawes
  „ Guns — 3 Heavy Guns
British „ — 4 Mowatt
  „ — 5 Robertson
  „ Cavalry — 6 H.A.
  „ Infantry — 7 H.A.
  —— Direction of Advance

Jungle

Line of Advance from Dingki

● MOULEANWALLA

CHILLIANWALLA

RUSSOOL ■

Jungle

Pennycuick

Campbell

Hoggan

Gilbert

Mountain

Godby

Lane
Pope

POSITION

TIBBA

SIKH ENTRENCHED

● LULLIANEE
● KOT BALAOO

● MOORO
● FUTTEH SHAH KNOREE
● SHADEEANWALLA
● LUCKNAWALLA

White

3rd Brigade.—Brigadier Penny:
> The 15th, 20th, and 69th Regiments N. Infantry.
Artillery Division, under Brigadier Tennant:
> Six troops of Horse Artillery under Brigadier Brooke, with Colonels Brind and C. Grant; the troops respectively under Lieutenant-Colonel Lane, Majors Christie, Huish, Warner, Duncan, and Fordyce.
> Two batteries of four 18-pounders and two 8-inch howitzers each, under Majors R. Shakespeare and Ludlow; Major Horsford commanding.
> Three field batteries: No. 5, commanded by Lieutenant Walker in the absence of Captain Kinleside, sick; No. 10, commanded by Lieutenant Robertson, in the absence of Captain Austin, wounded; and No. 17, commanded by Major Dawes.
The Foot Artillery, under Brigadier Huthwaite.

The European Infantry numbered about 900 each, and the Native Infantry about 700. Her Majesty's 24th, an exceptionally strong regiment, turned out 1000 men in the field. The Sikhs were lying with the Jhelum behind them, on the west, occupying a group of villages protected by jungle, with their left reaching to Russool, where there was a belt of hills. Chillianwallah, in advance of the line, was held only by their outposts. Lord Gough's intention was to march from Dinghi to Chillianwallah, drive in the outposts, and defer the attack till next day, when he had gained more accurate information of the position of the enemy.

At 7 a.m. on 13th January he advanced from Dinghi with his army formed in line of contiguous columns. By 12 o'clock he drove in the enemy's outposts. The Sikh position, which was entrenched, stretched from Russool on their left to Moong on their right, and Lord Gough decided to encamp, reconnoitre the position, and give battle on the following day. Whilst preparations for laying out the camp were in progress the Sikhs opened fire with their guns, and advanced beyond their entrenchments, whereupon the British general gave orders to prepare for immediate action. For the first hour the battle was an artillery duel, in which the enemy had the advantage both of position and of guns. At about half-past three in the afternoon our advance commenced.

The cavalry were on our flanks—White's on the left, Pope's on the right. Hoggan's brigade was on the left of the line, with Pennycuick's next, both under Colin Campbell; then came Mountain's, and then Godby's, both under Gilbert, with Penny's brigade (the 3rd of Campbell's division) in reserve. The artillery were ranged—in the centre the heavy batteries; attached to Campbell's division—3 troops Horse Artillery (Brind), and Walker's and Robertson's field-batteries, both under Major Mowatt; attached to Gilbert's division 3 troops Horse Artillery (Grant) and Dawes's field-battery.

On the enemy's side, the Sikh line extended for about 6 miles, covered by thick jungle, and with their right considerably overlapping the British left.

At the commencement of the general advance, Campbell, seeing the intricate nature of the ground to his front, covered as it was by thick jungle, directed his brigadier Pennycuick to act independently with his brigade, and he himself accompanied Hoggan with the other (left) brigade of his division. Robertson's field-battery, which should have acted with Hoggan's brigade, was sent off early in the action, by orders of a staff-officer, to the left of our line, to help the Horse Artillery who were trying ineffectually to silence the Sikh guns on their left front; at the same time Pennycuick's brigade advanced at such a rapid pace that it got in front of Mowatt's field-battery, which should have accompanied it, and consequently the latter could not give the required assistance to that brigade, but was enabled to render most important services to the other brigade (Hoggan's), which had lost its own field-battery (Robertson's) as above stated. This field-battery had silenced the Sikh guns which were engaged with Brind's Horse Artillery, and then tried to rejoin Campbell's division.

Pennycuick's brigade in their rapid advance soon got into very difficult ground, and came under a terrible fire, first of roundshot and then of grape, to which the centre regiment, Her Majesty's 24th, were principally exposed, and the enemy keeping behind trees and thick bushes was completely screened from view, so that the losses of that gallant regiment were most severe. Still, nothing daunted, the brigade pushed on, and at length came in view of the Sikh guns. There still remained some swampy and very difficult ground to be traversed before they made the final charge right up to the cannons' mouth.

Brigadier Pennycuick and many officers and men fell in this last attack, and although the 2 Native Infantry Regiments were advancing with the 24th Regiment, the brigade lost so heavily that it had to retire to a position clear of the jungle. The 24th Regiment had lost their

Colonel (Brookes) close to the guns, 13 of their officers were killed and 10 were wounded, while no less than 231 men were killed and 266 wounded. The Native Regiments also suffered heavy losses.

Meanwhile Mowatt's field-battery had covered the advance of Hoggan's brigade, led by Campbell, who had advanced with great care and regularity through the difficult ground he had to traverse. Her Majesty's 61st had scattered the Sikh cavalry on their front; the 36th Native Infantry were attacked on their flank by a large body of Sikhs, but rescued by 2 companies of the 61st Regiment, who captured 2 of the enemy's guns. The 46th Native Infantry were opposed on the left by a large body of Sikh cavalry, but repulsed them under their leader, Major Tudor. Later the Sikhs brought up fresh cavalry and 2 more guns against the right of Hoggan's brigade at the time it had first been driven back, but the brigade rapidly changed front and drove the enemy opposed to them off the ground. They captured in all 13 guns, after some very severe hand-to-hand fighting, in which the brigadier himself received a severe sword-cut on his right arm.

On our extreme left, White's cavalry brigade had advanced at same time as Campbell's division. The ground was wholly unsuitable to the action of cavalry, and they were exposed to a heavy fire of round-shot during their advance, and consequently no great success resulted. After remaining in support of the Horse Artillery for some time, Major-General Sir Joseph Thackwell had ordered an attack. It was at the time that the Sikh battery, as already related, had been silenced. The Grey Squadron of the 3rd Light Dragoons with the 5th Light Cavalry advanced, led by Captains Unett and Wheatley. The 5th Light Cavalry came upon a large body of Sikhs, and being exposed to heavy musketry fire, were repulsed, and had to retire; but the 3rd Light Dragoons, Unett's squadron, swept on gallantly right through to the enemy's rear, and after a splendid charge, had to cut their way back, suffering severe loss—23 men killed, 2 officers and 15 men wounded, 15 horses killed and missing, 7 horses wounded.

After this affair, Sir Joseph Thackwell detached a troop of Horse Artillery (Warner's) and a squadron of the 8th Light Cavalry to support Hoggan's brigade, and he himself with the remainder of his cavalry gave what support he could to Campbell's division, moving on its left for the rest of the day. Now to turn to the right and right-centre of the British line: we find that Sir Walter Gilbert was preparing to advance shortly after Campbell's Division had done so. On the extreme right was Pope's cavalry brigade with 3 troops of Horse Artillery under Colonel C. Grant; then Godby's (infantry) brigade, then Mountain's, with Dawes's battery between them. Brigadier Pope observing a considerable body of Sikh cavalry on the heights about Russool, detached a wing from each of the 1st and 6th Light Cavalry, a wing from the 9th Lancers, and 8 Horse Artillery guns, retaining the other wing of each regiment, and the whole of the 14th Light Dragoons with the rest of the guns; he sent the detached troops to his right flank under the command of Lieutenant-Colonel Lane, with orders to protect that flank and to act as occasion demanded. [13] The brigadier then advanced with his 9 squadrons and 10 guns on the right of Gilbert's Division in one line, without any supports or reserves, thus:

| 6 guns under Major Huish. | 4 guns under Major Christie. | 14th Light Dragoons, 4 Squadrons, under Lieut. Colonel King. | 6th Lt. Cavalry, 1½ Squadrons. | 1st Lt. Cavalry, 1½ Squadrons. | 9th Lancers, 2 Squadrons, under Major Hope Grant. |

ADVANCE OF POPE'S CAVALRY BRIGADE.

Very soon a body of Sikh horse was observed in front, and the guns were pushed forward, but, whilst they were getting into action, Pope came on with the cavalry, passed in front of them, and so masked their fire. The ground was particularly unsuited to the advance of a long line of cavalry, owing to its jungly nature and from being so full of obstructions, which made it very difficult for the squadrons to keep in touch and act in concert There was no real charge made by the cavalry, but they were advancing as best they could and as the difficult nature of the ground permitted, when all of a sudden there was a distinct order given to retire by the command 'Threes about,' which was heard proceeding from the centre of the line where the Native cavalry was posted.

The centre of the brigade went about, the command was quickly taken up by the whole line, and a retrograde movement took place which was carried out at an increased pace for a considerable distance before the line was halted and re-formed. This withdrawal of the cavalry left the Horse Artillery guns (commanded by Majors Christie and Huish) wholly unprotected, and they retired with the cavalry, but the Sikh horsemen coming up cut down several of the gunners,

13. This body of Cavalry and Horse Artillery under Lieutenant-Colonel Lane acted quite independently of the remainder of Pope's brigade, and no connection was kept up with the latter during the battle.

and captured 4 guns, 2 wagons, and 53 horses, besides rendering the 6 other guns useless for the day. The whole occurrence is shrouded in mystery: it may have been partly caused by a sudden panic to which the best of troops are at times liable, but it seems far more likely that the manner in which the brigade was handled was the real cause and origin of what happened.

The Horse Artillery suffered the greatest loss: Major Christie was badly wounded and died soon afterwards, 7 of his men were killed, and 2 were wounded; in Huish's troop 5 were killed and 5 wounded; in the cavalry brigade, Brigadier Pope was badly wounded and had to be conducted off the field; and the cavalry regiments lost 2 officers, 2 native officers and 11 men killed, 2 officers and 30 men wounded. Owing to the brigade having advanced without any supports or reserves whatever, there was no point for the retiring squadrons to rally on, which added considerably to the confusion, and rendered the matter far more serious than it otherwise would have been.[14] This incident occurred just as Sir W. Gilbert was leading his division to the attack, Dawes and his field-battery being in line with the skirmishers in the front; and Gilbert, when he perceived his right flank suddenly uncovered by the absence of the cavalry, had to refuse his right (Godby's) brigade in order, to some extent, to protect it.

The troops of this division behaved most steadily, and Mountain's Brigade (on the left) continued their advance covered by the fire of No. 17 Field Battery, charging and taking a Sikh battery in front of the village of Lullianee. Godby's brigade had also charged and carried some guns to its front, when their rear was suddenly attacked: this was caused by the unguarded flank left after the withdrawal of Pope's cavalry, hence Godby had to face his men to their rear, being literally surrounded by the enemy. At this juncture Dawes's battery came up and poured in a heavy fire on the Sikh horsemen who were about to charge, which drove them back. The 2nd Bengal Europeans[15] under Major Steele then charged a body of the enemy who were still threatening the rear, and after a sharp struggle successfully repulsed them. The same occurred in Mountain's brigade, which was also compelled to face about and drive off the enemy from its rear; and soon afterwards Colin Campbell with Hoggan's brigade and White's cavalry, as well as the whole of the artillery of the left, moved up and joined in the fight on the right.

---

14. See Appendix A.
15. Now the 2nd Battalion Royal Munster Fusiliers.

Penny's brigade, which had been ordered up from the reserve when the disaster happened to Pennycuick's brigade, lost its way in the jungle, and afterwards came up on the right of Godby's brigade about the time when it was attacked in rear by the enemy. This brigade was threatened on its right flank and in front by large bodies of Sikhs, but was rescued by the fire of Dawes's field-battery, which happened to be there at the right moment, and promptly drove the enemy off. The whole of the British artillery now opened fire on the masses of the Sikhs who were retreating in disorder upon Tupai, and Lieutenant-Colonel Lane, who had not taken any active part in the battle since he was detached, as already related, to the right flank, by Brigadier Pope's order, with his Horse Artillery and 5 squadrons of cavalry, [16] now appeared, and poured in a heavy fire where he observed the enemy in retreat, thus rendering valuable aid at the close of the battle. [17]

The losses of the Fourteenth at Chillianwallah were as follows:—

Killed:—1 Officer (Lieutenant A. J. Cureton).
    1 Man.
    2 Horses.
Wounded:—1 Officer (Major C. Steuart).
    14 Men.
    2 Horses.
Missing:—2 Men.
    4 Horses.

During the whole of the two days following the battle, being the 14th and 15th January, rain fell incessantly, and during this time the melancholy task of burying the dead was carried out by the troops. Afterwards the two armies lay at Russool and Chillianwallah watching one another, Lord Gough being determined to wait for the fall of Mooltan, so as to get the reinforcements from the south, especially as the enemy had already received large accessions of force under Chutter Singh. The Sikhs began to evacuate Russool on 11th February and fell back on the Jhelum. They subsequently turned and made an endeavour to cross the Chenab near Wazirabad, but Major-General Whish's column coming from Mooltan forestalled them there, and they had to take up a position on the plain between the two rivers

---

16. Two squadrons 9th Lancers and three squadrons from the 1st and 6th Regiments of Light Cavalry (one and a half squadrons from each). Lane also had his own 6 guns, and 2 guns detached from Christie's troop of Horse Artillery.
17. This account of the Battle of Chillianwallah is mostly taken from Gough's and Innes's *Sikhs and Sikh Wars*, some of it almost *verbatim*.

near Goojerat.

By the 14th the whole of the Sikhs had left their encampments at Russool. Accordingly on the 15th Lord Gough moved to Lassoorie, whence, pushing forward a column to guard the ford at Wazirabad, he moved on 16th to Pukee Nuggar and Sadulapore. By the 20th, Major-General Whish's troops from Mooltan (which city fell on 25th January) having come up, the army, now complete, was concentrated under Lord Gough at Shadiwal and Kunjah, the Sikhs being at Goojerat a little to the north of that position.

Our forces numbered 25,000 men with 96 guns. The combined Sikh armies under Chutter Singh and Shere Singh are believed to have numbered from 50,000 to 60,000 men, and they had 60 guns. Of the latter we subsequently captured or destroyed 53 guns at Goojerat.

The Battle of Goojerat was fought on the 21st February 1849, and the arrival of the Mooltan army gave Lord Gough that preponderance in artillery which he desired. The forces under his command were as follows:—

There were in the first place the same regiments which had been present at Chillianwallah. The divisional commanders were as before; but Brigadier Penny was now in command of what had been Godby's brigade in Gilbert's division, while Penny's and Pennycuick's brigades, in Campbell's division, were commanded by Carnegie and M'Leod.

To these were added the 1st Infantry Division, under Whish, with Brigadier Markham in command of the 32nd Foot and the 49th and 51st Native Infantry, and Hervey in command of the 10th Foot and the 8th and 72nd Native Infantry; also Dundas's Bombay column, 60th Rifles, 3rd Bombay Native Infantry, Bombay Fusiliers, and 19th Native Infantry.

The Scinde Horse and 4 regiments of irregulars were added to the cavalry. The artillery, under Brigadier Tennant, now numbered 96 guns, 18 being of heavy calibre. The engineers and sappers were under command of Major-General Cheape, who had returned with Major-General Whish from Mooltan.[18]

The Sikhs were drawn up in the form of a rough crescent, facing nearly due south. Their right flank lay across a deep dry *nullah* which curved round the city behind them and covered part of their front, then took a sharp turn south, and passed through the centre of the British encampment. Their left reached to a smaller *nullah* full of wa-

18. The above is taken almost *verbatim* from *The Sikhs and the Sikh Wars*, as well as much that follows in the account of the battle.

ter, which ran south into the Chenab. Their cavalry, Afghan horsemen chiefly, extended beyond the *nullahs* on right and left. The villages of Kalra and Chota Kalra, lying between the *nullahs*, had been occupied, fortified, and loop-hooled with great skill by the Sikhs.

The British faced them, looking north, their line divided by the great *nullah*. Gilbert's division was on the right next to this *nullah*, having Mountain's brigade on the left and Penny's on the right. Beyond Gilbert on the right was Whish's division, with Hervey's brigade in the front line and Markham's in the second. On the right flank were the cavalry brigades of Lockwood and Hearsey.

On Gilbert's left was the heavy battery of 18 guns; Whish was supported by 3 troops Horse Artillery, with Dawes's battery and 2 troops Horse Artillery for the time in reserve. The cavalry were supported by Warner's troop of Horse Artillery.

On the left of the *nullah* was Campbell's division, with Carnegie and M'Leod in the front line and Hoggan in second line, supporting Dundas and the Bombay column on the left. White's cavalry brigade, with Sir J. Thackwell, was on the left flank, supported by 2 troops of Horse Artillery. The Bombay column was supported by Blood's Bombay Horse Artillery; Campbell by the 2 light field batteries of Ludlow and Robertson. A reserve, consisting of the 5th and 6th Light Cavalry, the 45th and 69th Native Infantry, and the Bombay field battery, was in charge of the rear.

By half-past 7 the troops had started. The Sikhs opened fire, which showed the position and range of their guns. Our line halted, and the whole force of artillery was moved to the front covered by infantry skirmishers. By 9 o'clock the long line of guns was in position, about 800 yards from the Sikhs, and then the battle opened in earnest. For two and a half hours the artillery duel was continued. Both sides suffered considerably, but the enemy had by far the worst of it. Then at half-past 11 a general advance was ordered, the artillery still leading. Now followed some very stubborn fighting, when Penny's brigade, chiefly the 2nd European Light Infantry under their brigadier and Major Steele, stormed the village of Kalra. Chota Kalra, too, offered a desperate resistance to the 10th Foot in Hervey's brigade under Colonel Franks. Markham's and Hervey's brigades on our right had very hard fighting, but the fire of the Horse Artillery guns overwhelmed the enemy in that direction. The artillery on our left was most effective, and dominated the *nullah*, so that Campbell's infantry had little opposition.

On our extreme left the Afghan horsemen tried to turn our flank, but Thackwell brought his Horse Artillery to bear on them, and to cover a brilliant charge executed by the Scinde Horse, supported by the 9th Lancers, who drove back the enemy's squadrons in precipitate flight, and Thackwell was enabled to turn their flank. The ground prevented further action on the part of the cavalry on that flank, but the guns were brought forward and aided the rout of the enemy which was now beginning. On our right, the Afghan horsemen kept us constantly on the alert, but the ground there was very unfit for cavalry action owing to the wet *nullah* and the villages lying to our front.

By half-past 12 the whole Sikh Army was in full flight, and by 1 o'clock Goojerat itself, the Sikh camp, their baggage, and most of their guns were in possession of the British. On the left of the town, Dundas and Thackwell followed in pursuit, and on the right the cavalry under Lockwood and Hearsey, aided by infantry. The cavalry pursued for upwards of 12 miles, till it was dark, and the flying Sikhs had to drop most of the few guns they had carried off the field in their hurried flight. It was a thorough rout, and every branch of the army, horse, foot, and artillery, did its work thoroughly and with complete success.

The Fourteenth took a glorious part in the pursuit following upon this crowning victory of the campaign, and their steady conduct during the battle had the desired effect of holding in check and driving off those *goles* of Afghan horsemen which seriously threatened the right flank of our army. The Fourteenth were in the 2nd Cavalry Brigade, with the 1st Light Cavalry and the 11th Irregular Cavalry, commanded by Brigadier-General G. H. Lockwood, C.B., supported by Warner's troop of Horse Artillery, and the duty of this brigade was to defend the right flank. The Sikhs and Afghan horsemen were perpetually menacing this flank during the battle, and did their best to surround us by endeavouring to get to our rear. One troop of these audacious warriors did actually get round our rear, and threatened the commander-in-chief and his staff, but they were driven off most gallantly and cut to pieces by Lord Gough's escort, a troop of the 5th Light Cavalry, ably led by Lieutenant Stannus,[19] who was severely wounded on the occasion.

The successful manner in which these various were met by our cavalry on the right is best described in the following extracts from despatches relating thereto. Brigadier-General Brigadier G. H. Lock-

---

19. Afterwards General Henry James Stannus, C.B.

wood, C.B., writes:—

Camp Goojerat,
February 22, 1849.

On the morning of the 21st I deployed my brigade in the following manner:—In the first line,

5 troops of Her Majesty's 14th Light Dragoons,
2 squadrons 1st Light Cavalry,

with 1st troop 3rd Brigade Horse Artillery on the left, escorted by a troop of the 14th Light Dragoons and a *ressalah* of the 11th Irregular Cavalry; in support, the remainder of the 11th Irregular Cavalry; and in reserve (under Lieutenant-Colonel Doherty),

1 squadron 14th Light Dragoons,
1 squadron 1st Light Cavalry.

The enemy's horsemen appeared in great force upon our right, threatening to turn our flank, so I changed front to the right, directing the reserve to retain its front and communicate with the infantry on its left. Captain Warner's guns opened with great effect upon the horsemen and turned them, but they only retired a short distance, and then a regiment of their regular cavalry moved round by a circuitous route and got completely into our rear. I immediately detached towards them three guns with a squadron of the 14th Light Dragoons, who, in conjunction with Major Christie's corps of Irregular Cavalry, drove them off.

About this time a large *gole* of horsemen came on towards me and I prepared to charge, but as they turned at once from the fire of the guns, and as there was a *nullah* in our front, I refrained from advancing after them. The reserve also now advanced in support of Colonel Hervey's Brigade of infantry. I then received orders to bring on the brigade, and followed in the pursuit of the enemy.

In the pursuit the 14th Light Dragoons and 1st Light Cavalry cut down and shot a considerable number of the Sikh Infantry, and Corporal William Pain of the 14th Light Dragoons captured a red silk standard, killing in single combat the horseman who bore it. I beg to state to the major-general (commanding the cavalry division) that I had the greatest satisfaction in witnessing the steadiness of the troops composing the brigade in performing several manoeuvres under a heavy fire of artillery. My best thanks are due to Captain Warner, Horse Artillery; also to Lieutenant-Colonel Bradford, commanding 1st Light Cavalry; Lieutenant-Colonel King, commanding 14th Light Dragoons; and Lieutenant-Colonel Doherty, 14th Light Dragoons, who commanded the reserve.—*London Gazette*, April 19, 1849.

Brigadier-General Hearsey (commanding 4th Cavalry Brigade), who was commanding in the pursuit in which Brigadier Lockwood's (2nd) Brigade took part, says in his despatch, dated

> Camp, near Korea,
> 23rd February 1849.

The distance the cavalry under my command went over in pursuit was fifteen miles. I found Brigadier Lockwood, C.B., most zealous, and desirous of having an opportunity to charge at the head of the 14th Light Dragoons. The conduct of that regiment throughout the day was most exemplary and steady, and I have not the least doubt had an opportunity occurred it would have been most eagerly seized to the utter destruction of any body opposed to it.

In his despatch to the adjutant-general, dated Headquarters, Camp Goojerat, 25th February 1849, Major-General Sir Joseph Thackwell, K.C.B., commanding cavalry division, says:—

I am gratified to learn that both officers and men of Brigadier Lockwood's Brigade behaved greatly to his satisfaction, and that the 14th Light Dragoons, under Lieutenant-Colonel King, and the 1st Light Cavalry, under Lieutenant-Colonel Bradford, conducted themselves gallantly, and evinced every anxiety to close with the enemy. I am happy to observe that the brigadier has mentioned with great approbation the conduct of Lieutenant-Colonels Bradford and King in command of their regiments, and I cannot avoid here stating for the information of his Lordship that I observed with much satisfaction the zeal and judgment evinced by both officers when in command of considerable bodies of cavalry detached from the camp at Chillianwallah on important duties.

In his despatch, dated Headquarters, Camp Goojerat, 26th February 1849, His Excellency the Commander-in-Chief in India (Lord

Gough) says:—

> The determined front shown by the 14th (King's) Light Dragoons and the other cavalry regiments on the right, both regular and irregular, completely overawed the enemy and contributed in a very large measure to the success of the day: the conduct of all in following up the fugitive enemy was beyond all praise.'

This despatch was subsequently published by the Right Honourable the Governor-General of India in his general orders, for the information of the army after the battle.

The following reference to the pursuits at Goojerat occurs in Thackwell's *Narrative of the Sikh Wars:*—

> The brigades of Hearsey and Lockwood captured several guns in their advance, and committed awful havoc amongst the flying Sings. The 14th Light Dragoons were conspicuous in this bloody work of retribution. Captain Scudamore of that regiment was on the point of despatching a flying Sing when the cry of "Mercy!" arrested his arm. No sooner had the gallant officer passed him than he turned quickly round and shot his generous preserver. The zeal and activity of Lieut.-Colonel King in this pursuit were surpassed by no one.'

The casualties of the 14th Light Dragoons at Goojerat were as follows:—

Killed:—Lieutenant Ambrose Lloyd.
      4 horses.
Wounded:—Captain J. H. Goddard, severely.
      Captain A. Scudamore, dangerously.
      4 rank and file.
      2 horses.

In the pursuit on the day of the battle our cavalry and several troops of Horse Artillery tried hard to catch the Sikh cavalry and Afghan horsemen, but although the 9th Lancers, 3rd Light Dragoons, 14th Light Dragoons, and all the light and irregular cavalry of our army did their best, the enemy's cavalry was too fleet for them. However, the Khalsa Infantry were not so lucky: they were early overtaken on our right by Hearsey's and Lockwood's Brigades, in which were the Fourteenth, who simply drove the stubborn Sikhs from every garden, ravine, or hedge where they attempted to make a stand, and shot and cut them down without mercy. Shere Singh never halted in his flight till he had passed the Jhelum; guns, standards, the whole of his camp—left standing with all it contained—all the baggage of his army, ammunition, and several thousand head of cattle were the spoils of the victors.

The total losses of the British at Goojerat were 5 officers, 92 men, killed; 24 officers, 682 men, wounded.

In killed, wounded, prisoners, and missing, the Sikhs probably lost from 15,000 to 20,000 men, a great portion of their army having disbanded themselves.

Goojerat saw the Khalsa army completely shattered, and the victory was a glorious triumph for Lord Gough and the Army of the Punjaub. After the news of Chillianwallah reached England, popular feeling was very strong against Lord Gough and his 'Tipperary tactics,' as they were called, and the heavy loss of life incurred in his battles made him unpopular in the country. The government of the day determined to recall him, and on the 7th March 1849, Lieutenant-General Sir Charles Napier, K.C.B., was appointed Commander-in-Chief in India, with the local rank of General, but long before he arrived to assume command, the gallant old soldier he came to supersede had, by his brilliant victory of Goojerat, amply vindicated his reputation, and was restored once more to the confidence of his queen and country.

Immediately after Goojerat, Major-General Sir Walter Gilbert, K.C.B., a noted horseman and a very energetic officer, was despatched with 12,000 men of all arms, amongst whom were the Fourteenth, with orders from Lord Gough to pursue across the Jhelum, and to seize at once Rhotas, Attock, Peshawur, and the whole frontier up to the passes leading into Afghanistan. This force experienced very inclement weather, and had to make a temporary halt in consequence, on the 2nd March. Sir Walter Gilbert's orders were to grant no terms save unconditional surrender. By the 6th March the Sikhs, so hotly pressed by our troops and worn out with flight, without supplies of food or ammunition, restored all their prisoners, and finally, on the 12th March, at Rawul Pindhi, laid down their arms and surrendered at discretion to Sir Walter Gilbert.

The Fourteenth were present on this occasion, also at the capture of Attock, 17th March; whence, continuing their pursuit of the flying Afghan horsemen, they crossed the Indus, were at Peshawur on 21st March, and taking part in the expulsion of the Afghans beyond the Khyber Pass, encamped under Jumrood Fort till the 2nd April. The result of the victorious campaign now closed was the annexation to the British Crown of the whole of the Punjaub, from the Khyber Pass to the banks of the Sutlej, and this event took place on the 1st April 1849. The whole campaign, from the time the commander-in-chief actually took the field to the victory at Goojerat, occupied three months.

On 2nd April the Fourteenth left Jumrood on their march back; they left Peshawur 4th April, and arrived at Lahore 1st May, where, before the troops were dismissed to their lines, the 'muster' was held. On 7th May, Major-General Sir Walter Gilbert, K.C.B., inspected the regiment at Lahore, and again on the 17th October at the same station, and expressed satisfaction with all he saw. In the month of November, 109 men joined from England, making the strength present at headquarters up to 700 men.

The depot at Maidstone under Colonel C. Middleton, commandant of the Cavalry Depot there, consisted of 76 men on 1st December.

On 6th December the Marquis of Dalhousie, Governor-General of India, inspected the Fourteenth at Anarkullee (Lahore), on which occasion the new Commander-in-Chief in India, General Sir Charles James Napier, G.C.B., was present, and expressed his approbation of the movements of the Cavalry Brigade, in which the Fourteenth took part.

On 17th December the commander-in-chief inspected the regiment again at Lahore, and was pleased to express his satisfaction with what he saw.

1850

During the whole of this year the Fourteenth were stationed at Anarkullee,[20] Lahore. On 25th January, Lieutenant William Featherstonehaugh became Paymaster *vice* Rofe, who had served in that capacity ever since the year 1812, having then succeeded Mr. Flanegan, the first paymaster ever appointed to the 14th Light Dragoons.

On the 21st February and on 5th April the regiment was inspected by Major-General Sir. W. Gilbert, G.C.B.

On the 2nd March, Quartermaster G. Shenton died at sea.

On the 25th March, His Excellency the Commander-in-Chief in India, General Sir Charles J. Napier, G.C.B., made an inspection of the garrison at Lahore, seeing all the troops there, including the 14th Light Dragoons.

---

20. The military cantonment is now called Mean-Meer.

THE PUNJAUB
and
SURROUNDING DISTRICTS.

Scale of English Miles

KASHMIR

MAYNDHA Doab

DOAB

MALWA

BHAWALPORE

AFGHANISTAN

BELOOCHISTAN

RAJPUTANA

SCINDE

KABUL

PESHAWUR

Rawul Pindi

Attock

JAMMU
Sealkote

LAHORE
Umritsur

MOOLTAN

DELHI

R. Jumna

R. Indus

R. Chenab

R. Ravee

R. Sutlej

On the 6th July, Lieutenant-Colonel J. W. King, C.B., died at Lahore, and was succeeded in command of the regiment by Lieutenant-
Colonel H. E. Doherty, C.B.; on the 7th, Major C. Steuart became
2nd Lieutenant-Colonel; and on the 17th September, Captain J. H.
Goddard became Major.

On the 20th October, Major-General Sir Walter Gilbert, G.C.B.,
inspected the regiment, and expressed himself very much pleased with
the result. He saw the Fourteenth at 5.30 a.m. in 'marching-order,' and
at 5 p.m. in 'watering-order.'

1851

The Fourteenth left Lahore 19th January, and marched to Meerut,
arriving there 6th March.

On 1st February, headquarters were at Camp Loodiana; on 1st
March at Camp Mangal.

On 17th March the Fourteenth took part with the other regiments stationed at Meerut in a review held by Lieutenant-General Sir
Joseph Thackwell, G.C.B., K.H., at which His Excellency General Sir
William Gomm, K.C.B., Commander-in-Chief in India, was present
and was highly pleased; and on the same day His Excellency visited
the barracks, stables, regimental hospital, and the men's dinners, and
expressed to Lieutenant-Colonel Doherty, C.B., how satisfied he was
with everything he had seen.

On 22nd March, Lieutenant-General Sir J. Thackwell inspected
the Fourteenth very minutely, and he inspected a second time on
17th November, and on both occasions expressed satisfaction with all
he saw.

Lieutenant H. C. Reader was appointed Adjutant *vice* Lieutenant
R. P. Apthorp invalided home. Lieutenant M. C. Smith died at Meerut
4th March; and Cornet G. A. Francklyn died at the same place on 18th
December of pleurisy and lung disease. There is a very handsome silver claret-jug of a most uncommon pattern in the officers' mess which
was presented by the family of this young officer in his memory.

1852

The Fourteenth remained all this year at Meerut. On the 27th
March and 29th October, Lieutenant-General Sir J. Thackwell made
his inspections of the regiment, and on both occasions expressed himself satisfied with the appearance of the men, the condition of the
horses, and the interior economy of the corps.

On the 23rd July, Veterinary Surgeon A. W. Caldwell died.

General the Hon. Sir Henry Murray. K.C.B.
Colonel of the 14th Kings Light Dragoons.
1853-1860.

On 14th December authority was granted for the regiment to bear on its appointments the words 'Punjaub,' 'Chillianwallah,' and 'Goojerat,' in consideration of its services in the second Sikh campaign in the Punjaub, 1848-49.

1853

The Fourteenth remained at Meerut all this year. The strength of the service troops under Lieutenant-Colonel Doherty, C.B., at Meerut was 770 men; the depot troop at Maidstone, under the Commandant, Colonel F. Griffiths, consisted of 43 men.

Lieutenant-General the Honourable Henry Murray, C.B., was appointed Colonel of the regiment on 18th March, in succession to General Sir E. Kerrison, Bart., G.C.H., K.C.B., deceased.

On 20th July, Lieutenant and Riding-master John Holliday died at Meerut.

On 5th August, Cornet Charles Wemys Thesiger [21] joined the Fourteenth on transfer from the 5th Madras Light Cavalry.

On 30th December, Captain W. Wilmer became Major *vice* Clarke.

The Fourteenth were inspected at Meerut by Lieutenant-General Sir Joseph Thackwell on 30th March, and by Brigadier-General J. Scott, C.B., on 5th November. Both officers expressed their satisfaction at the efficient state in which they found the regiment.

1854

During the whole of this year the Fourteenth remained at Meerut. On 17th March, Brigadier-General Scott, C.B., inspected, and on 7th November, Brigadier-General George Brooke, C.B., and both officers seemed very pleased with what they saw.

Three officers died this year, *viz.* Lieutenant W. D. Boyd, at Bromley, Kent, on 14th January; Major J. H. Goddard, who had been wounded at the Battle of Goojerat, [22] at Simla, on 31st May; and Assistant Surgeon R. Wigstrom at Mazagon, Bombay, on 8th September.

On 1st June, Captain A. Scudamore became Major *vice* Goddard. The establishment was now—

9 Troops.	10 Farriers.	626 Privates.
57 Sergeants.	40 Corporals.	703 Troop-horses.
14 Trumpeters.		

21. Now Lieutenant-General the Hon. C. W. Thesiger, Colonel of the 14th (King's) Hussars.

22. Major Goddard was shot in the ankle at Goojerat.

A Saddler-Sergeant was included in the establishment this year for the first time.

His Excellency General Sir William Gomm, K.C.B., Commander-in-Chief in India, expressed his great satisfaction at receiving so good a report of the regiment from Brigadier-General G. Brooke, C. B., after his inspection held on 7th November at Meerut, as stated in a letter from Colonel Frederick Markham, Adjutant-General of Her Majesty's army in India, addressed to Brigadier-General Brooke, C.B., commanding at Meerut, which was notified to the officer commanding the regiment by His Excellency's desire. In an extract from General Orders, dated Headquarters, Shunishabad, 30th December 1854 (No. 91), His Excellency remarks with reference to the 14th Light Dragoons having been placed under orders to proceed to Bombay with all despatch, preparatory to embarkation for the seat of war in Turkey, as follows:—

> The commander-in-chief heartily congratulates the corps on its brilliant destination, and on the prospect this opens to it of early opportunity occurring for further ennobling its standards, rich already in the records of Peninsular and Indian victory. Her Majesty's Fourteenth will bring an accession, as we confidently trust, nothing short of 667 British sabres, with which it will quit Meerut, to the ranks of the heroic army, which in brief space of time has achieved exploits unsurpassed in the annals of British intrepidity and constancy. Sir William Gomm has pleasure in publicly recording the tenor of the half-yearly report made to him of the state of the regiment on 7th November last by an inspecting officer so competent in every respect to the duty as that by whom it was then visited. Brigadier Brooke reports in his "Summary of Remarks" as to the 14th Light Dragoons—
>
> > The regiment appears to be in a state of complete efficiency. The horses are in good working condition, and the appointments of both men and horses in excellent order.
>
> (Signed)　　　　　　　William Gomm, General,
> Commander-in-Chief, East Indies'

1855

On 8th January, at Meerut, the Fourteenth received orders for the Crimea, where the war between the Russians and the Allies was now in progress. On the 16th the march commenced from Meerut, but on

17th an order came countermanding the embarkation for the Crimea, and the regiment marched back to Meerut, and re-entered the station on the 19th January. On the same day orders were received from the governor-general direct by electric telegraph for the Fourteenth to march to Kirkee, and on 24th January the march to Kirkee, 75 marches and 884 miles distant, was commenced. The strength on leaving Meerut was 20 officers, 705 men, and 701 horses.

The Fourteenth entered Kirkee on 21st April, losing 2 men by death on the march. On the 28th April, Brigadier-General Trydell, commanding the Poona Brigade, made his inspection. He was much pleased, and said he could scarcely have expected to find the regiment in such an efficient state after their long march, as he did.

Lieutenant General the Honourable H. Murray, C.B., became General on the 16th February. On 28th June, His Excellency General Sir H. Somerset, Commander-in-Chief of the Bombay Army, reviewed the Fourteenth, and was very pleased with the manner in which the field movements were executed. The Right Honourable the Governor of Bombay, Lord Elphinstone, was present, and told Colonel Doherty that, as an old cavalry officer, he never saw a regiment 'trot past' better than the Fourteenth had done that day.

On 2nd November, Major-General F. Schuler, commanding the Poona Division of the army, made an inspection of the regiment, and was highly pleased.

1856

The Fourteenth remained at Kirkee this year.

Colonel Doherty, C.B., left India for England on leave of absence on 30th August, after commanding the regiment for six years, and he never rejoined it, as he retired on half-pay the following year.

On 7th November, Riding-master Joseph Raiker was appointed to the regiment.

His Excellency General Sir Henry Somerset, K.C.B., inspected on 20th March, and again on 17th December; Major-General Schuler inspected on the 28th October, and both expressed themselves perfectly satisfied.

On 31st October, Colonel Charles Steuart arrived from England and assumed command of the regiment during the absence of Colonel Doherty.

1857

On 20th February the regiment, under Colonel Steuart, left Kirkee for Persia on field-service with the expeditionary force commanded by Lieutenant-General Sir James Outram, K.C.B., and reached Bushire in March, where it disembarked and was encamped. The Fourteenth had moved by squadrons from Kirkee to Bombay, the last squadron marching on 24th February. The strength of the service troops proceeding to Persia was 25 officers, 614 men, and 649 horses. The headquarters embarked at Bombay 8th March, and landed at Bushire 31st March, and they left Bushire 30th April, landing at Bombay 15th May.

Captain Need's troop had embarked at Bombay in the ship *Raby Castle* with a strength of 76 horses on the 1st March, and landed on the 21st March at Bushire, where was an open roadstead with a very rough sea, in consequence of which many of the small boats used for landing were capsized and several horses drowned. Another troop sailed in the *Golden Era*, but was much delayed through grounding on a sandbank. Assistant-Surgeon J. H. Sylvester of the Indian Medical Service and Veterinary-Surgeon H. Dawson were attached to the regiment, and served with it in the Persian expedition.

The Persian expeditionary force proceeded by sea from Bombay in the months of February and March to the Persian Gulf, and landed at Bushire: it consisted of 2 divisions of infantry with artillery, sappers, and a cavalry division.

General Stalker commanded the 1st Division; Brigadier-General Henry Havelock, C.B., the 2nd Division; and Brigadier-General Jacob, C.B., the Cavalry Division; the two brigades of cavalry being commanded by Colonel Tapp, and Colonel Steuart of the 14th Light Dragoons.

One troop of the Fourteenth under Captain Prettejohn formed part of the force which started from Bushire towards the end of March and proceeded up the gulf with Lieut.-General Sir James Outram towards Shatta-el-Arab. Several of the vessels containing troops grounded on the bar at Shatta-el-Arab, the name given to the place at the mouths of the Tigris, Euphrates, and minor tributaries in the Persian Gulf, and thus considerable delay and inconvenience was caused, and most of the cavalry was late to be of efficient service partly in consequence of this, and partly owing to the small supply of boats for landing the troops. The forts of Mohamra were situated along the banks of the river, but the town of the same name lay 40 miles higher up, on the north side of the River Karoon, which at this point, near its junction with the Shatta-el-Arab, is from 600 to 800 yards wide.

Four armed steamers and two sloops of war, under Captain Young

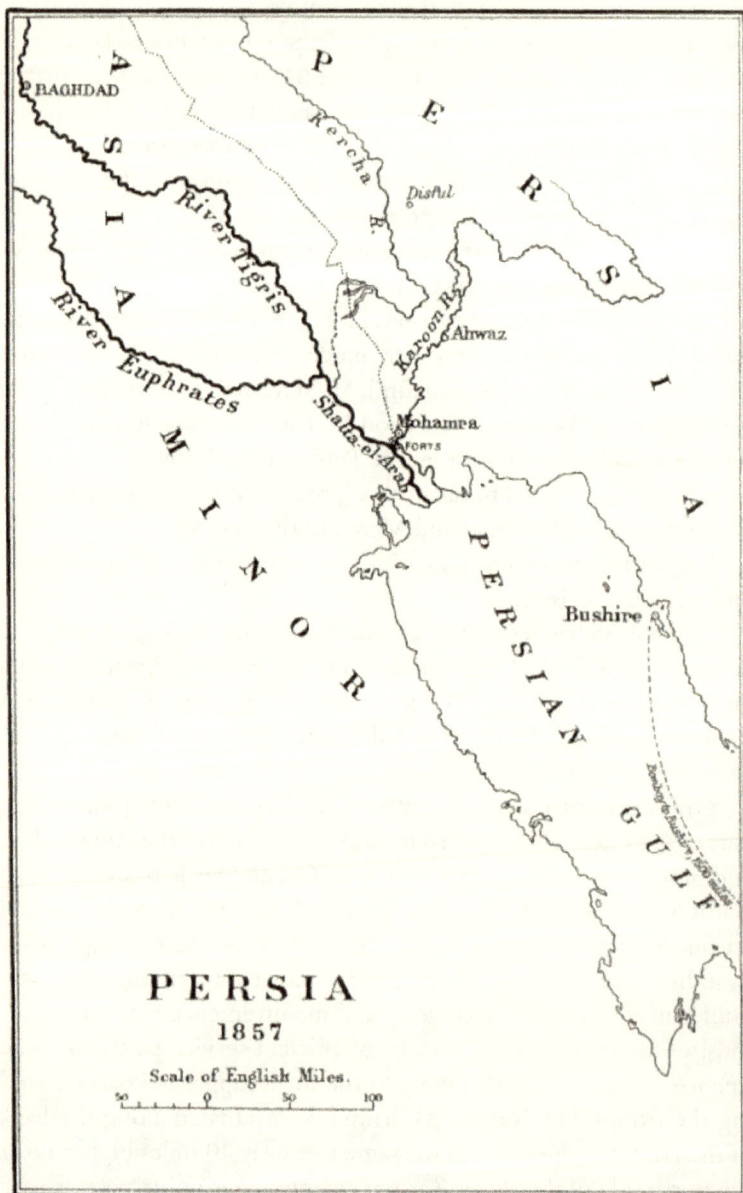

BAGHDAD

P E R S I A

Kercha R.

Disful

River Tigris

River Euphrates

Karoon R.

Ahwaz

Shatta-el-Arab

Mohamra

FORTS

A S I A   M I N O R

P E R S I A N   G U L F

Bushire

Road to Bushire 1200 miles

PERSIA

1857

Scale of English Miles.

50   0   50   100

of the Indian navy (acting commodore), had preceded the flotilla of vessels carrying the troops, and these successfully bombarded the forts and entrenched positions of the Persian army within gunfire, which had the effect of completely demoralising the enemy, as the fire was well directed; and subsequently, when the force landed under Sir James Outram, who was himself in the leading vessel, the *Feroze*, the whole Persian army evacuated their camp, leaving tents standing, and all their property, together with ammunition and 17 guns, which fell into our hands. The expeditionary force had to land in small boats, running the gauntlet of both gun and musket fire from some of the Persian batteries on the river bank, but so soon as ever the landing was effected and the advance on the enemy's camp 2 miles off actually made, the Persians fled, having first exploded their principal magazine.

Owing to the want of cavalry just when it was needed, no effective pursuit took place, although a detachment of the Sinde Horse under Captain M. Green did attempt it, but without much result, and the fugitives made good their escape, losing 200 killed. The only portion of the military forces engaged was the mortar battery under Captain Wogan, and a few European riflemen who were employed on board the war vessels when they bombarded the Persian earthworks and batteries lining the banks. There were 23 men killed and wounded altogether in the squadron during the bombardment, and the victory was really a naval one.

The strength of the Persian Army was 13,000 men, whilst the British and Indian troops numbered under 5000 men, as follows:—

	Men.
14th Light Dragoons,	89
Sinde Horse,	303
64th and 78th Regiments,	1534
2 Native Regiments,	1465
The Light Battalion,	920
Sappers and miners,	233
12 guns Horse Artillery and No. 2 Light Field Battery,	342
Total,	4886

The capture of Mohamra took place on 26th March. Sir James Outram had himself left Bushire on 18th March, reaching Shatta-el-Arab, 174 miles, on 21st March. He left a large portion of the expeditionary force, to the number of 3000 men, under the command of Brigadier -General Jacob, C.B., at Bushire, where General Stalker had unfortunately just died, and Commodore Ethersey of the Indian Navy, commanding the squadron, died in the Persian Gulf about the same time. The climate is a very pestilential one, and dysentery and fever are prevalent and very fatal to Europeans.

It was only Captain Prettejohn's, the 'H' troop of the Fourteenth, which was present at the taking of the town and fortress of Mohamra, as this troop happened to arrive first at Bushire and so was taken on first, as Jacob's Horse had not arrived, being delayed by the gales. The officers with Captain Prettejohn were Lieutenant Mackenzie, Cornet Ridley, and Assistant-Surgeon Fox.

The other troops of the Fourteenth and headquarters remained some time at Bushire, and some who left Bombay in sailing-vessels were sent back without even landing or doing any service in the expedition, much to their disappointment. The only losses suffered by the Fourteenth in Persia were 22 troop-horses by death, the result of accident or disease. After the affair of Mohamra some infantry with an armed flotilla were despatched up the river Karoon as far as Ahwaz, under command of Captain Rennie, Indian Navy, the detachment of the 78th Highlanders being commanded by Captain Hunt; but though the Persians numbered 7000 they retreated in hot haste before a body of 300 British infantry, 3 small steamers, and 3 gunboats.

Thus ended the war. The 64th Regiment and the troop of the 14th Light Dragoons were shortly afterwards sent back to Bushire, whilst the remainder of the force was kept some time longer in the unhealthy vicinity of Mohamra and Shatta-el-Arab, exposed alike to Persian sun and gulf fever. Sir James Outram himself did not finally quit Persia till 17th June, by which time the mutiny in India had broken out. The lieutenant-general says in his despatch, referring to the services of the military portion of his forces employed in this expedition:—

> Although not actively engaged with the enemy, I am not the less indebted to all ranks for their exertions and zeal, and especially for the great order and despatch with which the landing of the troops was effected under Brigadier-General Havelock, C.B. The highest spirit prevailed, and had the large Persian army only waited our approach out of the range of the ships' guns, I

---

23. The above is quoted from the *Biography of Sir James Outram*, by Sir F. Goldsmid.

feel confident it would have received a lasting lesson.[23]

The Fourteenth reached Kirkee in May and had scarcely settled down in their former quarters on return from the successful expedition to Persia, when they had to respond once more to the old familiar trumpet-call of 'Boot and Saddle.'

The 8th of June found the left wing of the regiment, 'B,' 'C,' 'D,' and 'E' troops, *en route* to Ahmednuggur and Nusseerabad; another troop, probably the 'A' troop, followed on the 11th, making the strength of those on field-service up to 10 officers, 300 men, and 305 troop-horses.

Major-General Schuler inspected the headquarters at Kirkee on 15th and 16th July, after the remainder of the regiment had left for service. 'G' and 'H' troops had been moved from Kirkee into Poona to be quartered there when the service troops left; but on 16th June, 'H' troop proceeded temporarily to Sattara in the southern part of the Bombay Presidency, followed by some more detachments of the regiment to the same town, their presence being urgently required there in consequence of an outbreak at Kolapore,[24] situated further south.

On 10th July the right wing began to take the field, and on that date 120 sabres (probably 'H' and 'K' troops) [25] marched to join the other portions of the regiment already on service in the Deccan, followed on 16th July by some more men of the right wing, so that by this time it may be said the whole regiment was fairly launched upon the campaign against the mutineers in the great *sepoy* revolt, which lasted till May 1859.

Since their arrival in India the Fourteenth had always worn the *puggrie* round their forage-caps, excepting when in full dress, and then the shako was worn; but now the latter was given up altogether, and the authorities gave permission for the men to wear turbans instead, which was a far more sensible head-dress for an Indian sun. Before the mutiny broke out the men of the Fourteenth were always called '*Puggrie Wallahs*' by the natives, having, it is believed, initiated the wearing of forage-caps with *puggries* round them.[26] Gloves and stocks were also discarded by the men at this time when going on field-service, as being useless encumbrances for actual fighting and hard work.

---

24. Kolapore, or Kolhapur, is in the Mahratta country.

25. Prettejohn's and Need's.

26. See *Scraps from my Sabretache*, by Stent, 1882, from which several quotations have been made in this *Record*. *Scraps from My Sabretache* by L E Warner & George Carter Stent is also published by Leonaur.

It was owing to the disturbed state of affairs throughout India generally just at this time, May 1857, that Lord Elphinstone, the Governor of Bombay, designed to form a column to secure and hold the great line of road between Bombay and Agra. This column was only a small one. It was placed under the command of Major-General Woodburn, C.B., and was intended by Lord Elphinstone to be used to open out communications with Central India and the North-West Provinces. It consisted of the following troops:—

5 troops of the 14th (King's) Light Dragoons,
The 25th Bombay Native Infantry,
Captain Woolcombe's battery of Horse Artillery,
A pontoon train.

The column started from Kirkee and Poona on 8th June, with orders to march at once to Mhow, in order to save that place and prevent the spread of the insurrection which had already taken place in the Malwa district and along the northern portion of the Bombay Presidency. The state of affairs at Mhow and Indore was very serious. Malleson says:—[27]

It was just possible that, making forced marches, General Woodburn might approach so near to Indore[28] as to baffle the plans of the discontented. Circumstances, however, occurred which baffled the hopes expressed by Lord Elphinstone, when, acting on his own unaided judgment, he pressed upon the military authorities the necessity for General Woodburn to advance.

The circumstances alluded to by Malleson were the revolts in Malwa and the Deccan, especially in Aurungabad, which latter city was once the capital of the kingdom of Ahmednuggur, and later the favourite residence of the Emperor Aurungzeeb. It is situated in the north-western corner of the *nizam's* dominions in Hyderabad, Deccan. On the second day's march of the column from Poona, it was joined by the 25th Bombay Native Infantry, under the command of Major Follett. The 25th Bombay Native Infantry was destined afterwards, in company with the 14th Light Dragoons, to perform the most brilliant services in Central India under Major-General Sir Hugh Rose, K.C.B., but just at the present crisis doubts were actually entertained

---

27. Vol. v.2

8. Malleson's Hunterian *nomenclature* is not adhered to in this *Record*, but the older spelling is generally preferred.

of its loyalty.

Subsequent events proved how utterly unfounded these were. The whole of this column, which has been called first the Deccan Field Force, secondly the Malwa Field Force, and thirdly the Nerbudda Field Force,[29] entered the city of Ahmednuggur at the same time, Captain Woolcombe's battery of Horse Artillery (native drivers and European gunners) having joined it simultaneously with the 25th Bombay Native Infantry.

The *nizam's* army was now in a very doubtful state of loyalty, and it was on the third day's march of Major-General Woodburn's column that intelligence came of the disaffection of the 1st Hyderabad Cavalry at Aurungabad, a day's march from the halting-place at Seeroor,[30] as well as of the alarming danger which threatened Mhow.

The monsoon had just burst, and naturally caused much inconvenience to the marching of the troops.

As the reports from Mhow were so serious, the order of march was altered to Malligaum, leaving Aurungabad to the right; but almost directly after the route was again changed, and the column recalled to proceed to Aurungabad to help the Europeans who were in such dire straits there, as the troops had mutinied. On the 19th June, Captain H. O. Mayne arrived in camp from Aurungabad with the ladies and children of that station.

After a wet march the column reached Aurungabad at 10 a.m. on 23rd June. Captain Abbott, commanding the 1st Cavalry of the Hyderabad Contingent, with the other officers and such of the men as had remained trustworthy, were posted in the mess-house, but the rebellious portion of the garrison, which consisted of the 1st and 3rd Hyderabad Cavalry, 2nd Hyderabad Infantry, and a battery of the artillery of the Hyderabad Contingent, had encamped themselves on high ground beyond the cantonment, on the Jaulna road. It was the 1st Cavalry who were mutinous. Malleson says:—[31]

> General Woodburn's column marched at once to the ground occupied by the mutineers, and ordered the men to give up their arms. With the exception of one troop of the 1st Cavalry,

---

29. The designation of the column was altered as it advanced and grew by reinforcements. When in the Deccan it was so called; leaving and entering Malwa it became 'The Malwa;' after quitting that territory and entering the valley of the Nerbudda it changed its name again.

30. Or Sirur.

31. Vol. v.

all obeyed. The general gave the men of that troop six minutes to consider the course they would pursue. When the time elapsed, the men, instead of submitting, put on a bold front, and attempted to ride away. In this attempt most of them succeeded. The next morning, some three or four, convicted of attempts at assassination, were hanged, and order was restored.

The formation of the column at the rebels' camp was, 14th Light Dragoons on the left, guns in the centre, 25th Native Infantry on the right. The 1st Cavalry fell in on foot, facing the column, with the native officers only mounted. The guns were previously loaded with canister, and pointed at the rebels; but during the six minutes' grace allowed, the men got on their horses and made off. Now, when too late, the guns were fired, knocking over a few horses left behind, and one native *syce*. Then the 14th Light Dragoons, with tired horses after a long forced march, were sent after the runaways, but they for the most part, as was to be expected under the circumstances, made good their escape. Captain Gall of the 14th Light Dragoons led his troop after those who were escaping by the Jaulna road. Captain Barrett pursued across the open country, and some of the loyal Native Cavalry under Captain Abbott joined the Fourteenth in their almost fruitless pursuit.

One squadron of the regiment under Lieutenant Leith, [32] with 2 guns, some of the 25th Native Infantry, and some sappers and miners, had been very judiciously posted near the bridge over the river leading to the cavalry lines, so as to prevent any disturbance occurring in the cantonment. In the end some few rebels were taken and brought back prisoners. Courts-martial were held, and several rebels were convicted and executed, either by hanging or else shot or blown away from the cannon's mouth; but there is no doubt that as a whole the mutineers on this occasion were treated too leniently, and without the necessary decision which is of paramount importance on such critical occasions, especially when dealing with the natives in India.

The next day a squadron of the 14th Light Dragoons, accompanied by 2 guns of Woolcombe's battery and some Native troops, were placed under command of Captain Gall, 14th Light Dragoons, and marched off at dusk for Boldana, in Berar, as there was a large sum of money in the treasury there under the guard of a troop belonging to the mutinous cavalry of the *nizam*. This column reached Boldana,

---

32. Afterwards Major Leith, V.C.

100 miles off, in three days, whence, after taking over from Mr. Bullock, the acting resident, the whole of the mutinous troop, previously disarmed, marched back under Captain Gall to Aurungabad, bringing the prisoners with them. They passed *en route* through Jaffarabad and Jaulna, and arrived on 6th July at Aurungabad. On 9th July news came to Aurungabad concerning the Mhow and Indore mutinies, and on the 12th the left wing of the Fourteenth and the rest of the column marched for Central India, Major Follett having assumed the command in consequence of Major-General Woodburn being incapacitated by illness.

A detachment of 50 sabres of the Fourteenth was left behind in Aurungabad for the protection of the place, as well as 2 guns. This troop of the regiment appears to have gone back to Kirkee in October when no longer required in the Deccan, and it remained there for a time with other details, forming a sort of depot under command of Brevet-Colonel C. P. Ainslie,[33] who had been reappointed on 26th August from half-pay to serve once more in the Fourteenth as second Lieutenant-Colonel. On 17th June, Lieutenant C. W. Thesiger[34] exchanged into the 6th (Inniskilling) Dragoons, which regiment he afterwards commanded. On 20th June, Captain Gaussen died in England, and on 26th August, Colonel H. E. Doherty, C.B. (in England), retired on half-pay, being succeeded in command Lieut.-Colonel of the Fourteenth by Colonel Charles Steuart.[35] On 18th September, Captain R. H. Gall became Major *vice* Wilmer.

The march of the column which started from Aurungabad for the relief of Mhow on 12th July, under the temporary command of Major Follett, 25th Bombay Infantry, and with which was the left wing of the Fourteenth under Captain Gall's command, lay through the Asseerghur jungles, which from June to November are very unhealthy and often prove fatal to Europeans, as there is much danger of malaria in that season.

At Edulabad, Major Follett fell a victim to cholera, and was buried at Burhampur.[36] When Major-General Woodburn fell ill at Aurungabad, Colonel C. S. Stuart,[37] of the Bombay Infantry, had been appointed as brigadier to command the force, and he assumed command

33. Colonel Ainslie commanded the station at Kirkee.
34. Now Lieut.-General the Hon. C. W. Thesiger, Colonel of 14th (King's) Hussars.
35. Afterwards Lieut.-General Charles Steuart, C.B.
36. See Sylvester's *Campaign in Central India.*
37. Afterwards General Sir Charles Shepherd Stuart, G.C.B.
38. Afterwards Sir Henry Marion Durand, K.C.B.

Colonel (afterwards Lieut. General)
Charles Stewart, C.B.
commanding 16th (King's) Light Dragoons.
1857-1861.

at Asseerghur, which was reached on 22nd July. Here also Lieutenant-Colonel Durand, R.E.,[38] Officiating Agent to the Governor-General for Central India (in the absence of Sir Robert Hamilton), Mrs. Durand, Dr. Henry Wilson, as well as several fugitive officers and ladies who had escaped from the mutiny at Indore, joined the column on the march.

On 27th July the troops crossed the Nerbudda in the vicinity of Hoosingabad, the 14th Light Dragoons swimming the river, [39] the infantry, guns, and baggage passing by the ford of Mokka-ka-Turr, near Burwai. As the force ascended the Vindhya range at a height of 1650 feet, all traces of cholera and malaria quickly disappeared, but the heavy rains continued almost incessantly during the greater part of the march.

On the 28th July the column was joined by the 3rd Regiment of Cavalry, Hyderabad Contingent, commanded by Major S. Orr; on the 31st it ascended the Simrol Pass, and the following morning entered Mhow. That night the monsoon came on with great violence, and very heavy rains set in and continued for the next two months. It was a most critical time: Holkar's troops at Indore, only 13 miles off, were in open mutiny; and there was no European infantry at Mhow, where the force, under Brigadier Stuart, consisted of 5 troops 14th Light Dragoons, 3rd Cavalry, Hyderabad Contingent, 1 horse battery of European Artillery, the 25th Bombay Native Infantry, and a pontoon train. A few days later, as related in Kaye and Malleson's *History of the Indian Mutiny*[40] 4 companies of the 86th Regiment [41] arrived to reinforce the column at Mhow; but no operations could be satisfactorily carried on during the heavy rains, so it was not till October that anything further was undertaken. On the 20th of that month Brigadier Stuart led forth his column, now the Malwa [42] Field Force, with a view to clear the rebels out of the surrounding districts where they had occupied some of the most important forts and towns of Malwa.

The first point of intended attack was Mundesor. This town is situated on a tributary of the River Chambal, about 120 miles from Indore. Malleson says:—[43]

In the month of July this place had been occupied by some of

---

39. Sylvester's *Campaign in Central India.*
40. Vol. v.
41. Now 2nd Battalion Royal Irish Rifles.
42. Malwa, in Central India, comprises the states of Gwalior, Indore, and Dhar.
43. Vol. v.

Sindhia's revolted troops, and these had been joined, and were being constantly further strengthened, by Afghan, Mekrani, and Mewati levies. In August the insurrection at Mundesor threatened not only to embrace all Western Malwa, but Neemuch as well. The leader of the Mundesor insurgents was Ferozshah, a *sháhzáda* or prince connected with the imperial family at Delhi. It was estimated in September that some 15,000 men, with 16 or 18 guns, had rallied round his standard, and this estimate was subsequently found to have been below the actual number.

The force under Brigadier Stuart at the time only consisted of about

> 200 of 14th Light Dragoons.
> 170 Artillery.
> 230 of 86th Regiment.
> 350 of 25th Bombay Native Infantry.
> 350 of 3rd Nizam's Cavalry.
> Madras Sappers and Miners.

Lieutenant-Colonel Durand, the political officer, saw the importance of striking a blow as quickly as could be; and accordingly, as Mundesor was too strongly held to be attacked immediately, it was determined first to march on the fort of Dhar. On the 14th of October an advanced party under Major Robertson, 25th Bombay Native Infantry, consisting of a troop of the 14th Light Dragoons, 3 companies Native Infantry, 2 guns, and some Hyderabad Cavalry, had been sent on from Mhow in the direction of Dhar to form a kind of advance-guard to the column, with orders to proceed *via* Gujri.

The main body, which left Mhow on 20th October, was divided into 2 columns, one under Major Keane, 86th Regiment, and the other under the brigadier. Each of these took a somewhat different direction, in order to try and clear the whole of Malwa of its rebels, and on the 22nd the entire force arrived in the vicinity of Dhar. Captain Mayne, 3rd Irregular Cavalry, who was attached to the force, had ridden forward with some *sowars*, and reported he had been fired on at a village about 4 miles from Dhar.

On coming in view of the fort and town the 86th Regiment advanced in skirmishing order, and it was ascertained that a large body of the garrison had sallied out from the fort to attack our force. Malleson says they had planted 3 guns on a hill south of the fort, from which

44 Kaye and Malleson's *History of the Indian Mutiny*, vol. v.

point they were extended along its eastern face in skirmishing order, and advanced boldly against the British.[44] The guns were charged and captured by some of the Fourteenth, acting with the 25th Native Infantry, led by Major Robertson, whose men promptly turned them on the rebels.

Almost simultaneously the four companies of the 86th Regiment and the sappers, flanked by Woolcombe's (Bombay) and Hungerford's (Bengal) batteries, advanced against the enemy's centre, whilst the cavalry threatened both flanks the dragoons under Captain Gall, the left, the *nizam's* cavalry under Major Orr, the right. Baffled in their advance by the action of the 25th Bombay Native Infantry and the play of the British guns on their centre, the enemy made a rapid movement to their left, and attempted to turn the British right. But the dragoons, led by Gall, and the *nizam's* cavalry led by Orr and Macdonald, Deputy Quartermaster-General of the force, charged them so vigorously that they retired into the fort, leaving 40 dead bodies of their companions on the field. On the British side 3 dragoons and 1 native trooper were wounded, a *jamadar* and a native trooper were killed. The fort was now invested, but the British force had to wait for their siege-guns, expected on the 24th. They arrived on the evening of that day; the next morning they were placed in position.[45]

During this action, as above related, the rebels' battery had been gallantly charged by a small body of the 14th Light Dragoons, led by Captain Gall and Cornet Giles, as well as by the 25th Bombay Native Infantry under Major Robertson. The 3 guns (brass 9-pounders of English manufacture) were captured and then turned on the enemy by the Native Infantry, who worked them, whilst our line advanced and the cavalry made their final charge. The enemy were thus driven from the outworks on all sides, pursued by the cavalry. Three standards were captured with the guns, and several acts of bravery were performed by the men of the Fourteenth, who behaved with great gallantry on this occasion. Sergeant G. Gardiner attacked, with only a few light dragoons, a party of the enemy who had fired at him from an ambush, killing several of them.

A division of 'D' troop charged a body of the rebels who threatened an attack on the baggage, when Troop Sergeant-Major Grainger

---

45. *Idem.*

displayed great resolution and courage, cutting down two of the rebel horsemen, one of whom was pressing a light dragoon very hard. In this *mêlée*. Troop Sergeant-Major Grainger received a spear-wound in the wrist, and his horse was wounded by two sabre-cuts. Most of the rebels took refuge inside the fort and town, and it was not till the 31st, at night, that the fort of Dhar was actually captured. The garrison for the most part had cleverly eluded us and made good their escape that night, quitting the fort between 9 and 10 p.m., and going to the north-west, in the direction of Mundesor. This occurred at the time the breach was entered by our men, the rebels escaping by the main gate. The outlying picquet of the 3rd Hyderabad Cavalry had a skirmish with the rearguard of the retreating enemy, but the main body had passed it and the dragoons unobserved; and although the cavalry pursued when the alarm was given, the rebels had got too far away, and only a few stragglers were captured.

It had unfortunately happened that the European picquet, which had been stationed near the spot where the garrison escaped for some days, and which knew the ground well, had been changed that morning, and when the men of the Fourteenth belonging to Captain Barrett's troop galloped up to where they heard firing going on, not knowing the ground well, several of them got hopelessly bogged in marshy ground. Moreover, the *sowar* sent by the *jamadar*[46] of the native picquet to give the alarm fell with his horse on the way, and was disabled. [47] A quantity of treasure and handsome elephant gear was found in the fort, and it was forwarded to Mhow under escort, the troops subsequently sharing in prize-money.

A large accession of troops came up for the British at this juncture in the shape of what was designated the Field Force, Hyderabad Contingent, consisting of troops of all arms sent by the *nizam*. These were placed under the command of Major Orr, and did good service now with the Malwa Field Force and subsequently with the Central India Field Force under Sir Hugh Rose's command.

These combined forces continued the march through Western Malwa in the direction of Mundesor and Neemuch, on the track of the rebels. There was nothing heard now but incessant reports of mutinies everywhere, and repeated massacres of Europeans took place. The rebels from Dhar had attacked Mehidpoor cantonment on the 8th November, and Captain Mills of the Native Cavalry fell in a charge against the

---

46. *Jamadar* or *jemadar*.
47. Lowe's *Central India*. Malleson, vol. v. and Sylvester's *Central Indian Campaign*.

mutineers made by half a troop of loyal *sowars*. The commandant, Major Timmins, with the adjutant, Lieutenant Dysart, escaped and reached the camp of the Malwa Field Force on 9th November, escorted by the loyal half-troop of Native Cavalry. On the 19th November the force crossed the Chambal River and reached Hernia.[48]

Whilst encamped on the banks of the Chambal, a parade was ordered to witness the execution of about 70 of the Mehidpoor rebels who had been taken, after a severe fight with a large body of mutineers, by Major Orr and his Hyderabad Cavalry, at the village of Rawal. A drumhead court-martial was held, and the rebels were shot. Owing to reports received of the siege of Neemuch by the rebels, the march of the Malwa Field Force was hurried on, and by the 21st November it encamped within 4 miles' distance of Mundesor.

Whilst the men were at breakfast that day, an alarm was given that the enemy meant to attack. A strong force had previously been posted by us on the heights immediately to our front, which hid the city from our view, and Major Robertson was in command of it. Seeing that we did not mean to attack them that day, the enemy were emboldened to attack us, and sallied forth in great numbers, crossing a small river in their passage, and began by attacking Major Robertson's position.

He opened his guns on them, and directed Lieutenant Dew of the 14th Light Dragoons to charge with the small body of cavalry he had: this he did most gallantly, and with a most successful result. Lieutenant Dew had only about 20 light dragoons of his outlying picquet with him, but he made a furious onslaught with these upon 300 footmen (*velaitees*),[49] and the latter were so taken aback by this sudden attack that they made a hasty retreat to the river they had previously crossed in their advance.[50] They were, however, pursued by the cavalry to its brink, and many were shot or cut down in attempting to cross. This success of the cavalry had an excellent effect on the attacking force, as the rebels all retired and left us quiet for the rest of that day.

It may fairly be said that this resolute charge of Lieutenant Dew's picquet was the main cause of the defeat of the enemy on this occasion, and contributed in no small degree to the success of Major Robertson's force in warding off from our camp the determined attack which

---

48. Lowe's *Campaign in Central India* gives an animated account of the troops crossing this river. See Malleson, vol. v.

49. *Velaitees* were matchlockmen.

50. Lieutenant Dew was well supported by some of the Hyderabad Cavalry on this occasion.

would otherwise have been made upon it. Lieutenant Dew's personal bravery was so conspicuous that he was recommended, though unsuccessfully, for the coveted distinction of the Victoria Cross, and several men of the Fourteenth were brought to notice for their gallant conduct on the same occasion.

Regimental Sergeant-Major Clark, who was severely wounded, did excellent work on the right flank, taking with him a party of skirmishers, following up the enemy and pursuing a considerable distance till they were finally driven off. Lieutenant Gowan was sent with a troop of the Fourteenth to support the skirmishers and cut off the rebels, and he reported very highly as to the admirable coolness and bravery of Private Buchanan when in presence of the enemy. It is believed 100 of the rebels were killed in this affair, and large numbers also were wounded. [51]

Next morning, 22nd November, the British force advanced, hoping to take Mundesor. The cavalry and artillery were in advance, and as we passed the large straggling town, surrounded by trees, a few shots reached our column. The rebel picquets fell in as we advanced, our long stream of baggage and native followers skirting round the town so as to reach the Neemuch road. About midday we halted in some *jowarree* fields, and the natives here told us that a large body of the rebels had left the town, but that the fort was still held by a garrison of 2000.

Shortly afterwards reports came that a body of rebels was advancing from a distance on Mundesor, and to meet these the wing of the Fourteenth under Captain Gall, together with the *nizam's* cavalry, were sent off. These crossed the river and dashed forward at a smashing pace across-country, through fields of standing grain, [52] but did not come in sight of the enemy for several miles, when they were seen making rapidly for the cover of the village of Peeplia. The Fourteenth and some of the Hyderabad Cavalry managed to get amongst the rebels' infantry, and cut up quite a hundred, pursuing them within matchlock range of the mud walls of the village, where they had a strong force under cover of the buildings; accordingly, as the cavalry had neither guns nor infantry with them, it was decided to rejoin the main body, especially as two officers and some men were already wounded, and the horses much fatigued after a long gallop.

During the retirement to camp, numbers of the enemy who had hidden themselves in trees and standing corn were killed by the cavalry. On the 23rd the force began to cross the Mundesor River, near

51 & 52. Sylvester.

which the camp lay on the preceding day, and whilst the baggage was being transported, an alarm was raised amongst the native followers. It soon appeared that the garrison of the fort had sallied forth and was advancing on our line of march. A troop of the Fourteenth was sent back across the river to endeavour to repulse this attack, which it apparently did most successfully, as the column now effected the passage of the river to the right bank, and then proceeded along the road towards Neemuch, 22 miles distant from Mundesor, for the relief of the Europeans there, who were in imminent danger, was the real object the brigadier had in view.

Soon, however, was heard a report of cannon to the right front, and an alarm was also raised from the rear that an attack was imminent on our rearguard and baggage, where Lieutenant Fenwick of the 25th Bombay Native Infantry was in charge. The guns heard to the front were from the village of Goraria, about 4 miles distant, where the rebel force which had come from Neemuch had taken up a strong position, 'their right resting on the village, their centre on a long hill, and their left well covered by fields of uncut grain, with broken ground and *nullahs* in their front, full of water and mud.'[53] To meet the attack from the Mundesor garrison on our rear a troop of the Fourteenth, with Lieutenants Leith, Redmayne, and another subaltern was immediately detached, and endeavoured to keep the enemy at bay for a time, as the rearguard had not actually been engaged, but was only threatened.

The guns of our force meanwhile opened on the enemy in front: the 14th Light Dragoons under Captain Gall were on the right, the Hyderabad Cavalry under Major Orr on the left, Hungerford's and Woolcombe's batteries formed our right centre, the Hyderabad bullock-battery the left centre, the 86th Regiment and 25th Bombay Native Infantry the centre, with the Hyderabad Infantry and Sappers on the left of the *nizam's* battery. Our guns and the fire of the infantry— especially that from the Enfields of the 86th Regiment soon weakened the fire of the enemy's field battery, which had been carefully placed near his centre, masked by date, palm, and other trees;[54] and behind it, sheltering the mutineer Mehidpoor Cavalry and rebel infantry, were some ruined huts on the edge of the village, whilst on the left of the village was a gharry road constructed in a deep cutting.

53. Malleson, vol. v.
54. Sylvester.
55. This battery opened fire at 900 yards' range, and then made a forward movement to its right to enfilade the enemy's line. Sylvester.

It was now that Lieutenant Martin placed himself at the head of 19 troopers of the Fourteenth, who were escort to Woolcombe's battery,[55] and with these gallant fellows charged across the deep cutting into the midst of the rebels' guns and actually took them, but so hot was the musketry-fire from the infantry posted in the huts in rear of the battery that the party had to retire, Lieutenant Martin being himself severely wounded. Captain Gall with a squadron of the Fourteenth, composed of 'B' and 'D' troops, quickly came to the rescue, making a gallant and most successful charge, and captured the battery of 5 guns. He cut down the gunners, and then pursued and cut up 200 of the rebel infantry. Not long after this the enemy retired, though slowly, still clinging tenaciously to the village of Goraria, which they continued to occupy when night fell.

Malleson states that the British loss was considerable on this occasion, amounting to not less than 60 killed and wounded. The enemy lost on a much larger scale, especially in the outskirts and in the surrounding country, for our cavalry pursued round the village in every direction and cut up hundreds of them.

Captain Gall went to the right with the Fourteenth, Major Orr with the Hyderabad Cavalry went to the left. They found a large quantity of loot and plunder on the rebels, which the latter had brought from Neemuch, where they had raised the siege and were hoping to rescue Ferozshah and the garrison of Mundesor, when they were thus so opportunely caught and defeated at the right moment by our column at Goraria.

To return now to the movements that had been going on in rear of the column whilst this fight had been carried on in front. A party of infantry, some Hyderabad Cavalry under Captains Abbott and Murray, as well as 2 guns, had been sent back to the rearguard to reinforce the troops of the Fourteenth under Lieutenant Leith already there. The baggage and rearguard had been attacked by a large force, about 2000, from the Mundesor garrison. Our guns immediately opened fire on the rebels, the cavalry charged—both the Fourteenth and the Hyderabad Horse—and drove them back, pursuing and sabring a large number.

The pursuit was continued up to a point where a small pond of water and some shallow pits or stone quarries joined: here the enemy drew on our cavalry into broken ground, and Lieutenant Redmayne, who was leading in front, followed by a few men, wheeled round

56. Sylvester.

70

the pond, and was shot down in a tremendous volley fired by some men hidden in the gravel quarries.[56] Poor Redmayne met a soldier's death. His body was mercilessly cut up by the rebels, his charger and accoutrements instantly carried off, and several of his men belonging to the Fourteenth were wounded at the same time. [57] Private O'Neill behaved most gallantly in this affair, and was shot through the chest by a jingal-ball of great size; he lived and recovered from his wound. At this critical juncture Captain Abbott luckily arrived by a different route, on the other side of the water and gravel pits, which caused the enemy to retire within the fort.

During the night our cavalry surrounded Goraria, and the remainder of the force encamped, the enemy keeping up a continuous matchlock fire even after darkness set in.

On the morning of the 24th our heavy guns were brought to bear on the village, and at last, about noon, some 200 of the rebels, the *velaitees*, came out under a flag of truce and surrendered themselves prisoners. Those that still remained inside Goraria were the brave Rohillas, and they stuck to the last brick in the place. [58] At about 4 p.m. the 86th Regiment and the 25th Bombay Native Infantry stormed the village at the point of the bayonet, when those who rushed out of the houses were cut down by the cavalry, and several hand-to-hand fights took place in the sugar-cane plantations outside. [59] The village was set on fire, and the Madras Sappers and Miners fought nobly with the rebels amongst the fire and smoke.

On the morning of the 25th November not a living man remained in Goraria. Neemuch was now successfully relieved, and Captain Mayne was able to ride in safely, returning there with an escort of loyal *sowars*.

Malleson says:—

The stern defence of the Rohillas did service to their cause. Whilst the British force was dealing with them, the *sháhzáda* and his 2000 Afghans and Mekranis, as panic-stricken as they had been bold, evacuated Mundesor and retreated on Nangarh, whither the cavalry, worn out by four days of unremitting exertion, was unable to pursue them. They [the rebels] fled through the country, endeavouring to seek refuge in the jungles.'

---

57. The charger was subsequently recovered at the capture of Rathgur Fort, 28th January 1858, by Sir Hugh Rose, who bought the charger.
58. Malleson, vol. v.
59. Sylvester.

Some of these were afterwards killed by loyal natives at Partab-gharh, in Rajputana, and the remnant escaped across the Chambal River towards the east. Mundesor having thus fallen into our hands, the fort was subsequently dismantled and the guns destroyed. Thus our troops had been most successfully engaged in the western district of Malwa; Dhar, Neemuch, and Mundesor were cleared of rebels, and the Malwa Field Force had finished its appointed work. The column was henceforth to be designated the 1st Brigade of the Nerbudda Field Force under the same brigadier, Colonel C. S. Stuart, Bombay army, and still accompanied by the Officiating Agent to the Governor-General, Lieutenant-Colonel Durand.

The march of this brigade was accordingly continued to Indore, passing through Mehidpoor on the banks of the Sipra in Western Malwa, and itself the scene of a recent mutiny, where Major Timmins had been defeated by the mutinous troops and several European officers and sergeants murdered, the whole native garrison, with few exceptions, going over to the rebels. After passing through Oujain, [60] another town on the Sipra, Indore, Holkar's capital, was reached about 14th December.

Here Holkar's disaffected regular cavalry were disarmed in the presence of Lieutenant-Colonel Durand and the Nerbudda Field Force, the disarmed soldiers being placed under the care of the Sikh cavalry of the late Bhopal contingent. One thousand six hundred men of Holkar's infantry were also disarmed the same evening by the Maharajah's chief minister at the request of Lieutenant-Colonel Durand. On the following day, 15th December, Sir Robert Hamilton, Agent to the Governor-General, arrived and relieved Lieutenant-Colonel Durand, and at the same time the 1st Brigade occupied the cantonments.

Major-General Sir Hugh Rose, K.C.B.,[61] having on 17th December assumed command of the forces in Central India, they were designated the Central India Field Force and the Hyderabad Contingent Field Force, the former consisting of the two brigades of the late Nerbudda Field Force, under the same brigadiers, [62] and Major Orr

---

60. Or Ujjain.

61. Sir Hugh Rose marched from Poona to Mhow in company with C G' troop of the Fourteenth under Captain W. McMahon, who brought up some horses left there sick by other portions of the regiment when they started on service.

62. Colonel C. S. Stuart, 1st Brigade, and Colonel Charles Steuart (14th Light Dragoons), 2nd Brigade.

being commandant of the *nizam's* contingent. Sir Hugh, shortly after assuming command, ordered the 1st Brigade from Indore to Mhow, where it remained till 30th December.

Sylvester says:

> Long after these events the despatches appeared in which Lieutenant Martin's gallantry was noticed, and he well deserved it. Brigadier Stuart was made a Companion of the Bath, Lieutenant-Colonel Durand became colonel, and Captains Gall, Robertson, Woolcombe, and Hungerford, received the rank of brevet-major for their services.

This brings to an end the campaign of 1857, in which the left wing of the Fourteenth under Major Gall played such a prominent part whilst with the Deccan Field Force, and afterwards in the 1st Brigade of the Malwa and Nerbudda Field Forces, commanded by Brigadier C. S. Stuart of the Bombay army.

The right wing of the Fourteenth had meanwhile marched from Aurungabad and the Deccan under Major Scudamore, on 31st October, in order to reach Sehore, a town in the Bhopal state, Central India, where a mutiny had broken out amongst the Bhopal contingent. They marched by way of Asseerghur and Hoosingabad, Lieutenant Travers acting as staff officer. The town at Sehore is a large one, and is situated 22 miles to the west of Bhopal. After a long march Scudamore's wing reached Sehore the 23rd November, and formed part of the 2nd Brigade of the Nerbudda Field Force under Brigadier Charles Steuart. On the 17th December this wing became a part of the 2nd Brigade, Central India Field Force, commanded by Major-General Sir Hugh Rose, K.C.B., as already related.

Active preparations for the coming campaign in Central India were carried on during the remaining few days of 1857, both at Mhow and Sehore: the siege-train was hurried on to completion, and the transport improved, while camels in abundance were easily procured in the surrounding districts of Malwa and Rajputana.

The small portion of the Fourteenth, representing the depot or headquarters of the service troops, remained at Kirkee till the end of the year, under command of Colonel C. P. Ainslie, and on 29th November sent some detachments from Kirkee to Sattara in the southern part of the Bombay Presidency, where they were required for temporary duty. During 1857 the depot troop in England remained under the commandant of the Maidstone Cavalry Depot, Colonel C.

M. Balders.

The establishment of the Fourteenth had been augmented in June from 9 to 10 troops, and consisted of—

59 Sergeants.	40 Corporals.
14 Trumpeters.	626 Privates.
10 Farriers.	703 Troop-horses.

1858

This proved a very memorable and eventful year in the history of the Fourteenth, owing to a succession of most brilliant services performed by them in Central India, Gwalior, Bundelcund, and the North-west Provinces, during the suppression of the Indian Mutiny. 'The Fighting Fourteenth,' a *sobriquet* gained nearly fifty years earlier in the Peninsular campaign, was most amply justified in this campaign by the successors of the men who gained it; and these by their gallantry and valour, displayed in many an action, siege, and pursuit in which they took part, during these operations conducted against the rebels, have added to the long list of honourable distinctions already earned by the regiment yet another name—that of 'Central India.' [63] During the whole year of 1858 and for several months in 1859 the Fourteenth were continuously in the field, either in brigade or movable column, hunting up the rebels, and most of these services were performed under the command of those two able leaders, Major-General Sir Hugh Rose, K.C.B., [64] and Major-General Sir Robert C. Napier, K.C.B. [65] Central India

The Central India Field Force consisted of 2 brigades, as follows:—

At Mhow, 1st Brigade, commanded by Colonel C. S. Stuart, Bombay Army, as Brigadier, consisting of—

Left wing, 14th Light Dragoons under Major Gall.
1 Troop 3rd Bombay Light Cavalry.
2 Regiments of cavalry, Hyderabad Contingent.
2 Companies 86th Regiment (Royal County Down).[66]
25th Regiment Bombay Native Infantry.

---

63. 'Central India' is borne on the appointments of three other cavalry regiments, *viz*. 8th Hussars, 12th Lancers, and 17th Lancers.
64. Afterwards Field-Marshal Lord Strathnairn, G.C.B., G.C.S.I.
65. Afterwards Field-Marshal Lord Napier of Magdala, G.C.B., G.C.I.E.
66. The remainder of the 86th Regiment joined this brigade later, on 16th March, the day before the attack and capture of Chanderi.

1 Regiment of infantry, Hyderabad Contingent.
3 Light Field Batteries—1 Royal Artillery.
1 Bombay Artillery.
1 Hyderabad Contingent.
Detachment of sappers.

At Sehore, 2nd Brigade, commanded by Colonel C. Steuart, 14th Light Dragoons, as Brigadier, consisting of—

Right wing and headquarters 14th Light Dragoons,
> under Major Scudamore.
Headquarters 3rd Bombay Light Cavalry,
1 Regiment of cavalry, Hyderabad Contingent.
3rd Bombay European Regiment.[67]
24th Bombay Native Infantry,
1 Regiment of infantry, Hyderabad Contingent,
1 Battery Horse Artillery,
1 Light Field Battery,
1 Battery Bhopal Artillery,
1 Company Madras Sappers.
Detachment of Bombay Sappers.
Siege-train, with guns worked in action by drafts from
> field batteries.

The recent hard work and privations to which most of these troops had been exposed during their services in the Malwa and Nerbudda campaigns necessitated some repose before starting on a fresh campaign. We have recounted what they did at Aurungabad, Boldana (in Berar), Dhar, Mundesor, Goraria, and Mehidpoor; it now remains to record their gallant deeds in Central India.

Malleson bears ample testimony to the good services of the Fourteenth, and particularly of that gallant officer, Major R. H. Gall, afterwards Major-General Gall, C.B., who commanded the left wing of the regiment at this period. [68] He says, when referring to the Malwa campaign and operations carried on towards the close of the year 1857:—

Many officers distinguished themselves in this campaign. One

---

67. Now the 2nd Battalion of the Prince of Wales's Leinster Regiment (Royal Canadians), late 109th Regiment.
68. *History of the Indian Mutiny*, by Kaye and Malleson (Longmans, Green, and Co., 1898), from which work many quotations have been made in these records. See vol. v.

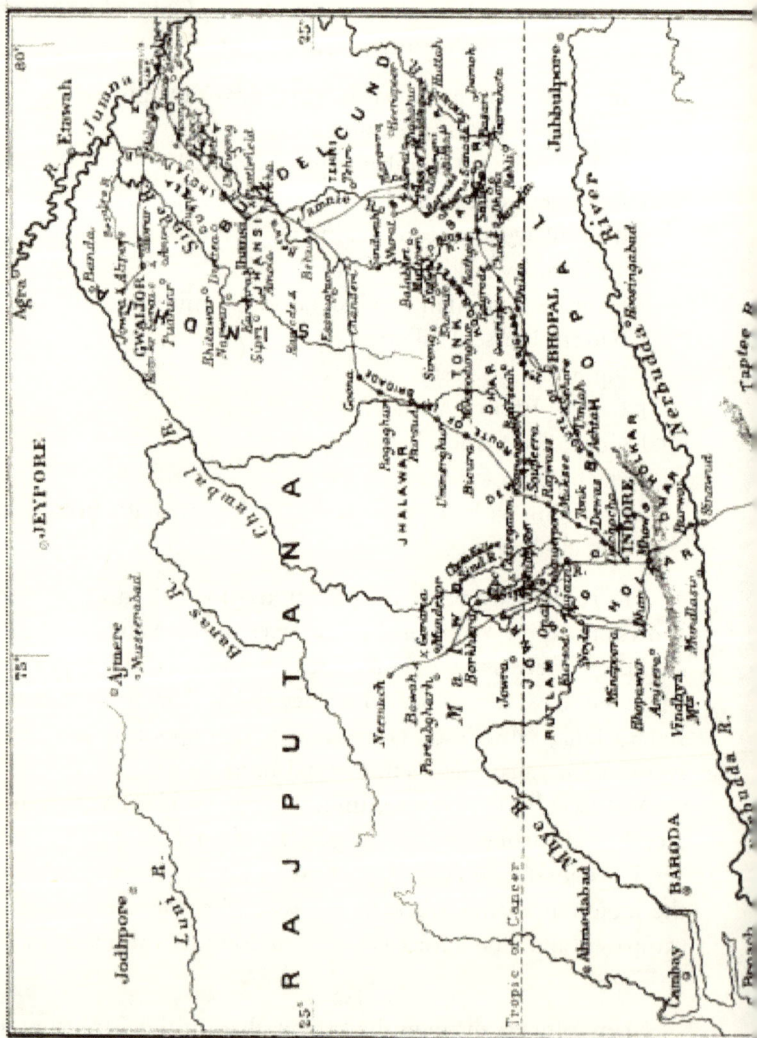

CENTRAL INDIA

Scale of English Miles.

London: Longmans, Green & Co.

Stanford's Geogical Estab. London

of these, who for his daring, his gallantry, and his brain power, was especially noticed by Colonel Durand, requires mention here. "Much of the success in quelling this insurrection," wrote Durand[69] to Lord Canning at the end of November 1857, "is due to the judicious daring, the thorough gallantry with which, whenever opportunity offered, Major Gall, his officers and men, sought close conflict with the enemy—a bold one, who often fought most desperately. I feel it a duty to Major Gall and Her Majesty's 14th Light Dragoons, men and officers, thus especially to beg your lordship's influence in favour of officers and men who have merited, by conspicuous valour, everything that Her Majesty's Government may be pleased to confer. They deserve most highly."

After a rest of three weeks at Mhow and Indore, Major-General Sir Hugh Rose, K.C.B., took the field with the Central India Field Force and the Hyderabad Contingent Field Force. He left Mhow on 6th January escorted by a troop of the Fourteenth and some Hyderabad Contingent Artillery, and accompanied by the Agent to the Governor-General at Indore, Sir Robert Hamilton, who was the political officer for the whole of Central India. On arriving at Sehore on 8th January, the Major-General found there the 2nd Brigade of the Central India Field Force, under command of Brigadier Charles Steuart, C.B., 14th Light Dragoons, in which was the right wing of the Fourteenth under command of Major Scudamore. Brigadier Steuart had just been awarded the Companionship of the Order of the Bath for his services in Persia in 1857.

On 15th January, Lieutenants Leith and Dew with 'E' troop of the 14th Light Dragoons arrived at Sehore from Mhow, escorting the much-needed siege-train for the 2nd Brigade. Sir Hugh Rose on arrival at Sehore lost no time in bringing the mutineers of the Bhopal contingent to punishment. There were about 150 of them, who were put to death after having been found guilty by a drumhead court-martial. They were all shot. Stent, in his *Scraps from my Sabretache*, relates how that the number to be shot was 149, but that after the execution 150 bodies were counted, and he accounts for it by saying that 'a brother of one of the prisoners came to see the last of him, and in the *mêlée* must have shared his brother's fate, whether by accident, or purposely, no one knew.' It is said by the same authority, that as the

69. Colonel Henry Marion Durand, R.E., Officiating Agent to the Governor-General for Central India.

rebels knew our words of command perfectly, when the word 'Fire!' was given many threw themselves down uninjured on the ground, the shots passing harmlessly over them, and these had to be afterwards despatched by men placed near for the purpose with muskets and carbines.

The 2nd Brigade and the Hyderabad troops left Sehore on 16th January. They had been reinforced by 800 men of Bhopal levies, contributed by the loyal *begum* of that principality, and all marched for the relief of Saugor, where the garrison was besieged by rebels; but Rathgur had first to be reduced.

Malleson says:—

The 1st Brigade left Mhow on the 10th January, and then marched in a line parallel with the 2nd Brigade upon Chanderi, a very famous fortress in the territories of Sindhia.'

The operations of the 1st Brigade will be referred to further on. We will now follow the fortunes of the 2nd Brigade, with regard to which Malleson[70] writes:—

Rathgur,[71] distant only 25 miles from Saugor, is situated on the spur of a long high hill and commands the country surrounding it. Near its base runs a deep and rapid river, the Bina. Altogether it was a most formidable position. Sir Hugh Rose arrived before this place on the morning of the 24th January. He at once, with small loss, drove the enemy from the outside positions they had occupied in the town and on the banks of the river, and then completely invested the place. Fronting the eastern face he posted the Bhopal levies, facing the northern the 3rd Bombay Light Cavalry and the Hyderabad Contingent Cavalry. With the remainder of the force he occupied the plain across which runs the road to Saugor. He then reconnoitred the ground preparatory to selecting sites for his breaching batteries.

Early on the morning of the 26th Sir Hugh Rose made a move forward. Crossing the Saugor road with the 3rd Europeans, followed by the 18-pounders, howitzers and mortars, and the guns of the Hyderabad Contingent, he entered the jungle. But no sooner had these troops reached a point well within its thick covering than the enemy, who had been working near, fired the

---

70. Vol. v.
71. Or Ratghur.

jungle-grass on all sides. For a few moments the position was perilous, but Sir Hugh, turning back beyond the range of the flames, sent his sappers to cut a road for the guns up the height to the north of the town. This operation and the bringing up of the guns occupied the greater part of the day. Meanwhile the remainder of the force had occupied the town of Rathgur, and driven the enemy within the fort.

During the 26th, 27th, and 28th, Sir Hugh besieged the fort with his mortar battery and other artillery, whilst the 3rd Europeans employed their Enfield rifles to suppress the matchlock fire of the enemy. By 10 p.m. on 28th, a large breach had been made in the fort. That same night, as related by Malleson:—[72]

> The Rajah of Banpur advanced on the rear of the besieging force with a considerable body of revolted *sepoys* and other levies. He came on with great boldness, his standards flying and his men singing their national hymns. Instead of ceasing his fire against the fort Sir Hugh Rose redoubled it, but at the same time detached a small force, consisting of a detachment of the 14th Light Dragoons, the 3rd Bombay Light Cavalry, the Horse Artillery, and the 5th Hyderabad Infantry, to deal with the Rajah of Banpur and his followers. They did not wait to be charged, but throwing away their arms and ammunition, made off with such celerity that, though hotly pursued, a few only were cut up.'

After this relieving party of the rebels had been driven off those within the fort apparently lost heart. The garrison was said to number from 500 to 600 men—*Velaitees,* Mekranies, and Bundeelas, all fighting-men from their boyhood; but they silently evacuated the fort during the night. When Sir Hugh discovered the precipitate flight of the garrison he gave orders for a pursuit, but the rebels had gone too far, and no great results came of it. About noon on the 30th January information came that 'the Rajah of Banpur, reinforced by the garrison, had taken up a position near the village of Barodia, about 15 miles distant.' [73]

Sir Hugh, with a considerable portion of his of the force of all arms, including the greater part of his cavalry (3 troops Fourteenth and a squadron of Bombay Cavalry), went in pursuit.

---

72. Vol. v.

73. Malleson, vol. v.

About four o'clock in the afternoon he came upon them posted on the banks of the Biná, and prepared to dispute his passage. Sir Hugh at once attacked, and, though the rebels fought well, he forced the passage of the river. The country on the other side was thick and bushy, and the rebels took every advantage of it. From the river to Barodia, Sir Hugh had to fight his way step by step. He did not do this without loss.[74]

Captain Neville, R.E., [75] was killed, and numerous other casualties of officers and men occurred in killed and wounded. The *rajah* himself escaped, but his followers were completely defeated, and the column returned to Rathgur about 2 o'clock on the morning of the 31st January. Malleson remarks:—

The fall of Rathgur had effected two most important objects. It had cleared the country south of Saugor of rebels, had re-opened the road to Indore, and had made it possible for the general to march to the relief of Saugor, now beleaguered for nearly eight months.[76]

Amongst the rebel chiefs who fell into the hands of the British at the capture of Rathgur was Mahomed Fazil Khan, one of the Delhi Royal Family. He was captured, when hiding, by a native servant in the employment of Captain Need, 14th Light Dragoons. This fortunate native servant obtained a handsome pecuniary reward which had been set on Mahomed Fazil Khan's head by the government, and the luckless chieftain was doomed to be hanged over the gate of the fort, where his body was seen suspended by the side of Khamdar Khan, a former adherent of the British in Kolara, who had recently thrown in his lot with the mutineers.

The charger of Lieutenant Redmayne, 14th Light Dragoons, who fell in action at Mundesor on 23rd November 1857, was recovered here when the British captured the fort. The animal had received a severe shell-wound over the eye, and was purchased by Sir Hugh Rose. The Shahzadah of Mundesor took possession of it when Lieutenant Redmayne fell, and had brought it to Rathgur, but he abandoned it in his flight.

Our cavalry pursued the fugitive garrison from Rathgur, and suc-

---

74. Malleson, vol. v.
75. This officer had only just joined the force. He had served with distinction in the Crimean campaign.
76. Malleson has 'Sagár,' 'Indur,' 'Rátgarh' or 'Ráhatgarh.'

ceeded in cutting up several chieftains as well as about 70 rebels, and nearly 100 followers were taken prisoners. [77]

The standards taken here, as at Mundesor, were marked with the crescent and bloody hand. Before leaving Rathgur the fortifications and defences were laid waste by the Engineers, and Sir Hugh Rose led his troops in triumph to Saugor.[78]

The 31st Native Infantry had remained loyal, so the houses and property in the cantonments of Saugor were intact. Stent remarks:—

As we passed under the walls of the fort we were greeted by the ladies, who thronged the battlements, with the waving of hands and handkerchiefs (I will not be positive that they did not even cheer us), and we were proud to think that our timely arrival had saved them from the clutches of the rebels. Saugor had been from six to seven months beleaguered, and the poor creatures shut up there had heard with intense delight the pounding of our guns at Rathgur, which is only 22 miles distant.[79]

The relief of Saugor took place on the 3rd of February, and the column rested there several days. On the 8th a small force was sent under command of Captain Hare, Hyderabad Contingent, to destroy the fort of Sanoda. On the 9th, Sir Hugh Rose marched with his troops towards the fort of Garrakota, [80] standing on an elevated plateau 25 miles east of Saugor, with the wide river Sonar flowing past it. According to Malleson the fortifications were strong. He says:—

It was held by the revolted *sipahis* (*sepoys*) of the 51st and 52nd Native Infantry and other rebels, well supplied with ammunition.[81]

'G' troop of the Fourteenth, under command of Captain William McMahon, together with 2 companies of the 24th Bombay Native Infantry, was left for the time in Saugor to protect the station when the remainder of the Central India Field Force marched on Garrakota.

Sir Hugh Rose with his force arrived in sight of Garrakota on the afternoon of the 11th, and made a thorough reconnaissance of the

77. Sylvester.
78. Sylvester.
79. *Scraps from my Sabretache.*
80. Garhakota (Malleson).
81. Vol. v.

place. He drove in the rebels from the village of Basari, [82] where they occupied a position, and next day commenced his attack. A steady fire from our guns and mortars was kept up all day: this silenced the enemy's guns, but under cover of darkness the garrison slipped away by the Paunch Ghat towards Dumoh and made good their escape, as, owing to the smallness of our besieging force, it was unable to guard this part of the fort.

As soon as the flight of the garrison was reported, early on the morning of the 13th, Captain Hare with the Hyderabad Cavalry, 2 Horse Artillery guns under Lieutenant Crowe, and 2 troops Fourteenth under Captain R. J. Brown and Captain Arthur Need, followed in pursuit. They came up with the rebels at the Bias [83] River, a tributary of the Sonar, near the village of Bias. The cavalry and guns crossed the river, and the latter opened fire, then the cavalry charged and pursued for a considerable distance. Captain Need highly distinguished himself by his bravery and swordsmanship. The cavalry slew nearly 100 men, and of these Captain Need himself killed 5. [84]

The 2 troops of the Fourteenth engaged were 'A' and 'K' troops, the captains of which were Need and Brown, with Lieutenants Leith and Dew. In Captain Hare's report of the affair he speaks of Captain Need, 14th Light Dragoons, as 'a good and dashing cavalry officer,' and he specially mentions in terms of the highest praise the gallant conduct of Captain Need and his troop, adding, 'Captain Need pursued with his gallant troop until dark.' Sir Hugh Rose recommended Captain Need to the favourable consideration of His Excellency the Commander-in-Chief in India for his services on this occasion.

A large quantity of supplies fell into our hands at Garrakota, as the place was well stored with provisions of grain, flour, etc. There was also a collection of all sorts of loot, evidently derived from English sources, and plundered by the natives from the houses of the English. Sir Hugh had a portion of the fortress destroyed under direction of Major Boileau and the Madras sappers and miners, and then marched back to Saugor, arriving there 15th February. Captain McMahon's troop of the 14th Light Dragoons then rejoined the right wing of the regiment under Major Scudamore.

Malleson [85] says:—

---

82. Or Bassaree.
83. Or Beas.
84. See Appendix B.
85. Vol. v.

Jhansi, 125 miles distant to the north, was the next point to be aimed at. But between Saugor and Jhansi lay the passes of Malthone and Muddenpore, the forts of Surahi and of Maraura, the towns of Shahgarh and Banpur.[86] After overcoming the obstacles which these places would probably offer, Sir Hugh would have, before marching on Jhansi, to effect a junction with his 1st Brigade under Brigadier Stuart. He could scarcely move from Saugor until he should hear that Brigadier Whitlock's column had started from Jubbulpore[87] for that place. Meanwhile he would have time to repair damages and to store supplies.

At length news came that Whitlock had left Jubbulpore. Sir Hugh's preparations were now as complete as they could be made.'

He had, according to Malleson, caused to be collected large supplies of sheep, goats, oxen, grain, flour, tea, soda-water, an additional supply of elephants, and summer clothing for his European soldiers. In addition he had transferred the sick and wounded to the Saugor Field Hospital, and re-supplied the siege-train with ammunition, strengthening it by the addition of heavy guns, howitzers, and large mortars from the Saugor arsenal. On the 26th February a start was made; on the 27th the fort of Barodia was shelled and taken.

On 3rd March the pass of Malthone was sighted, but it was resolved to force the pass of Muddenpore, making simultaneously a feint on Malthone Pass, which was fortified and held in force by the rebels. For this purpose Major Scudamore, with a squadron of the Fourteenth, some guns, some native infantry and other details was detached, whilst with the main body of his force Sir Hugh moved rapidly on the pass of Muddenpore. He soon came under the fire of the defenders, supposed to number 9000 men, chiefly composed of Bundeelas and Velaitees, as well as some Bengal Sepoys.[88]

For a time the British advance was checked and the fire was so heavy that their guns had to be retired some distance, and Sir Hugh's horse was shot under him.

Later on the superior tactics of the British prevailed, and a deter-

---

86. 'Maraura lies 37 miles north of Sagar, and 22 west by north of Shahgarh. Shahgarh lies 40 miles north-east of Sagar. Banpur is in the Lalitpur district' (Malleson).
87. Jabalpur (Malleson).
88. Sylvester.

mined bayonet charge by the 3rd Europeans,[89] aided by the Hyderabad Infantry, completely carried the day. The enemy fled in disorder into the town, but our howitzers drove them out of that, and they fled to the jungles pursued by the cavalry, amongst which were 3 troops of the Fourteenth, who drove them up to the fort of Saralic. Major Scudamore received the thanks of the Major-General for the able and successful manner in which he had conducted the feint on Malthone.

Malleson writes:—[90]

The effect of this victory was very great. It so daunted the rebels that they evacuated without a blow the formidable pass of Malthone, the fort of Narhat to the rear of it, the little fort of Sarahi, the strong fort of Maraura, the fortified castle of Banpur (the residence of the rebel *rajah* called after it), and the almost impregnable fortress of Tal-Bahat on the heights above the lake of that name. They abandoned also the line of the Bind and the Betwa, with the exception of the fortress of Chanderi, on the left bank of the latter river.

It will now be necessary to return for a time to the operations of the 1st Brigade, Central India Field Force, which we left at Mhow in January of this year, under command of Brigadier Stuart, Bombay Army, and in which Major Gall with the left wing of the Fourteenth was serving. Stuart left Mhow on the 10th January, and marched along the Agra Trunk road as far as Goona. About 70 miles to the east of Goona are situated the fort and important town of Chanderi. The former is situated on a lofty hill, and during the month of February 1858 numbers of the rebel *sepoys* already defeated by the 2nd Brigade of the Central India Field Force, as above related, flocked thither for refuge, and with a firm determination to make a last stand there against the British troops.

On the 5th of March, Stuart arrived in the vicinity of Chanderi, and the men encamped near a small village 6 miles short of the town, in order to give time for a thorough reconnaissance of the position. A party of the 14th Light Dragoons and Irregular Horse,[91] accompanied by Major Gall of the Fourteenth, Captain Fenwick, R.E., Major Keatinge[92] of the Bombay Artillery, the political agent, and Assistant-

89. Now the 2nd Battalion Leinster Regiment.
90. Vol. v.
91. Sylvester.
92. Afterwards General Keatinge, V.C.

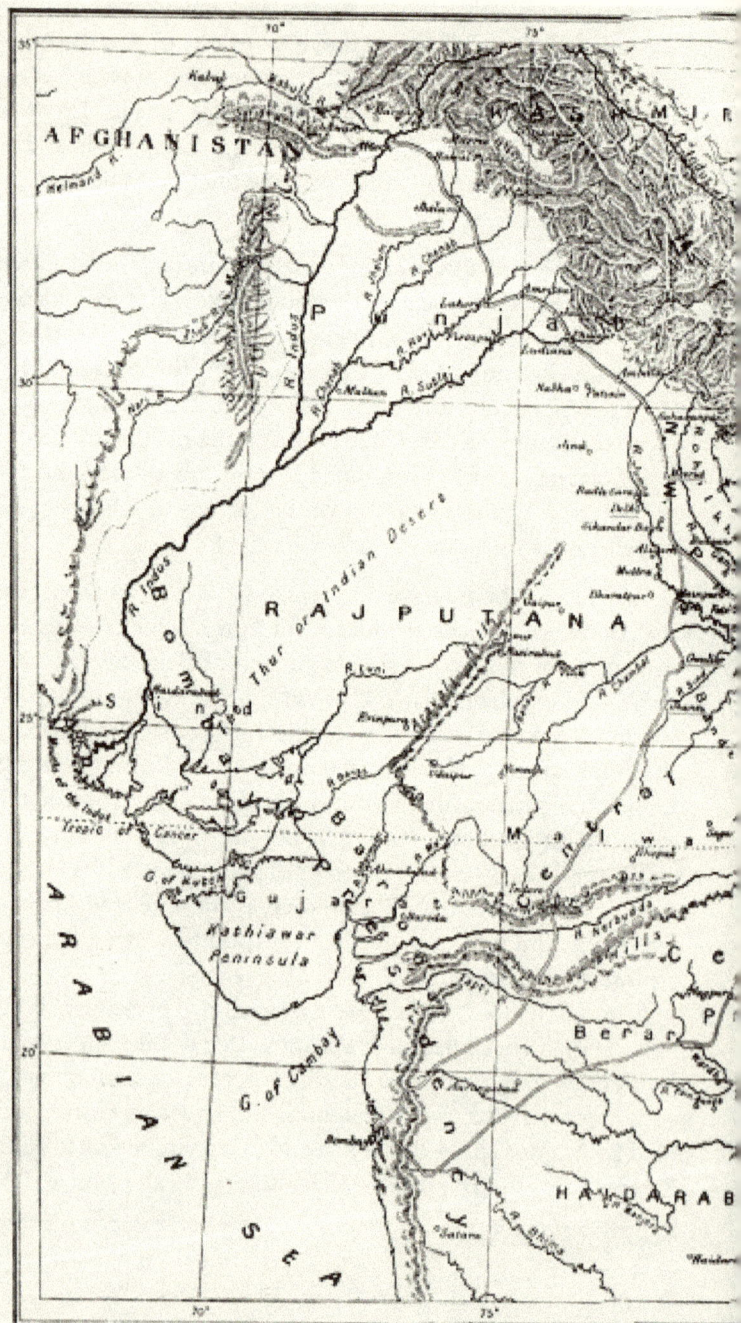

AFGHANISTAN

KASHMIR

Kabul

R. Helmand

R. Indus

R. Jhelum

R. Chenab

R. Ravi

R. Sutlej

Multan

Amritsar

Lahore

Ludhiana

Nalka Yatrain

Amd.

Delhi

Mathra

Bharatpur

Thar or Indian Desert

R A J P U T A N A

R. Luni

Brinpura

Udaipur

R. Banas

R. Chambal

R. Indus

Haidarabad

od

S i n d

Tropic of Cancer

Mouths of the Indus

G. of Kutch

Kathiawar
Peninsula

G u j a r a t

G. of Cambay

Bombay

Satara

R. Narbuda

M a l w a

Hills

Berar

HAIDARABAD

R. Bhima

A R A B I A N   S E A

NORTHERN INDIA
THE MUTINY 1857-9.

English Miles

REFERENCE

The principal centres of the Mutiny are underlined thus, *Benares*

Railways are shown thus,

The line from Calcutta to Ranigonj was open in 1857,

that from Allahabad to Cawnpore in 1858.

The Grand Trunk Road is shown thus,

Other Main Roads are

Surgeon J. H. Sylvester,[93] attached to the 14th (King's) Light Dragoons, were sent forward through the dense jungle to reconnoitre. After proceeding a considerable distance the party was fired upon by a volley of musketry, and as it would have been the height of folly to proceed further, the presence of the enemy having been ascertained, the party returned to camp.

Next day, 6th March, with a strong advance-guard under Major Robertson, Bombay Army, we advanced on this once famous place. It is said that Chanderi[94] was very important in the prosperous days of the Moghul Empire. Malleson says there was a proverb in the time of Akbar, '*If you want to see a town whose houses are palaces, visit Chanderi.*' It has been described as being in those days a city possessing 14,000 houses built of stone, 384 markets, 360 *caravansaries*, and 12,000 mosques. The oppression of the Mahrattas subsequently brought it to a very different state, added to which its manufactures had suffered from competition with Manchester. Although its former splendour had departed, much that was picturesque remained at the time it fell into our hands.

There was a good deal of fighting outside the fort on the 6th as our advance-guard moved forward. The infantry advanced in skirmishing order, 2 companies 86th Regiment and 25th Bombay Native Infantry, whilst the artillery opened with round-shot and shell, driving the rebels from the outlying ruins and summer-houses, out of which they had been firing upon us as we passed through an intervening gorge. The enemy then took shelter behind a loop-holed wall, which defended the fort and town at the point where we advanced to the attack. After a while this position was taken by our men, and the enemy retired within the town and fort, half a mile distant. Our brigade subsequently encamped on one of the hills which commanded the fort on the west side.

For the next few days our men were employed in clearing out the surrounding villages, in reconnoitring, and in placing guns in favourable positions. The cavalry were kept busy reconnoitring, but the ground was not suitable for horsemen to act in. The 24-pounder guns were dragged up by elephants on the 10th March, and by the 13th of that month the breaching batteries commenced to fire. On the next

93. Mr. Sylvester was in medical charge of the left wing of the Fourteenth throughout this campaign. He belonged to the Indian Medical Service, and served later in Beatson's Horse and Mayne's Horse (and Regiment).
94. Chanderi is in the Gwalior State.

day a breach was effected, and on the 17th the fort was stormed by the men of the 86th Regiment (now the 2nd Battalion Royal Irish Rifles, formerly the County Down Regiment), who had been augmented by the arrival of their other wing the day before, as well as the 25th Bombay Native Infantry.

The assault was eminently successful: the rebels for the most part hurled themselves over the parapets and made a hasty retreat. Our cavalry was not numerous enough to prevent the escape of the garrison, as the fort and town were so extensive and of such great size. A magazine exploded during the capture, by which several men of the 86th Regiment were killed and others badly injured and burned.

Most of the enemy effected their escape through the town; any that remained were shot down or bayoneted. The 3 troops of the Fourteenth which were present under Major Gall had been chiefly employed in patrolling and reconnoitring, but the country at Chanderi was not in any way suitable for the action of cavalry. On the night before the assault Lieutenant Gowan with 'C' troop of the Fourteenth was posted in a selected position, and at the signal for the assault at daybreak on the morning of the 17th, made a very successful feint by firing some rounds of blank ammunition so as to draw away the attention of the garrison from the real point of attack.

This duty was most satisfactorily carried out, and Lieutenant Gowan and his troop received the thanks of the brigadier for its complete success. The fort of Chanderi alone was 4 miles in circumference, and occupied a very commanding situation, with a fine view over the surrounding country. All the guns as well as stores of grain and salt fell into our hands, but nothing of value, and only about 100 of the rebels were killed.[95] The British loss was 29, including 2 officers.

On the 15th, Lieutenant Dowker and 30 *sowars* of the Hyderabad Contingent Cavalry had arrived with despatches for the brigadier from Major-General Sir Hugh Rose, who was anxiously looking for our junction with him and the 2nd Brigade in front of Jhansi.

As it was the 17th March, the bands all played 'St. Patrick's Day' whilst the troops marched through the now deserted town to their camp, and of course the men of the 86th (Royal County Down) Regiment were the heroes of the hour. As soon as the fort had been dismantled the 1st Brigade moved away to join Sir Hugh Rose in the vicinity of Jhansi.

On 19th March the left wing of the Fourteenth was ordered from

---

95. Sylvester.

Chanderi to Jhansi to join the right wing and headquarters of the regiment, which were with the 2nd Brigade, and had arrived there on the 20th inst. Accordingly Major Gall made all haste, and by forced marches his 3 troops covered 70 miles in 2 days, arriving in front of Jhansi on the 21st March, in good time to take part with the rest of the regiment in the investment and ultimate capture of that important city and fortress.

According to Malleson, both Lord Canning, the Governor-General of India, and Lord Elphinstone, the Governor of Bombay, attached the very greatest importance to the fall of Jhansi. Jhansi was regarded as the stronghold of rebel power in Central India, the main strength of the formidable rebel force on the Jumna. Here, too, English men and women about 9 months earlier had been slaughtered under circumstances of peculiar atrocity.

It was on the 20th March that Brigadier Steuart with the cavalry and artillery of the 2nd Brigade of the Central India Field Force had arrived and invested Jhansi. With this brigade were 5 troops of the Fourteenth, being the right wing of the regiment, under Major Scudamore's command, numbering 325 rank and file; and it was on the following day that the other 3 troops of the regiment, composing the left wing, under Major Gall, numbering about 200 rank and file, also arrived.

On the 22nd March the city and fortress were completely invested by our cavalry.[96] When Sir Hugh Rose arrived in front of Jhansi with the 2nd Brigade, the latter was halted for a time in the plains at some distance from the town, and the Major-General with his staff and escort proceeded to reconnoitre the position thoroughly. This was not done without attracting the fire of the enemy's batteries from all sides. Malleson[97] says:—

It was at 9 a.m. on 21st March when Sir Hugh Rose arrived at Jhansi, and he did not finish his reconnaissance of the place till 6 p.m., so completely did he do the work. The city was walled in; the fortress, standing on a high granite rock, was due north of the city, overlooking it. The fortress commands the city and surrounding country; it is built of excellent and most massive masonry; it is difficult to breach because, composed of granite, its walls vary in thickness from sixteen to twenty feet. It has extensive and elaborate outworks of the same solid construction,

96. See Appendix B.
97. Vol. v.

with front and flanking embrasures for artillery-fire, and loop-holes, of which in some places there were five tiers, for musketry. Guns placed on the high towers of the fort commanded the country all around. On one tower, called the "white turret," then recently raised in height, waved in proud defiance the standard of the high-spirited *ranee*. [97]

The fortress is surrounded on all sides by the city of Jhansi, the west and part of the south face excepted. The steepness of the rock protects the west; the fortified city wall springs from the centre of its south face, running southeast, and ends in a high mound or *mamelon*, which protects by a flanking fire its south face. The mound was fortified by a strong circular bastion for five guns composed of solid masonry, round part of which was drawn a ditch twelve feet deep and fifteen broad.

The city of Jhansi is about four miles and a half in circumference. It is surrounded by a fortified and massive wall, from six to twelve feet thick, and varying in height from eighteen to thirty feet, with numerous flanking bastions armed as batteries, with ordnance, and loop-holes, and with a banquette for infantry. [98]

According to Malleson, the town and fortress were garrisoned by 11,000 men, composed of rebel *sepoys*, foreign mercenaries, and local levies, and they were led by a woman who believed her cause to be just, and who, classified according to Channing's definition of greatness, was a heroine, though of the third order.

In his long reconnaissance of the 21st March, Sir Hugh Rose had noted all the strong points of the defence, and had examined the nature of the ground. He noted the many difficulties presented to the attack by the fort perched on a lofty granite rock, with its three lines of works, its flanking fire, its thick and solid walls. He had discovered that it would be necessary to take the city prior to assailing the fortress, a work involving double labour and double danger. In this reconnaissance, however, he had decided on his plan of attack. That night he was joined by the cavalry of the 1st Brigade: the next day he completely invested the city and fortress with his cavalry.[99]

The cavalry investment was carried out with great tact and discre-

---

97. *Rani* (Malleson).
98. The above description, Malleson says (vol. v. footnote), is taken from Sir H. Rose's despatch of 30th April 1858, where it is stated, 'a remarkable feature in the defence was that the enemy had no works or forts outside the city.'
99. See Appendix B.

tion. There were seven flying camps of cavalry established with their chain of outposts and vedettes on duty round the city day and night. Stent's [100] description of the part taken by his troop gives a good idea of what the work was:—

> My troop (of the 14th Light Dragoons), the "K," under Captain Brown, numbered about 60 men. We were expected to cover a certain portion of the city, to see that none escaped, or to turn out at any moment, and on any emergency. Consequently we were never out of harness, sleeping in front of our horses, which were always ready saddled and bridled never having the bits taken out of their mouths, night or day, except a few at a time for feeding purposes, or to give them a drink in comfort, so that it came harder on the horses than it did on us. As for ourselves, I don't think we were able to change our clothes, or have a wash, for about a fortnight, and it may be imagined that we were rather dirty, and that a bath would have done the whole of us good; but we couldn't even wash our faces, to say nothing of the elaborate luxury of a bath. Yet somehow, in spite of this and the dreadful heat, none of us fell sick, and all of us seemed to enjoy the life we led.
>
> One day, six privates and myself were out in charge of a young Irish officer of the regiment, belonging to " K " troop, named Beamish, and we had caught a party of *sepoys* in a small building. They had retreated up a narrow staircase which was only wide enough for one to go up at a time, and could easily have kept us at bay if they had not been apparently panic-struck at our appearance. We had all dismounted, and our leader was soon busily engaged pulling the *sepoys* one by one down the stairs by their "hind-legs" (as a comrade observed), and handing them over to our tender mercies. This amusement highly delighted Cornet Beamish, who, when he had finished, declared it was much better fun than "drawing badgers,"
>
> One cavalry flying camp was commanded by Major Gall with a squadron of the Fourteenth from the 1st Brigade. One was commanded by Captain Thompson, 14th Light Dragoons, and it was posted near the water palace and lakes of Jhansi. Another was under Captain Forbes, 3rd Bombay Light Cavalry. Three more were commanded by Captains Abbott, Murray, and

---

100. *Scraps from my Sabretache.*

Clarke, Hyderabad Contingent Cavalry, and Major Scudamore commanded the seventh, and he was placed in command of the whole of the investing force of cavalry, and on the night before the battle of the Betwa (31st March) he had command of the whole of the troops employed in the investment of the city and fortress. Brigadier Stuart with his 1st Brigade from Chanderi arrived about 24th March and was encamped about 2 miles from the 2nd Brigade, and 1 mile from the fortress of Jhansi.

The siege commenced on the 22nd March, and what was called the besieging force was divided into two attacks. The right attack was near the water palace and was carried on by the 2nd Brigade. The left attack was placed opposite the *mamelon*, and being carried on by the 1st Brigade, it was not thoroughly commenced until 25th March. From this date the siege was carried on with great vigour, and the system of investment by the "flying camps" of cavalry was most admirably conducted— it was said a cat couldn't pass their lines. Day after day the same routine was rigidly enforced. No quarter was given: those attempting to escape from the city were cut off by our vedettes and sentries, or attacked by our ambush parties posted at night. There was not a night passed but a large number of prisoners were taken by our cavalry picquets, and many of these were summarily disposed of.

Malleson says:—

For 17 days the fire from the besieging batteries and from the walls of the city and fort was incessant. Shot and shell were poured into the city, and the enemy's guns never ceased to reply. The labour imposed upon the small force of the besiegers was tremendous. During the period of which I have spoken, the men never took off their clothes, and the horses were not unbridled except to water. Nor were the exertions of the besieged less determined. Women and children were seen assisting in repairing the defences of the walls, and in carrying water and food to the troops on duty, whilst the *ranee* constantly visited the troops and animated them to enthusiasm by her presence and her words.

As we had only 2 18-pounders for breaching purposes, the progress made against the massive masonry of the walls was somewhat slow, but by the 29th March the *mamelon* guns were silenced by the fire of our left attack, and on 30th and 31st our cannonading was continued with renewed vigour so that a breach, not, however, yet practicable, had been made.

Unluckily, just at this juncture Sir Hugh received intelligence of the advance of a relieving army, which was the so-called army of the Peishwa, advancing on Jhansi from the north. Tantia Topee, the agent of Nana Sahib, was leading this army at the entreaty of the *ranee*, and it was said that he had in his ranks *sepoys* from numerous mutinous regiments, as well as levies from several rebel *rajahs*, and some of the finest regiments of the disaffected Gwalior contingent. His numbers were estimated at 22,000 men and 28 guns.

Such a sudden and unexpected danger placed Sir Hugh Rose in a most perilous position: he saw that to withdraw the troops then investing the fortress for the purpose of attacking this new enemy would be a most unwise and dangerous step. So he determined to gather together all the men he could who were not actually on duty in the siege, and face the foe with these, whilst at the same time the siege should be continued with unabated vigour by the others. Under this arrangement only 1500 men, including 500 British, were available to march against Tantia Topee's thousands. The force selected was furnished by detachments taken from both brigades. The detachments from the 1st Brigade were led by Brigadier C. S. Stuart, whilst Sir Hugh Rose himself led those supplied by the 2nd Brigade.

On the night of the 31st March the men bivouacked in their clothes with everything ready at hand for immediate action. At 4 o'clock on the morning of the 1st April, Tantia Topee advanced towards the British encampments around Jhansi, hoping to sweep us from the face of the earth. Half an hour later, according to Malleson, our picquets fell back and gave the British general warning of the approach of the enemy, who came up to within 800 yards, completely overlapping our small line, and apparently hoping to envelop our flanks. The rebel guns immediately unlimbered and opened fire. The immense line of Tantia Topee's looked as if it would completely hem in and crush not only the small force brought out against it by Sir Hugh, but also the whole investing force round Jhansi, in which case we should have been placed between two fires—Tantia Topee's on the one side, and the guns of Jhansi on the other.

Luckily Sir Hugh was able to grasp the situation, and in an instant he took the necessary steps to ward off this impending danger. He placed Captain Lightfoot's field battery on his left with a squadron of

the Fourteenth under Captain Prettejohn: these were ordered to attack the enemy's right. In the centre he placed his heavy guns and infantry: the latter consisted of the 3rd Europeans[101] under Lieutenant-Colonel Liddell, the 24th Bombay Native Infantry, and the Hyderabad Contingent Infantry. Of these the 24th were formed as a support, which materially weakened the first line, but was unavoidable. The 1st Brigade detachments under Brigadier C. S. Stuart had been intended for Sir Hugh's second line, but he had subsequently ordered them off by a circuitous route to our left to watch some fords of the river and to prevent any portion of the rebels' forces from doubling back on Jhansi, in which case they would have cut off Colonel Scudamore's flying camps of cavalry.

The infantry in the centre of our first line were placed behind some rising ground, and were lying down to avoid the heavy fire poured forth by the enemy at his first attack, and their orders were to advance so soon as the cavalry and artillery attacks on both our flanks were well developed.

On his right flank Sir Hugh placed Captain Need with a troop of the Fourteenth, as well as a troop of the Nizam's Cavalry under Clarke, and the Eagle Troop of Horse Artillery (the 1st troop of Bombay Horse Artillery), commanded by Lieutenant Colonel Turnbull.[102] These were to attack the enemy's left. Sir Hugh Rose himself took command of the right of his line. At first it looked as if our guns would prove powerless to check the onward rush of the enemy, who so greatly outnumbered us, but Sir Hugh's tactics, as it happened, turned out to be exactly suited to the exigencies of the moment. In order to enfilade the enemy's left he sent forward 2 guns from the Horse Artillery on our right under Lieutenant T. C. Crowe,[103] who moved diagonally to his right, and although one of the guns was disabled, the fire of the other was so rapid and so correct that the enemy's left was shaken.[104] The enemy's centre advanced very steadily, and poured in a heavy fire upon our centre which began to tell on our men around the heavy guns, and it was at this time that the infantry, who were lying down, had been ordered to advance, when the cavalry charges were being executed.

---

101. The 3rd Bombay European Infantry, afterwards the 109th Regiment, now the 2nd Battalion Leinster Regiment.
102. Now 'N' Battery, Royal Horse Artillery.
103. Now Major-General Crowe, late Royal (Bombay) Artillery.
104. Malleson, vol. v. where 'enemy's right' is printed for 'enemy's left.'

Speaking of the infantry advance, Malleson says:—

> The infantry sprang to their feet, advanced a few yards, then poured in a volley, and charged. The result was magical. The first line of the enemy at once broke and fled in complete disorder towards the second line, abandoning several of their guns.

The charges of the cavalry brought the battle to a speedy and successful issue, concerning which Sylvester says:—

> The Horse Artillery gun having been disabled was more than Sir Hugh Rose could bear: the major-general, at the head of Captain Need's troop of dragoons,[105] dashed into the enemy's left, while Prettejohn and McMahon, with Lieutenant Dew, led their troops[106] against the enemy's right, and doubled them up. This was a magnificent sight, and in a moment the enemy's ranks were a mass of confusion: they were shaken and disorganised, and commenced a disastrous retreat. They were hurled back on the Betwa by the irresistible attack of the dragoons.[107]

The *nizam's* troop of Hyderabad Cavalry on our right also did good service in supporting Captain Need's charge, and Sylvester says that before this charge the same troop under Clarke had been ordered by Sir Hugh Rose to charge the battery which had disabled Lieutenant Crowe's gun, but that Clarke was thrice driven back by showers of grape and volleys from the *Velaitee* [108] matchlockmen, losing some men and horses and receiving a wound himself. Stent, who was present as a non-commissioned officer in the regiment, gives the following account of the charges of the Fourteenth on this occasion:—[109]

> It was a glorious sight to see them thundering along, headed by the general and Captain Prettejohn, the latter of whom was bareheaded, and who fought and shouted like a demon. One minute, and they were among the enemy, and all that was to be seen was a confused mass of flashing swords and bayonets, struggling men and horses, and hoarse shouts of rage. From

---

105. The 'A' troop 14th Light Dragoons.
106. The 'H' and 'G' troops 14th Light Dragoons.
107. Sylvester.
108. The word *Velait* or *Welait* is Hindustani for 'foreign' a Velaiter is a *foreigner*. The *Velaitees* were native mercenaries, generally armed with matchlocks and *tulwars*. They were the best fighting-men amongst the rebels, and were composed of cut-throats, '*budmashes*,' and first-class scoundrels. (Sylvester.)
109. *Scraps from my Sabretache.*

this seething, struggling mass our men emerged victorious, for the result of the charge showed that an act of daring and personal bravery on the part of a leader (an act not often done—a commander-in-chief to lead a charge) will sometimes change defeat into victory as it did in this case.

The rebels were thoroughly routed in this charge, and turned and fled; were rallied, formed up again, to be again charged and routed; and yet again, only to undergo the same infliction, losing all their guns, and finally bolting in the greatest confusion, pursued by our men, who cut up great numbers of them, stopping only at the River Betwa from sheer exhaustion. Many of the enemy who escaped our swords were drowned in attempting to cross the river; the whole of the ground passed over by our men was strewed with their bodies, and at the lowest estimate it was calculated that 1500 of them must have been slain, and no doubt the wounded were at least as many more. Our cavalry and artillery bore the brunt of{ this severe engagement, my regiment[110] suffering the most, from the nature of the conflict being a succession of charges and hand-to-hand fights.

We must now leave for a moment the routed first line of Tantia Topee, pursued by their victors, to glance at the movements of those detachments of the 1st Brigade under Brigadier C. S. Stuart, C.B., to whom allusion has already been made, and to show what an important effect their movements had on the fortunes of the day.

Brigadier Stuart had moved round the hill into the plain on the right of the enemy, in order to check a large body of them who were taking advantage of the battle raging in front of the line to move off towards Jhansi. Stuart attacked, defeated them, and drove them back, hotly following them. So close indeed was the pursuit that they had no time to re-form, but fled in confusion, leaving gun after gun in the hands of the victors, and numbers of their men dead or dying on the field.[111]

This affair of the 1st Brigade was most opportune, for had this body of rebels not been cut off it is highly probable they would have worked round to Jhansi, and made the position of Colonel Scudamore's flying camps of cavalry very perilous. Lieutenant Giles, 14th Light Dragoons, with 30 or 40 of his troop, distinguished himself very

110. 14th Light Dragoons.
111. Malleson, vol. v.

highly in this pursuit, and cut up a large number of the enemy; but his force was too small and quite inadequate against the dense masses of matchlockmen that confronted him. The ground, too, was most unsuitable for cavalry and utterly impracticable for artillery, and the infantry could not keep up from sheer fatigue after their long march. The rebels sheltered themselves behind the adjacent rocks and caused several casualties in Lieutenant Giles's troop, killing 1 man, wounding 5, and placing 10 horses *hors-de-combat*, so that, notwithstanding the dauntless courage and gallantry exhibited by this officer, he could not do more than content himself with cutting up outsiders.

As it was, however, 250 of the rebels had been killed by Stuart's attack, and many more wounded, besides which 6 guns, 2 elephants, some camels, ammunition and treasure fell into his hands. Malleson says:—

> Tantia beheld in dismay the men of his first line rushing helter-skelter towards him, followed by the three arms of the British in hot pursuit; but he had scarcely realised the fact when another vision on his right flank came to add to his anguish.'

This vision was the rout of a large body of the enemy, caused by the very successful flank movement executed by Brigadier C. S. Stuart, and in which Lieutenant Giles, with his small troop of the Fourteenth, played such a conspicuous part. The second line of the rebel army was commanded by Tantia Topee in person. That crafty leader had occupied a selected position about 2 miles in rear of his first line, and here he placed his second line and reserve upon rising ground, with its front covered by jungle. Thus he was able to descry in an instant the reverse that had happened to his first line. Malleson says:—

> It had the effect of forcing upon him a prompt decision: the day, he saw, was lost, but there was yet time to save the second line and his remaining guns. The jungle was dry and easily kindled: Tantia Topee at once set fire to it, and under cover of the smoke and flames commenced a retreat across the Betwa, hoping to place that river between himself and the pursuers. His infantry and horsemen led the retreat, his guns covered it. Right gallantly and skilfully they did it, and he did succeed in crossing the Betwa with his reserve and guns and some of the fugitives of the first line.'

When the first line of the rebels was routed, as we have already

described, the pursuit became general. Our cavalry and artillery, with Prettejohn[112] and Need[113] at the head of the Fourteenth, dashed at a gallop through the burning jungle, cutting up hundreds of the rebels in their onward course, and determined to capture every gun of the enemy that had opened fire upon them. The flying enemy often rallied in a mass or '*gole*,' and many hand-to-hand fights between them and our cavalry took place, as in the swamps about Dhar; but the further the pursuit continued the thinner and fewer these rallying masses became, till at last little squares and groups, and then only single fugitives, dotted the plain.

The pursuit did not cease till 2 troops of the Fourteenth and a troop of the Nizam's Cavalry had actually crossed the Betwa, and here they became exposed to the heavy fire of the enemy, both in crossing the ford and also in ascending the steep road on the opposite bank. The rebels made great efforts to carry off their guns, elephants, and ammunition, but the greater part fell into our hands. Eighteen guns, 2 standards, and large stores or ammunition were captured, and after the capture of the last gun, an 18-pounder, about a mile and a half on the other side of the Betwa, Sir Hugh withdrew the cavalry from pursuit. They had been marching and fighting incessantly for many hours, and both men and horses were quite exhausted.

Nine miles remained to be traversed back to Jhansi, but the troops returned to camp amply compensated at having achieved so brilliant a victory over their vaunting foes. Malleson says 1500 rebels were killed and wounded that day. The British losses were 81 men and 29 horses, of which 15 men and 13 horses were killed. The Fourteenth suffered in proportion more heavily than any other regiment or corps. Their losses were: killed, 5 men, 11 troop-horses; wounded, 25 men, 16 troop-horses.

In Appendix B, extracts from Sir Hugh Rose's despatch, dated 30th April 1858, are inserted *verbatim*, and in these the reader will find officially recorded the gallant part taken by the regiment in this important victory over the Peishwa's army. The names of three officers of the Fourteenth—Captain Need, Captain Prettejohn, and Lieutenant Leith—are brought to notice for their important services on this occasion, as well as that of one non-commissioned officer, Sergeant Gardiner, who also, on a former occasion at Dhar, behaved so gallantly.

112. Afterwards Major-General R. B. Prettejohn, C.B.
113. Afterwards Lieutenant-Colonel Sir Arthur Need, Lieutenant of the Yeomen of the Guard.

Lieutenant Leith, who was in charge of the 'A' troop, led by Captain Need, performed an act of bravery and devotion for which he was recommended by Sir Hugh Rose for the Victoria Cross, and received that much-coveted decoration subsequently.[114]

In that charge Need, who was a great swordsman, dashed up rocks where no horse could keep its footing, and was in great danger; but Leith saw his perilous position and came to his captain's help at the right time and saved his life. Need was not actually unhorsed, but was almost surrounded by the enemy's infantry. His saddle, and even his jacket, which was loose and large, was slashed in several places, and his reins were cut.

The following copy of the telegram forwarded by Sir Hugh Rose to the government gives a very clear and concise account of this battle, and is taken from Stent's *Scraps from my Sabretache:*—

This morning, at daybreak, the force under my of the Betwa. orders fought a general action with the so-called Peishwa's army, and, by the blessing of God, gained a complete victory. The rebels are stated to have numbered from 20,000 to 25,000 men: they were under Tantia Topee, Nana Sahib's relative, and their object was to relieve Jhansi. I did not discontinue the siege or investment of Jhansi, consequently the force with which I fought was extremely weak. The rebels, amongst whom were the grenadier regiment and another regiment of the Gwalior contingent, fought, except the cavalry, desperately; but I turned their left flank with artillery and cavalry, and after making two stands they broke and fled, after defending themselves individually to the last.

I pursued them to the River Betwa, taking all their guns, eighteen in number, and an English 18-pounder of the Gwalior contingent drawn by two elephants; an 8-inch mortar, and quantities of ammunition, including shells, 18-pounder shot, ordnance park, and two elephants. Two standards were also taken. The enemy tried to stop our pursuit by setting the jungle on fire, but nothing could check the ardour of the artillery and cavalry, who galloped in pursuit across the country in flames. I cannot calculate at present the enemy's loss in killed, but it must have been very great, as the country is strewed with dead bodies, chiefly those of *sepoys*. As I now shall be free from the at-

---

114. See Appendix B.

tacks of a numerous attacking army I hope to conclude speedily the siege of Jhansi.

The remnant of the Peishwa's army, with Tantia at their head, made their escape towards Calpee,[115] and the victors resumed their former positions round Jhansi the same evening. During the time this battle had been raging the besieged had redoubled their fire; they manned the walls, poured down volleys of musketry, shouting and yelling hideously, and seemed to threaten a sortie. It seems incredible that no effectual attempt was made by the garrison to come out and attack the attenuated lines of besiegers, but perhaps they were deterred by the increased vigour displayed by our batteries, and also by a feigned attack which was purposely made by a body of troops under Major Gall, 14th Light Dragoons, and Lieutenant Lowrie, Royal Artillery, upon a distant part of the city wall, where a party of rebels did make some slight attempts at a sortie, but were effectually driven back by a 9-pounder and howitzer, together with some native infantry and dragoons acting under Major Gall.

Sir Hugh Rose determined to take advantage of the discouragement which it was well known the defeat of the relieving army would undoubtedly produce on the minds of the *ranee* and her garrison. Accordingly the siege was prosecuted with renewed vigour, and when it was known that the breach in the city wall was just practicable, he determined to storm the place on 3rd April. His plan of attack, according to Malleson, was this: to make a false attack on the west wall with a small detachment under Major Gall, 14th Light Dragoons. As soon as the sound of his guns should be heard, the main storming-party was to debouch from cover and enter the breach, whilst on the right of it attempts should be made to escalade the wall. His dispositions were as follows:—

1. The right attack, composed of the Madras and Bombay Sappers, 3rd Bombay Europeans, and infantry of the Nizam's Hyderabad Contingent, was divided into two columns and a reserve:—
The right column under Lieutenant-Colonel Liddle, 3rd Europeans; the left column under Captain Robinson, 3rd Europeans; the reserve under Brigadier C. Steuart, C.B., 14th Light Dragoons.
This attack was to attempt to gain the town by escalade.

2. The left attack, composed of the Royal Engineers, the 86th Foot, and the 25th Bombay Native Infantry, was similarly divided into two

115. Kalpi (Malleson).

columns and a reserve:—

The left column, commanded by Lieutenant-Colonel Lowth, 86th Regiment, was to storm the breach; the right column, led by Major Stuart, 86th Regiment, to escalade the rocket-tower and the low curtain immediately to the right of it. The reserve was commanded by Brigadier C. S. Stuart.

At 3 o'clock on the morning of the 3rd April, the storming-parties marched to the positions assigned them, to await there the signal from Major Gall's party. No sooner was it given than the stormers dashed to the front.

The left attack was successful, but on the right the escalading party suffered very heavily, and their ladders were too short and too weak. Lieutenants Dick and Meiklejohn of the Bombay Engineers, while nobly leading, were killed, and Lieutenant Bonus of the same regiment was hurled down from the wall struck in the face by a log or stone, Lieutenant Fox of the Madras Sappers was shot in the neck on the wall; but at length the stormers got a footing on the rampart, and owing to an opportune rescue made by a party from the left attack under Captain Brockman, who with some men of the 86th Regiment took the defenders in flank and rear and drew them off, the right attack was enabled to hold its own and to join the left attack in dispersing the defenders, so that eventually, after a sanguinary contest, the city and palace were successfully captured.

The resistance in the stables of the palace, as well as in the apartments, was very determined, and severe conflicts ensued here and in some of the streets leading through the city, where desultory fighting continued during the night and following day, as well as in the suburbs. Whilst the palace was being captured a body of rebels, about 400 in number, driven from the city, took refuge on a hill to the west of the fortress, where they were surrounded by our cavalry.

On hearing of this Sir Hugh ordered a mixed force, under command of Major Gall, 14th Light Dragoons, to storm the position and capture the rebels. Major Gall, with his usual skill and courage, took the position with the 24th Bombay Native Infantry, and all the defenders were either killed or blown up, with a loss of 1 officer and a few men of the 24th Bombay Native Infantry. Another body of 1500 men held out in a suburb, but these also were driven out with a loss of 300. Sir Hugh now bethought himself to make plans for capturing the fortress, but the *ranee* saved him all trouble on that score. She had fled there for safety when the palace was taken, but on the night of the

4th of April, despairing of success, she evacuated the fortress and fled to Calpee, intending to join Tantia Topee there.[116] She was reported to have escaped on horseback with her child before her, and a drawn sword in her hand, accompanied by her few remaining followers and a cavalry escort of *sowars*, along the Banda road. The following description of the Ranee of Jhansi is from Stent:—

> She was a very handsome woman about 24 years of age, a perfect Amazon in bravery, heading her troops, mounted like a man just the sort of daredevil woman that soldiers admire. She was finally killed, fighting against us at Gwalior.[117]

It is believed she was wounded by a carbine bullet in the fighting at Morar, June 1858, and was carried to the rear, where she expired, and was burned according to the Hindoo custom. At the time of her death she was attired as a cavalry soldier.[118]

As soon as the flight of the *ranee* was known, a cavalry force was sent in pursuit, but she had got too great a start and made good her escape to Calpee. Lieutenant Dowker with some *sowars* went in hot pursuit, and actually got near her at one time, but he was wounded by her escort whom he engaged, killing a large number of them and capturing the *ranee's* tent. Sir Hugh's force occupied the fortress on 5th April. Our losses in and around Jhansi, including the action fought on 1st April, amounted to 343 killed and wounded, of whom 36 were officers. The enemy's loss was computed at 5000: 1000 bodies were actually burned or buried in Jhansi itself.[119]

During the last few days of the siege, and for some time after the capture of Jhansi, Major Gall, 14th Light Dragoons, had been given the command of 'The North Outpost,' with a force under him of 2 and sometimes 4 pieces of ordnance, a squadron of the Fourteenth, and about 200 native infantry. He had constantly to move out of camp to his right or to his front, either to support the picquets near or to attack the enemy in the city lying to his front, and to prevent them from escaping. During the day of the Battle of the Betwa, on 1st April, he was employed with this force in making an attack on the city wall, and preventing an expected sortie of the garrison.

On the day the city was stormed, 3rd April, he made the feigned

---

116. Malleson, vol. v.
117. *Scraps from my Sabretache.*
118. Sylvester.
119. Malleson.

attack on the bastion of the north-east wall, so as to divert attention from the real attack on the south-east, and thus gave the signal to the storming-party to enter the breach.

On the 5th April, taking 150 of his infantry, Gall moved out of camp, and swept the ground along the city walls on the north side. Lieutenant Gowan, 14th Light Dragoons, with a small party of his men was also employed on the same duty. These parties sabred or shot down a large number of fugitive rebels who had secreted themselves in the cornfields and gardens about, not having been able to escape through the cavalry picquets when the city was taken. Most of the cavalry were thus employed on the day after the *ranee* escaped, when the fort was evacuated. By this means six or seven hundred of the enemy are said to have been cut up or shot. Cornet Beamish, 14th Light Dragoons, accounted for about 300 in this way with his party of dragoons, and a very large number, about 220, were disposed of by the Hyderabad Cavalry under Captain Abbott. Major Gall's infantry killed 100, Lieutenant Gowan's men, 30.

After the fall of Jhansi, Sir Hugh Rose remained there nearly 19 days, partly to rest his troops and partly to make the necessary preparations for another campaign. His next object was to march on Calpee: this was the arsenal of the rebels. Rao Sahib, the nephew of Nana Sahib, was there, with large supplies of artillery and warlike stores, and a numerous garrison. Calpee was situated on the river Jumna, 102 miles north-east of Jhansi, and 46 miles south-west of Cawnpore.[120]

On the night of the 22nd April a column under Major, now Brevet Lieutenant-Colonel Gall, 14th Light Dragoons, consisting of 3 troops (B, C, and E) 14th Light Dragoons, Lightfoot's battery of artillery, some companies of 3rd Europeans, some companies of 25th Native Infantry, and some Hyderabad Cavalry, was sent off from Jhansi to a place on the Calpee road. This force reached Pooch, 14 miles from Koonch, on 1st May.

On 25th April, at midnight, Sir Hugh left Jhansi for Koonch with the 1st Brigade, leaving orders for the 2nd Brigade to follow in two days. Major Orr with the bulk of the Hyderabad Contingent troops had been sent previously to cut off some rebels from crossing the Betwa and so doubling back southwards, and he too was to march on Koonch. On 1st May Sir Hugh with the 1st Brigade came up to Pooch, and joined Lieutenant-Colonel Gall's column, and by the 5th May Sir Hugh was joined by his 2nd Brigade, now augmented by the

120. Malleson.

arrival of the 71st Highlanders. The whole force now marched on Lo-hari, 10 miles nearer to Koonch, but on arrival there it was ascertained that the rebels had possession of the fort. Lieutenant-Colonel Gall with his column was detached to take it. This he successfully achieved after a stiff fight and some loss.

The 3rd Europeans and the 25th Native Infantry had severe hand-to-hand fights, but the whole garrison was destroyed and the fort cap-tured. Lieutenant-Colonel Gall and 4 other officers were wounded, and we lost 1 man killed and 13 wounded. One brass gun was captured in the fort. Lieutenant-Colonel Gall himself personally led the storm-ers, and was afterwards highly complimented by the Major-General for the able manner in which he had conducted the capture. [121]

After the flight from Jhansi, Tantia Topee and the Ranee of Jhansi had both escaped to Calpee. Here Rao Sahib, at the *ranee's* request, reviewed the whole of his army, and then placed Tantia Topee in com-mand of it, and ordered him to take it forward at once against the British. Tantia accordingly proceeded to Koonch on the Jhansi road, 42 miles from Calpee, and there entrenched himself in a strong posi-tion covered by woods and gardens, with temples at intervals, and sur-rounded by a strong wall. Meanwhile, as we have seen, the main body of the Central India Field Force and Hyderabad Contingent Force was advancing on Koonch under Major-General Sir Hugh Rose to confront the rebels.

The major-general had decided to make a flank march, and so to turn the enemy's position by attacking him in flank instead of making the usual frontal attack so dear to Asiatics. Accordingly on 6th May he broke up his camp and proceeded towards Koonch, so as to gain a position facing the unfortified side of the town, and hoping thus to cut off the enemy's line of retreat in the direction of Calpee.[122] On 7th May Sir Hugh's force came in sight of Koonch by 7 a.m., having marched 14 miles. Here he halted and drew up his line 2 miles distant from the town: the 1st Brigade formed on the left, the 2nd Brigade were in the centre, and the Hyderabad troops, under Major Orr, were on the right. Preparatory to the attack the troops were served out with a dram of grog and some biscuit. At 8 a.m. Lieutenant-Colonel Gall was sent forward with some cavalry to reconnoitre the wood, gardens,

---

121. See Appendix B.
122. Malleson, vol. v. In Sir Hugh Rose's despatch the date of the battle at Koonch is 7th May. Malleson's *History* has 6th May. Sylvester, who was present, confirms Sir Hugh's as the correct date.

and temples, and his advance was covered by artillery fire. At the same time the siege-guns were moved to a position whence they could effectually play upon the town.

Lieutenant-Colonel Gall soon returned and reported that the enemy had retreated through the wood nearer to the town, that they had cavalry in their rear, that the fire of the siege-guns had driven the rebels from the right of the wood into the town, but that some outworks were still held by them. The major-general determined to clear the wood and the outworks with his infantry, and then to storm the town. This was well and successfully carried out, and the fort was occupied by the men of the 1st Brigade, led by Sir Hugh, the fighting and skirmishing in the wood, however, causing several casualties.

The enemy were ultimately driven from the wood, gardens, and outworks, through the town, out of the town, and along the plain on the road leading towards Calpee. This was on the north side. Steuart with the 2nd Brigade, arriving from the west and occupying the centre of the line, had attacked a body of rebel infantry strongly posted to his front, directly in his intended line of advance. He met with a very determined resistance, and it was not till a body of the 1st Brigade came to his assistance by a well-delivered flank attack on the rebels that he was enabled to disperse them.

In this attack of the 2nd Brigade the 2 troops of the 14th Light Dragoons, under Captains Thompson and Gordon, took a prominent part, and at the critical moment Captain Gordon led his troop forward and made a gallant charge against a mass of the enemy, whom he broke and cut up, for which he was specially mentioned by Sir Hugh Rose in his despatch of the 24th May 1858.[123] Steuart then endeavoured, but ineffectually, to cut off the rebels from their line of retreat, but instead of working on through the town as he had been expected to do, his Horse Artillery and Cavalry moved round to the south side of it and joined in the general pursuit. Major Orr, with the *nizam's* troops, arriving from the south, had acted on the right of the line in the attack, and also joined in the attempt to cut off the fugitives in the direction of Calpee.

The action was over in about an hour, but the heat of the sun was so terrific that the infantry were not in a fit state to be sent in pursuit. The fugitives at once commenced a well-organised and orderly retreat. The greater part of the cavalry, including the Fourteenth and some of the Pursuit at Hyderabad Cavalry, together with the Horse Artillery

123. See Appendix B.

and light field guns, were launched forth in hot pursuit, the guns pouring volleys of grape on the retiring masses. Malleson says:—

> The manner in which the rebels conducted their retreat could not be surpassed. They well remembered the lessons they had learned from their European officers. There was no hurry, no disorder, no rushing to the rear; all was orderly as on a field-day. Their skirmishers fired, then ran behind the relieving men and loaded, the relieving men then fired and ran back in their turn.[124]

Captain William McMahon's squadron and Captain Blyth's troop of the Fourteenth charged the enemy's skirmishers magnificently. The former officer had to lead his men over a piece of very heavy ploughed land under a heavy fire: several of his men and horses were killed and a large number of saddles emptied. When the squadron got to close quarters the enemy fought fiercely. After firing they used their bayonets and native knives, with which they cut and slashed desperately at our men and horses. Captain McMahon received 3 sabre wounds, but continued to lead his squadron through the pursuit. These 3 troops of the Fourteenth cut up almost to a man the rearguard, which the enemy had thrown out in skirmishing order. Captain Blyth charged on another occasion and captured a gun under a very heavy fire; and Captain Prettejohn, by Sir Hugh's personal order, gallantly led a troop of the Fourteenth against an enfilading line of the enemy's skirmishers, also under a very heavy fire—'an order,' says Malleson, 'carried out by that most daring officer with great gallantry and success.'

This pursuit was continued up to 7 miles from Koonch in the burning sun, and the men and horses suffered intensely from the exposure. Even the major-general was so much overcome at one time by the heat that he had to dismount and seek shade, where Dr. Vaughan attended him, but he subsequently resumed his duties in the pursuit.[125] Sylvester, who was present on the occasion, says:—

> The heat was terrible; I never recollect suffering so much from thirst, and there was little water to be had. The Fourteenth were never better than on this day; they charged like a body of demons straight into the huge masses of revolted *sepoys* until Scudamore screamed "Halt! it is perfect madness." I counted 34 dead *sepoys* in one spot. The enemy got away with an 18-pounder and a

124. Vol. v.
125. Sylvester.

24-pounder gun along the Jaloun road to Calpee.

The rebels never gave in till nearly all their guns were captured, and they then crowded along the road a helpless mass of fugitives. At length our tired troops were recalled from pursuit and brought back to bivouac at Koonch, having been 16 hours marching, fighting, and in pursuit. It was 8 o'clock before the cavalry returned in the evening. We captured 9 guns and a large quantity of ammunition. The enemy lost about 600 men in the action and pursuit. Our losses were 3 officers and 59 men killed and wounded, besides a large number struck down by the sun.[126]

The Fourteenth lost heavily:—

Killed:—5 Men.
          3 Troop-horses.
Wounded:—Captain McMahon, severely.
                  (Sabre-cuts on leg and right hand.)
          17 Men.
          6 Troop-horses.
Missing:—4 Troop-horses.

In addition to these killed and wounded, the 14th Light Dragoons had 2 officers (Captain Need and Lieutenant Travers) and 16 men struck down by the sun, of whom 2 men died subsequently. In his despatch about Koonch,[127] Sir Hugh Rose brings the gallant services of the regiment into very prominent notice, and specially mentions the following officers for the favourable consideration of the Commander-in-Chief: Captain Gordon, Captain McMahon, Captain Prettejohn, Captain Todd (Staff Officer to Brigadier Steuart, C.B.), and Captain Blyth.

The Ranee of Jhansi, present during the action, had fled from Koonch to Calpee, attended by her cowardly horsemen, who turned tail, having never faced us at all; and Tantia Topee, always foremost in flight, escaped to a place near Jaloun, where his parents dwelt.[128] Our men had nothing to eat till 8 p.m. at night, except what they carried in their haversacks.

The 8th of May was a day of rest for both brigades. Their tents were pitched at daylight, and men and horses pulled themselves together for the coming march on Calpee. The men of the Fourteenth

126. Malleson.
127. See Appendix B.
128. Malleson.

110

were in a splendid state of physique at this time, being well inured to the climate, so they suffered less than the other Europeans, of whom the newly arrived 71st Highlanders lost more men by sunstroke than any other corps present, but even in the Fourteenth there were nearly 150 men, including sick and wounded, belonging to the left wing only, under medical treatment on the day after the Battle of Koonch.

At 2 a.m. on 9th May the major-general moved off with the 1st Brigade, followed next day by the 2nd Brigade. The march to Calpee was a most trying one, owing to the intense heat and the want of water. The rebels had thrown up elaborate fortifications along the direct road leading from Koonch to Calpee, hoping to make short work of us as we passed; but Sir Hugh got timely notice from spies, and from reports brought in by Lieutenant-Colonel Gall, 14th Light Dragoons. As a result of his reconnaissance it was ascertained that the enemy was entrenched in large numbers to our left. Sir Hugh took a circuitous route, and moved towards Golowlee, on the right bank of the Jumna, 6 miles from Calpee, avoiding the direct road, and thus outflanking the enemy, who found himself completely outwitted and his great defences on the main road turned and useless. [129]

There was another advantage too in this plan of campaign, for Sir Hugh had received an intimation that a column under Colonel G. V. Maxwell, with the 88th Foot and other details, would co-operate with him, and had already reached the left bank of the Jumna opposite Golowlee. On the 13th May, owing to the illness of Brigadier C. Steuart, C.B., 14th Light Dragoons, the command of the 2nd Brigade devolved for a time upon Lieutenant-Colonel Campbell, 71st Highland Light Infantry. On the 15th, Sir Hugh with the 1st Brigade reached Golowlee, and established communication with Colonel Maxwell's column on the opposite bank by means of pontoons, as no boats could be found.

On the 16th, Lieutenant-Colonel Campbell brought up the 2nd Brigade, which had been menaced by the enemy on the march from Etora. This brigade encamped near Golowlee, on the left flank of Major Orr's Hyderabad Force, and opposite the village of Diapora. The 1st Brigade had also been harassed by large bodies of the rebels on their last day's march to Golowlee, when their rearguard was attacked by cavalry.

On the 16th, after the 2nd Brigade had reached camp, the rearguard was attacked; it was commanded by Major Forbes, 3rd Bombay

129. Sylvester.

Cavalry, who had with him 170 of his own *sowars*, a weak troop of the Fourteenth under Lieutenant Beamish, 2 guns Royal Artillery, 200 Irregular Horse, a company of 3rd Bombay Europeans, a company of Bombay Sappers, and 116 men of the 24th Bombay Native Infantry, under Lieutenant Estridge. It seems that 6000 of the enemy, who had occupied the village of Etora as soon as the brigade moved out, had cut off some of our baggage in rear. They followed up to within 600 yards of camp, and fired on our men with artillery shots and volleys of musketry, whilst their cavalry seemed threatening a charge.

We lost some men of the 24th Bombay Native Infantry and of the 3rd Bombay Cavalry, whilst an artilleryman had his pouch shot off his belt, and one of the Fourteenth had his turban shot off,—the latter was replaced with the most perfect nonchalance! Major Forbes handled his force most skilfully, and, notwithstanding his critical position, brought it safely into camp. The whole force was eventually turned out under the major-general, and desultory firing went on till dark, when the enemy, tired out like ourselves, gradually ceased firing and left us quiet.[130] The position of the 2nd Brigade camp was 6 miles from the Jumna, and was much exposed to attacks from the enemy; the 1st Brigade was encamped within a mile of the river's bank nearer Golowlee.

There was a village called Muttra near the camp of the 2nd Brigade, and it was here that the enemy was constantly endeavouring to attack us and to get round the left rear of the position. The determined fire of Captain Field's battery, however, kept him at a respectful distance, though his round-shot would occasionally roll in among the tents of the Fourteenth, and in an attack made by the rebels on the 17th May several troops of the Fourteenth, with infantry and artillery, had to be employed to drive them off and to keep up connection between the 2nd Brigade and village of Muttra, which lay to our left.[131] There were incessant skirmishes going on and threatened attacks by the enemy on the 18th, 19th, and 20th May. The heat of the sun was terrific, and in consequence our men suffered dreadfully from the exposure and harassing work, for the enemy knowing this persisted in making attacks.

A mortar battery in front of the 1st Brigade was established by the 19th, and on the 20th, Colonel Maxwell, from the other side of the

---

130. The above account is from Sylvester's *Recollections of the Campaign in Malwa and Central India under Major-General Sir Hugh Rose*, G.C.B.
131 Appendix B. (Lieutenant-Colonel Campbell's report).

Jumna, sent over 2 companies of the 88th Regiment and 120 Sikhs to reinforce Sir Hugh. By the 21st, Maxwell's batteries opened on the town of Calpee. There was a move forward of all the camps on 19th, after which both brigades and the *nizam's* troops rested on the right bank of the River Jumna, encamped one behind the other, with Golowlee in front, and a mile of ravines lying between them and the river bed.[132] In the forthcoming attack on Calpee, Sir Hugh intended Maxwell to shell the fort and city, whilst he would clear the ravines and other obstacles and attack the fort on the left side.[133] The left of the British force nearly touched the road running from Calpee to Banda. Malleson describes the fortress of Calpee as being protected by five lines of defence to its front, and by the River Jumna to its rear. These five were—

1st. A series of entrenchments with flank defence;

2nd. 84 temples of solid masonry, with walls round them of the same;

3rd. An outwork of ravines;

4th. City of Calpee;

5th. A second chain of ravines; and lastly came the fort itself, built on a precipitous rock.

The rebels at Calpee were commanded by the Nawab of Banda, a fugitive from the defeat inflicted on him by General Whitlock at Banda, and he was aided by the brave Ranee of Jhansi, driven from Koonch. They had a large number of *sepoys* as well as 2000 horsemen from Banda, besides guns and numerous followers.

It would be difficult to describe all the suffering our men and horses went through at this period of the campaign, especially on the march from Koonch, and in the operations about Calpee, both from the fierceness of the sun and the great scarcity of water, which prevailed until the camps were moved within reach of the Jumna. The sick-list was enormous, and the cases of sunstroke which occurred incessantly had a most depressing effect on the whole force. A foraging-party of 33 men belonging to the Fourteenth left camp one day, and of this number only 19 returned on their saddles.

Of the infantry, the 71st Highlanders suffered most. They had only recently come to India, before which they had been in the Crimea. The rebels well knew how fatal the exposure to the sun's rays was to

132. Sylvester.
133. Malleson.

Europeans, and so they invariably arranged their fights to take place at the hottest time of the day. On the 22nd May, the date of the capture of Calpee, the enemy commenced the attack by marching in masses along the Banda road about 10 a.m. and threatening the British left near Golowlee. Another body opened fire at the same time against our centre.[134] According to Sylvester, the disposition of the British forces was as follows:—

Brigadier C. S. Stuart, commanding 1st Brigade, posted himself by 8 a.m. at the mortar battery in front of the camps, taking with him half Woolcombe's battery and a party of the 3rd European Regiment. On his right, extended as a line of skirmishers reaching along the ravines to the Jumna, was the 86th Regiment under Colonel Lowth; on the left of the Brigadier was a wing of the 25th Native Infantry; in rear as a support was a troop of the Fourteenth, as well as a troop of the 3rd Bombay Light Cavalry.

Towards the centre of the line was Colonel Robertson, with the other wing of his corps (the 25th Bombay Native Infantry), the remaining half of Woolcombe's battery under Lieutenant Strutt, and the 21st company Royal Engineers; on the left centre Lightfoot's troop of Horse Artillery, and 2 troops of the Fourteenth, our heavy guns, the Royal Artillery field battery, 71st Highlanders, and main body of the 3rd Europeans. On the extreme left were the Hyderabad Contingent force, Maxwell's camel-corps riflemen and Sikhs. Here, too, as the ground was more suitable for cavalry than on our right, was a squadron of the Fourteenth under Lieutenant-Colonel Gall, and 3rd Hyderabad Cavalry under Captain Abbott.

Such was the disposition of Sir Hugh Rose's little army when the enemy commenced their attack, as already stated above. By 9 a.m. our vedettes began to fire and fall back, but owing to the nature of the ground, especially in the direction of the ravines, a good half of the approaching rebels came on without being visible to us. The mass of their cavalry and artillery were on the right of their line, the ravines being impracticable to their left. Our infantry began to advance, and our guns opened fire at the same time.

The enemy's attack on our left was only intended as a feint. It was led by the Nawab of Banda and Rao Sahib, the nephew of the Nana. It proved, however, in the end serious. It was pushed well home, and our left became heavily engaged. Sir Hugh, notwithstanding, being fully persuaded in his own mind of the real intention of the enemy,

---

134. Malleson, vol. v.

did not move a man from his right, and his forecast was correct. Suddenly, as if by magic, the whole line of ravines became lighted up by a mass of fire, both artillery and musketry, which was brought to bear with overwhelming force on the British right. As Malleson says:—

The suddenness of the attack, the superior numbers of those making it, and the terrible heat of the day, gave the rebels a great advantage.

The sun had struck down an unusual number of Europeans, and some of our men's Enfield rifles having become clogged by constant use in all weathers, were difficult to load, so that at one time things looked very critical when the enemy, starting up in great numbers from the ravines, pressed forward with loud yells and caused the British to fall back to the position where our light field-guns and mortar battery were posted. It was here that Brigadier Stuart made a gallant stand; himself dismounted, and standing by the guns, he bade the gunners defend them with their lives.[135] The 86th Regiment and 25th Native Infantry in a thin extended line made a good resistance, and disputed the advance step by step. Malleson says:—

Still the rebels pressed on, and it seemed as though from their very numbers they must prevail, when Sir Hugh, to whom news of the attack had been conveyed, brought up the camel-corps, which had opportunely crossed the river that very morning, at their best pace; then, dismounting the men, and leading them forward himself at the double, charged the advancing foe, who was then within a few yards of the British guns. For a moment the enemy stood, but only for a moment. A shout, a dash forward from our whole line, and they went headlong into the ravines below.

Not only was the attack on our right repulsed, but the battle was won. The attack on our left collapsed when it was seen that that on the right had failed, and our guns, gaining the rebels' flank, inflicted great loss on them as they fled. Sir Hugh followed them up so closely that he cut off a number of them from Calpee. The fire from Maxwell's batteries made those who reached that fort feel that it was no secure place of refuge. They evacuated it accordingly. The main bulk of the enemy, pursued by the Horse Artillery and cavalry, lost their formation and dispersed, losing all their guns and baggage. Even the Ranee of

135. Malleson.

Jhansi, who fled with them, was compelled to sleep under a tree!

The numbers of the defeated army are computed by an eyewitness[136] as being 'ten times our number.'

Next morning Sir Hugh marched into Calpee. The 1st Brigade under Brigadier C. S. Stuart went through the ravines, following the course of the Jumna, whilst Sir Hugh led the 2nd Brigade himself along the Calpee road, and Colonel Maxwell's batteries shelled the fort and villages in front. There was, however, no resistance offered, and both brigades entered the town and fort, whence the rebels had fled, leaving their great arsenal replete with all the munitions of war entirely in our hands.[137]

Lieutenant-Colonel Gall with all the available men of the Fourteenth, Horse Artillery, and Hyderabad Cavalry was immediately sent in pursuit, and, as related in Sir Hugh Rose's despatch of 22nd June 1858, extracts of which are printed in Appendix B, this duty was most ably carried out. The enemy was pursued as far and as closely as possible: the whole of his guns and 6 elephants were captured, and large numbers of the rebel *sepoys*, especially the Sind Velaitees and mercenaries of the Nawab of Banda, were cut up by the Fourteenth and the Nizam's Cavalry.

In Sir Hugh Rose's despatch of 13th October 1858, the services performed by the regiment, the privations undergone from exposure to the sun, want of water, and scarcity of forage, are fully recorded, and Lieutenant-Colonel Gall's name is specially brought to notice for his gallant conduct in the pursuit of the rebels after their defeat at Golowlee and Calpee, in which 5 troops of the Fourteenth took part. In this pursuit the cavalry, who had been 13 hours in the saddle, pursued 8 miles on the Jhansi road. The names of Captain Barrett, Captain Need, Lieutenant Giles, Surgeon Stewart, Acting Regimental Sergeant-Major Clark, and Private Winton of 'B' troop were specially mentioned by Lieutenant-Colonel Gall in his report of the 25th May as having performed gallant services on the same occasion. Captain Need led a charge against the rear of an infantry column, in which the Fourteenth captured 3 guns and cut down 200 rebels.

On this occasion Lieutenants Giles and Beamish used their revolvers with great effect. A charge led by Lieutenant-Colonel Gall with Captain Barrett, 14th Light Dragoons, and Captain Abbott, Nizam's

---

136. Dr. Lowe, author of *Central India During the Rebellion of 1857-58*.
137. Malleson, vol. v.

Cavalry, at the head of their respective troops, went straight into a line of the retiring enemy and cut up about 300 rebels, losing only 2 men wounded, with 3 horses killed and wounded, and also captured 4 elephants.[138] The *ranee* and the Nawab of Banda both made a precipitate flight from Calpee, at midnight, after the battle. It was said that a shell from Maxwell's battery burst in the *ranee's* room and killed two of her attendants, which somewhat hastened her departure. [139]Subsequently, on 1st June, she was in the vicinity of Gwalior when the *maharajah's* troops deserted him, and, after his flight to Agra, took possession of the city and fort of Gwalior together with Rao Sahib and Tantia Topee.

On the 25th May, Sir Hugh despatched a 'pursuing column,' in consequence of the information brought by Lieutenant-Colonel Gall on his return from the pursuit, that he was certain a very large body of rebels had retreated along the Jaloun road to reach a ford across the Jumna, heading to the north. With this column a troop of the Fourteenth was despatched at first, and shortly afterwards, on the 29th May, 2 squadrons of the Fourteenth and a wing of the 86th Regiment followed from Calpee as reinforcements.[140]

Lieutenant-Colonel Robertson reported soon after that there was no doubt the main body of the Calpee rebels had taken the road to Gwalior, and the 1st Brigade under Brigadier Stuart set off on the 1st June in hot haste after them: 2 troops of the Fourteenth went with this brigade.[141] On the 6th June the major-general himself started for the same destination, with a part of the 2nd Brigade, in which were 2 more troops of the Fourteenth. Thus the whole of the Fourteenth once more set out on the march for further fighting and campaigning in the very hottest time of the whole year, and as the rains were nearly due, every endeavour would have to be made to reach Gwalior before they regularly set in.

This march of the Central India Field Force on Gwalior was mostly carried out at night, to avoid the terrific heat of the day. The men usually left camp at 11 p.m., reaching their camping-ground by sunrise. Brigadier-General R. Napier, C.B., arrived from Lucknow about the 14th June, and assumed command of the 2nd Brigade. Notwithstanding the great heat,[142] Sir Hugh Rose made forced marches, and reached the vicinity of Morar cantonments by 16th June. Here the

---

138. Malleson, vol. v.

139. See Appendix B.

140 & 141. Sylvester.

142. It was 130 Fahrenheit in the shade at times.

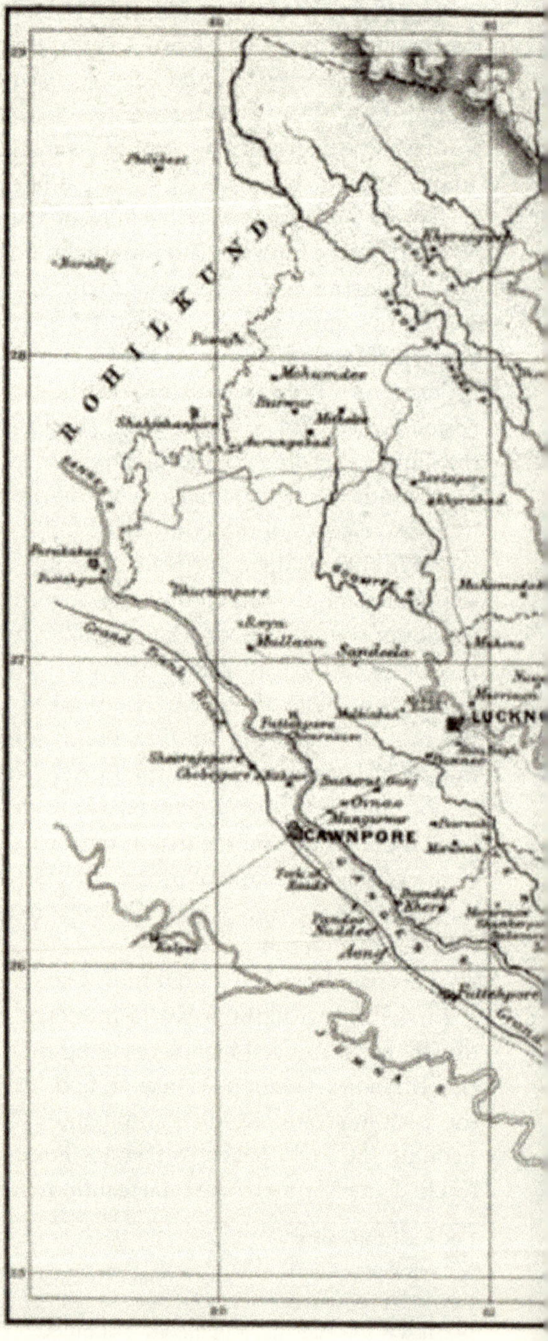

ROHILKUND
Mohumdee
Aurungabad
Mullaon
Sandeela
Grand Trunk Road
CAWNPORE
Oonao
Kalpee
Futtehpore
JUMNA

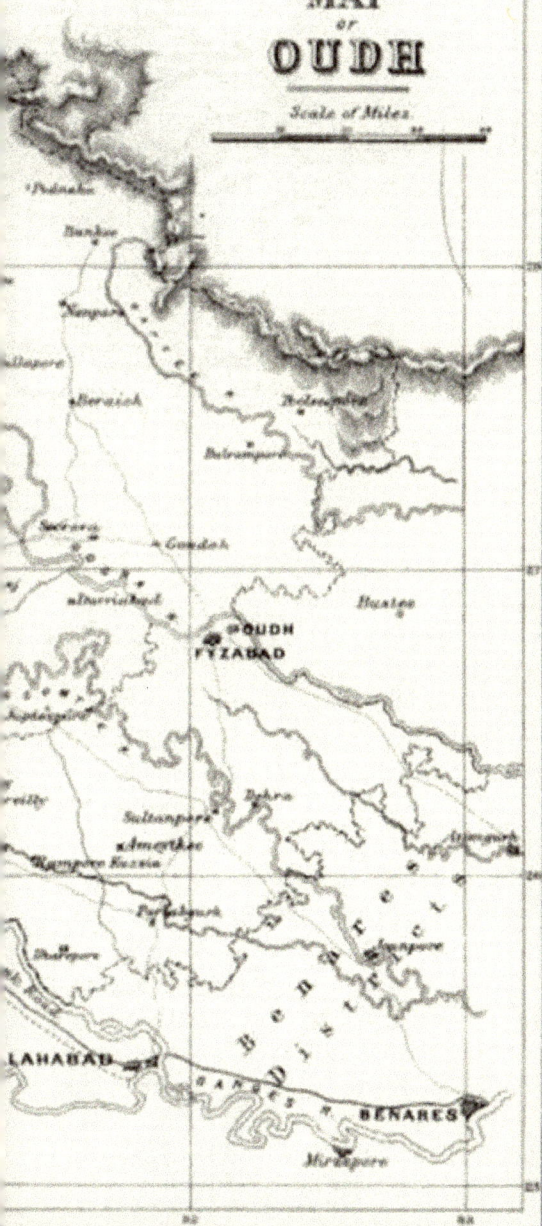

MAP
OF
OUDH

Scale of Miles.

OUDH
FYZABAD

ALAHABAD

GANGES R.

BENARES

Mirzapore

rebels were ready to receive us in force, but, tired though his men were, the major-general, with his usual dash, engaged them, and took the cantonments after some severe fighting. He first reconnoitred the position carefully, and ascertained the enemy's strength, then decided to attack.

The Fourteenth and Nizam's Cavalry were placed on either flank, guns and infantry in the centre; the 2nd Brigade supported, the 1st was in front. Sir Hugh moved somewhat to his right and turned the enemy's left. The enemy being taken thus unexpectedly, gave way on all sides, but a considerable number took shelter in a dry *nullah* with ravines, in rear of the cantonments and a village adjoining, and here the 71st Highland Light Infantry, under Lieutenant-Colonel Campbell, lost an officer and several men in clearing out the rebels. The enemy was eventually driven by our men right through the cantonments, and the rout was completed by a very successful charge of a wing of the Fourteenth led by Captain P. S. Thompson. He caught the fugitives in the plains and cut up a large number of them. One troop of the Fourteenth under Lieutenant Gowan also charged a body of rebels as they fled from the ravines, and destroyed a considerable number. [143]

On the 17th, Brigadier Smith, coming from Rajputana with a column to join the Central India Field Force round Gwalior, had arrived near Kota-ke-Serai, 5 miles to the southeast of Gwalior, and had been fighting all day with strong bodies of the rebel infantry. He had reported his need of assistance, and Sir Hugh sent off immediately, as a reinforcement, the 25th Bombay Native Infantry, 4 guns of artillery, and 3 troops of the Fourteenth, all under command of Colonel Robertson.

During a cavalry charge made by a squadron of the 8th (King's Royal Irish) Hussars belonging to Brigadier Smith's column, which was led by Colonel Hicks and Captain Heneage of the 8th Hussars, the Ranee of Jhansi met her death. She was slain by a trooper, her horse having fallen, and he being quite ignorant of her rank or sex. She was dressed as a cavalry soldier. Her body was picked up and burned that night by some of her devoted followers, in accordance with the Hindoo custom. On the following day, 18th June, Sir Hugh started with the 1st Brigade from Morar cantonments (which were left in charge of Brigadier-General Napier and the 2nd Brigade), and

---

143. Brigadier-General R. Napier, C.B., mentions in his report (see Appendix B) the gallant part taken on this occasion by the right wing of the Fourteenth.

marched in the afternoon to join Brigadier Smith.

It was a long, circuitous march, very trying, especially to the infantry, who knocked up in considerable numbers. At night they bivouacked on the Morar River, and in the morning Scindiah had arrived from Agra to witness the result of that day's fighting, which was destined to restore to him his lost principality with the city and fort of Gwalior. After an early reconnaissance, Sir Hugh Rose decided to attack as speedily as possible. During the whole of the previous day, the 18th, the enemy's guns, posted on a ridge to the left of Brigadier Smith's camp, had been pounding our troops. A canal lay between the two forces, and this had to be bridged over by us. This duty was performed with alacrity by the Madras sappers and miners, whilst all the time the enemy's battery on the ridge kept up a heavy fire on the working parties, and masses of their infantry were seen moving to take up positions from which they could act with the best advantage to oppose our advance.

Sir Hugh lost no time in sending his infantry, 86th and 95th British Regiments, as well as the 10th and 25th Bombay Regiments, across the canal to seize the ridge and attack both flanks of the opposing rebel infantry. He directed Brigadier Smith to be ready to attack the enemy's positions at the Phool Bagh[144] and beyond it with a troop of Horse Artillery and a squadron of the Fourteenth, whilst he sent a light field battery, escorted by 2 troops of the Fourteenth, to the heights as a covering party for his advanced line, intending these guns to reply to the enemy's batteries in position in front of Gwalior.[145]

The infantry attack was admirably carried out. Several of the enemy's guns were taken in position, and turned on themselves by the men of the 86th and 95th Regiments, whilst the Bombay Regiments also captured some guns. 'The day was won,' says Malleson; 'the heights were gained, Gwalior lay, as it were, at the feet of the British.' To their right, looking down from the heights above across the plain, lay the Phool Bagh and the old city, surmounted by the fort; to their left lay the Lushkar (literally 'encampment,' but really the 'New City'), with the Maharajah's palace, and its spacious streets and houses. On the plain were visible the enemy, who had been driven from the heights, endeavouring to seek refuge in one or other of the fortified places or walled enclosures at hand. Sir Hugh at once ordered a general advance.

---

144. 'Flower-garden.' A garden and palace at the foot of the fort.
145. See Appendix B.

Gwalior Fort

The 1st Bombay Lancers were sent round the rear of the heights by a circuitous road, and were thence to make an attack on the New City (the Lushkar). The 3rd Bombay troop of Horse Artillery and a squadron of the Fourteenth protected the right flank of the troops attacking the grand parade, and also turned the enemy's left. The 86th Regiment advanced on the left, the 95th on the right. The rebels appeared paralysed. It is true their guns replied, but their infantry fell back. The charge of the Bombay Lancers added to their dismay, after which our infantry came up and completed the capture of the Lushkar.

Meanwhile, on the right, Brigadier Smith had taken the Phool Bagh, killing large numbers of the rebels, and, as a considerable body of them, including some cavalry, fled towards the British Residency, which lay about 8 miles from Gwalior in the direction of Agra, he launched forth after them his cavalry and guns in pursuit, which was carried on till long after dark, inflicting great loss on the fugitives, and capturing most of their guns. Brigadier Smith speaks very highly of the steadiness with which the 2 troops of the Fourteenth, escorting the 3rd troop Bombay Horse Artillery, stood the enemy's artillery fire of 'shot and shell, and of the ardour with which they afterwards fell on the guns and the retreating enemy.' [146] Sylvester says:—

> The enemy was taking away a large number of guns and ammunition wagons, but Brigadier Smith with the mounted part of his brigade gave pursuit, overtook, fought, and captured several guns, and only allowed the remnant to escape because the exhausted men and cattle could go no further in the darkness, for night had not closed the work. Here, as ever heretofore, did the 14th Light Dragoons and Bombay Horse Artillery add to their now weighty crown of laurels.

Two troops of the Fourteenth had been held in support on the lower slopes, during the final attack on the two cities of Gwalior. The fort still remained unconquered. It was owing to the gallantry of a young officer, Lieutenant Rose, 25th Bombay Native Infantry, assisted by Lieutenant Waller of the same regiment, who had under them a detachment of their own men, and who were posted on duty near the main gateway of the rock fort, that this important and formidable fortress fell into our hands on the 20th June, the day following the Battle of Gwalior. It was 'a deed of unsurpassed daring,' says Malleson. Lieutenants Rose and Waller with a party of *sepoys* and some of Scin-

---

146. See Appendix B.

diah's police (*kotwallahs*) forced the gate, passed through the other six gates, charged a gun at the archway of the fortress, and closed with the rebel garrison opposed to them. Here they were engaged in a hand-to-hand contest.

A desperate fight ensued, and many fell on both sides, when, just in the hour of victory, Rose fell mortally wounded by a musket-ball fired from behind the wall. The man who fired it was despatched by Waller, but Rose died a hero's death. The rock fortress was gained. Sir Hugh Rose thus mentions the circumstance in his despatch:

> But the gallant leader, Lieutenant Rose, who has been twice specially mentioned by me for good and gallant conduct, fell in the fort mortally wounded, closing his early career by taking the fort of Gwalior by force of arms.

Tantia Topee, as usual, had deserted his post and fled when the battle was at its height, drawing off numbers of the rebel cavalry with him as a guard, 'and setting to his men a base and cowardly example, which went unpunished till a later period, when the halter encircled his "Bunniah"-born neck at Sipri.'[147] Thus Morar, the two cities and the fort of Gwalior were all in our hands by the 20th of June, and the total losses of the British arms were less than 100 men killed and wounded.

A squadron of the 8th Hussars and a squadron of the 14th Light Dragoons, 'honourable representatives of my force,' says Sir Hugh Rose, [148] 'escorted His Highness the Prince of Gwalior to his palace in the Lushkar.' This ceremony was attended by the Major-General and his staff, who received Scindiah with every possible mark of respect upon his arrival, in company with Sir Robert Hamilton, Agent to the Governor-General for Central India, with a large and imposing retinue. Scindiah was everywhere greeted with enthusiasm by the populace, and after eighteen days' occupation by the rebels the city, fort, cantonments and states of Gwalior were restored to their ruling prince. Subsequently, as a mark of his appreciation of the great services rendered to him, Scindiah presented to the officers and men of the Central India Field Force the Gwalior Star, an elegant design in frosted silver, bearing on it a snake of gold, the crest of the Prince of Gwalior, and the figures '1858,' worn with an orange ribbon; and the royal authority was afterwards granted for its issue to, and acceptance

---

147. Sylvester.
148. See Appendix B.

by, the troops engaged.

In Appendix B are extracts from the despatch of Sir Hugh Rose, dated 13th October 1858, giving full particulars of the recapture of Gwalior and Morar.

After the victory at Gwalior, Sir Hugh Rose proceeded to Bombay to assume command of the army of that Presidency. He issued the following farewell order:—

> The Major-General commanding, being on the point of assuming the command of the Poona Division of the Bombay army, bids farewell to the Central India Field Force, and at the same time expresses the pleasure he feels that he commanded them when they gained one more laurel at Gwalior. The Major-General witnessed with satisfaction how the troops and their gallant comrades-in-arms, the Rajputana Brigade under Brigadier-General Smith, stormed height after height, and gun after gun, under the fire of a numerous field and siege artillery, taking finally by assault two 18-pounders at Gwalior. Not a man in these forces enjoyed his natural health or strength: an Indian sun and months of marching and broken rest had told on the strongest; but the moment they were ordered to take Gwalior for their Queen and country they thought of nothing but victory.
>
> They gained it, restoring England's true and brave ally to his throne, putting to rout the rebel army, killing many of them, and taking from them in the field, exclusive of those in the fort, 52 pieces of artillery, all their stores and ammunition, and capturing the city and fort of Gwalior, reckoned the strongest in India. The Major-General thanks sincerely Brigadier-General Napier, C.B., Brigadier Stuart, C.B., and Brigadier Smith, commanding brigades in the field, for the very efficient and able assistance which they gave him, and to which he attributes the success of the day. He bids them and their brave soldiers once more a kind farewell. He cannot do so under better auspices than those of the victory of Gwalior.

On the 19th June, at Gwalior, immediately Sir Hugh saw that success was certain, he sent off an express to Brigadier Napier at Morar requesting him to pursue the rebels as far and as closely as he could. Napier received this order between 5 and 6 o'clock on the morning of the 20th June, and started within two hours, taking the following troops of his 2nd Brigade with him!:——[149]

	Men
Lightfoot's troop of Bombay Horse Artillery,	99
Captain Prettejohn's troop 14th Light Dragoons,	62
Captain Abbott's Hyderabad Cavalry,	245
3rd Light Cavalry, 2 troops,	104
Meade's Horse,	180
Total,	690

This force, after a fatiguing march of 25 miles exposed to a terrific sun, rested for the night, and next morning, shortly after sunrise, came up with Tantia Topee and a strong body of the rebels at Jowra-Alipore.

In his *Sepoy Revolt*, General Innes, V.C., gives the following account of the engagement which ensued:——

> The routed and flying enemy were forthwith pursued by a light column under Brigadier-General Robert Napier, C.B., who next day overtook them at Jowra-Alipore, drawn up 12,000 strong in two lines. Holding his cavalry in hand in their front, but sheltered from them by intervening high ground, he sent the horse artillery to enfilade their lines from their left flank. This speedily shook and began to roll up their lines, when the cavalry were let loose and made a frontal charge. On this the enemy broke and fled, losing 25 guns, all their equipment, and 300 killed. The rout was complete, and from that time, the end of June, Tantia Topee's force became a fugitive one: it gradually dwindled away, though it never surrendered.

This force, which was so effectively dealt with by Brigadier-General Napier's column, was composed of the remnants of the Calpee army, with considerable additions picked up at Gwalior, and was headed by Tantia Topee, Rao Sahib, and the Nawab of Banda. Malleson says:——

> The result was decisive. Prettejohn's distinguished valour and Abbott's gallant leading were especially conspicuous. The dash of Lightfoot's Horse Artillery was superb to look at. "You cannot imagine," writes an eye-witness, a cavalry officer, "the dash

---

149. See Brigadier Napier's report, Appendix B.

of the artillery: it was wonderful. We could scarcely keep up with them." But, in fact, every man behaved like a hero; each vied with his comrade. After a brief resistance the rebels broke and fled, hotly pursued. They lost 25 guns, all their ammunition, elephants, tents, carts, and baggage, and had 300 to 400 men killed. Never was a rout more complete.

The Fourteenth had only one man (Private G. Staple) wounded in this affair. Captain Prettejohn, Captain Todd, and Surgeon Stewart were specially mentioned in the brigadier's despatches, [150] and he recommended for the Victoria Cross Private Novell, of 'H' troop, for an act of conspicuous bravery in charging alone, under a heavy fire, into a village and killing one of the enemy. The pursuit was continued by the cavalry for 6 miles from the scene of their first attack.

The following is a brief recapitulation, taken from Malleson, of what the Central India Field Force had accomplished in less than six months:—

On 6th January, Sir Hugh Rose had left Indore.

On 24th January, he laid siege to Rathgur.

28th January, he defeated the Rajah of Banpur.

29th January, he took Rathgur.

3rd February, he relieved Saugor.

13th February, he took the strong fort of Garrakota.

4th March, he forced the Muddenpore Pass.

17th March, his 1st Brigade stormed the fort of Chanderi.

22nd March, he invested Jhansi.

1st April, he defeated Tantia Topee on the Betwa.

3rd April, he successfully stormed Jhansi.

6th May, he defeated Tantia Topee and the Ranee of Jhansi at Koonch.

23rd May, he beat the rebels at Golowlee near Calpee and occupied that fort the following day.

16th to 20th June, he recaptured from the rebels the Morar cantonments, the heights, cities and fort of Gwalior, and reinstated Scindiah on his throne.

---

150. See Appendix B.

The Central India Field Force was now to a great extent broken up. Brigadier-General R. Napier, C.B., took command of the Gwalior Division. The larger portion of the infantry remained at Morar and Gwalior with some cavalry and artillery, and a brigade of native infantry, with cavalry and artillery, was sent to hold Jhansi. Of Brigadier Smith's brigade a part was sent to Sipri, a part to Goona, and part remained at Gwalior. The distribution of the Fourteenth was as follows: 3 squadrons at Gwalior, 1 squadron at Jhansi.

Many of the officers and men of the Fourteenth had suffered from illness and sunstroke during the operations about Koonch, Calpee, and Gwalior. Colonel Charles Steuart, C.B., Brigadier of the 2nd Brigade, became ill at Koonch, and during the month of May he, together with Captain Brown, Lieutenant Leith, Lieutenant Travers, and Veterinary-Surgeon Dawson went home to England on medical certificate, owing to illness caused by the hardships and exposure they had undergone in the campaign. At Golowlee, on 22nd May, Major Scudamore, who was in command of the Fourteenth, was struck down by the sun's rays, and Brevet Lieutenant-Colonel Gall assumed temporary command of the regiment, and was senior officer with the five troops taking part in the pursuit on that day and at the capture of Calpee.

In the operations about Calpee the Fourteenth had lost, from sunstroke, 12 men: 8 of these were in the left wing with the 1st Brigade, and 4 were in the right wing with the 2nd Brigade.

The tired and enfeebled men of the late Central India Field Force were now looking forward to some rest and repose, and as the rains had begun to fall in torrents this gave them relief from the oppressive heat. But their rest was destined to be cut short. Tantia Topee had still to be pursued and the rebels must be hunted down: indeed, for several months to come there was plenty of work for the British troops in various directions over Central India and other provinces. Brigadier Napier operated with his detached parties first in Gwalior, then in the districts to the west and south-west of Gwalior, bordering on Rajputana, up to the end of November.

In December a new enemy invaded Gwalior. The pseudo-prince, as Malleson calls Ferozshah, who was expelled by our troops from Mundesor in November 1857, had now determined to join Tantia Topee in his struggles against the British. Accordingly he crossed the river Jumna on 9th December, coming from Etawah, and proceeded in the direction of Jhansi. Previous to this, in the month of August, a column had been sent out from Jhansi under Captain P. S. Thompson, 14th Light Dragoons, in which was included a squadron of the Fourteenth consisting of 'C' and 'E' troops. This column was employed in various operations against the rebels, and had an engagement on 23rd September at Garotha. For his services on this occasion Captain Thompson subsequently received the thanks of His Excellency the Most Honourable the Viceroy and Governor-General of India in Council.

From the 10th September to the 4th October, Major Scudamore had command of a column in the field against the rebels, in which a squadron of the Fourteenth was included, consisting of 'A' and 'H' troops; and again from the 5th October to the end of the year 1858, Major Scudamore was hunting down the enemy in command of another column, included in which was a squadron of the Fourteenth, composed of 'B' and 'D' troops. This column, like the previous one, took the field and operated in various directions throughout the districts surrounding Gwalior.

In the month of December, owing to reports received by Brigadier-General Sir Robert Napier, K.C.B., about the advance of Ferozshah, as alluded to above, he sent off several detachments to watch the roads by which that chieftain would probably come. [151] On the morning of the 12th December he received from the commander of one of these, Captain William McMahon, 14th Light Dragoons, who was posted with a detachment of his men near the confluence of the Jumna, Chambal, and Sind Rivers, information that the rebels had passed into the Lohar district of Kuchwaghar, a marshy spot, and were advancing up the jungles of the Sind River. The major-general, hoping to intercept them, marched that day from Gwalior to Antri, on the Jhansi road, his force consisting of the following details:—

	Men.
1 squadron 14th Light Dragoons,	150
Mahratta Horse,	100
71st Highlanders,	117
25th Bombay Native Infantry,	50
40 camels, Gwalior Camel Corps,	—
2 Bombay light field battery guns,	—

The squadron of the Fourteenth consisted of the 'A' and 'H' troops under Captain Prettejohn, and there were also 25 men of the Balandshar Horse, who joined Sir R. Napier's force at Narwar (for he had

151. Malleson, vol. v.

marched to the south from Antri, owing to fresh intelligence received of the rebels' movements), and by the 17th, marching with all speed, he reached Ranode, which is a large town 50 miles north-east of Goona.

As it happened, Ferozshah was marching from a different, though parallel, direction on Ranode that very same morning, with an intention of sacking the place. He was quite ignorant of the arrival of the English, and his army, a somewhat irregular mass, extended with a front of nearly a mile.[152] Sir R. Napier had scarcely time to form up the Fourteenth when the rebels were within a few yards of him, as the other portions of his little army were delayed by the camels in crossing a ravine. The troops actually engaged in the action were Prettejohn's squadron 14th Light Dragoons; Mahratta Horse, under Captain F. H. Smith; and 38 men of the 71st Highlanders under Captain Smith, mounted on camels, guided by Captain Templer.

Prettejohn, directly he saw the opportunity for charging, dashed with his squadron into the midst of the rebels, and the blow completely doubled them up. They turned and fled before the Mahratta Horse were upon them, but the latter were in time for the pursuit. Captain Prettejohn and 13 men of the Fourteenth were wounded in the charge, which was carried out with special dash and complete success. The pursuit was continued for 7 or 8 miles. The rebels, who as a mass made no resistance, fought bravely in individual cases. We captured 6 elephants, several horses and ponies, and a quantity of arms. There were 150 dead bodies of the enemy left on the scene of this charge at Ranode. As Captain Prettejohn was wounded, the command of the Fourteenth devolved upon Captain Need, who estimated the loss of the rebels in the subsequent pursuit at 300.[153]

The following extract from a letter written by Brigadier-General Sir R. Napier, K.C.B., to Major Scudamore, then commanding 14th Light Dragoons (owing to the absence on sick-leave in England of Colonel C. Steuart, C.B., and Colonel Ainslie being employed elsewhere in India), has reference to the affair of Ranode:—

This morning the enemy were beaten and pursued with slaughter for eight miles, your glorious Fourteenth going a mere handful into the mass without looking twice, Prettejohn leading, as you would expect.

---

152. Malleson, vol. v.
153. See Appendix B, Captain Need's report and Sir R. Napier's despatch.

For their gallant conduct on this occasion the following officers and men of the Fourteenth were specially brought to notice in despatches:

Captain Prettejohn.
Captain Need.
Captain Todd.
Lieutenant Giles.
Regimental Sergeant-Major Thomas Clark.
Corporal George Best ('H' troop).

Captain Prettejohn's wound was a severe sabre-cut on the outside and back of his left thigh, three inches above the knee. In addition to the 13 men wounded, the Fourteenth also had 1 officer's charger wounded and 1 missing, 5 troop-horses wounded and 13 troop-horses missing.

Lieutenant Hugh Gough[154] of the Mahratta Horse was present in this affair, and was mentioned in despatches for his gallant conduct on the occasion. He has very kindly allowed the following extract from a book written by him to be inserted here:—[155]

We (2nd Mahratta Horse) arrived at our destination, Morar (Gwalior), just in time to take a share in Sir R. Napier's dashing pursuit of Ferozshah, ending with the action and complete dispersal of his followers at Ranode on 1 7th December. Sir R. Napier had received intelligence at Morar that Ferozshah, with about 2000 rebels, was endeavouring to make his way across Bundelkund towards Central India, endeavouring to join forces with the famous Tantia Topee, about the most energetic and restless of the rebel leaders. Hoping to cut off Ferozshah, Sir Robert organised a movable column, consisting of a squadron of the 14th Light Dragoons, 100 men of the 71st Highland Light Infantry (as a camel corps), the 2nd Mahratta Horse, and the Torvanna Horse (independent Punjaub Cavalry) under a native leader, Jehan Khan.

With this small force, about 350 all told, Napier left Morar on, I think, December 13, 1858, starting down the Jhansi road. On arriving near the village of Ranode in the early morning of the 17th December, our little force was carefully distributed in am-

154. Now General Sir Hugh Gough, G.C.B.,V.C. 155. *Old Memories*, by General Sir Hugh Gough, G.C.B.,V.C. Blackwood, 1897.

bush, and as the enemy approached, when thoroughly exposed to our attack on an open plain, the order was given to "Advance and charge." We were down on them like lightning, and in an instant all was confusion, slaughter, and flight. Ferozshah was the first to bolt, and being well mounted, he got away; but most of the leaders were killed, and little resistance was made. It was a case of *sauve qui peut* from first to last.

Our newly raised recruits (Mahratta Horse) were not in it with the 14th Light Dragoons, who rode like mad and pursued for seven miles over a most break-neck country. We cut up numbers, and dispersed the whole gathering, besides capturing six or seven elephants. Prettejohn of the Fourteenth got a severe sabre-cut across the thigh, and on my way back I passed him, much distressed, not at being wounded, but at being unable to get at his cigars, which, being in his holster, had disappeared with his horse! After this affair at Ranode, the column marched for a time about the jungles in pursuit of Tantia Topee, and we passed through Goona and Augur where "Meade's Horse"[156] were, and subsequently we returned to Morar.

1858–59

In the subsequent pursuit of the rebels by Brigadier-General Sir R. Napier's column, Major Prettejohn's men endured some very harassing marches, continuing, as they did, for a prolonged period.

On 1st March 1859, the 'B' troop joined this column, and all were employed actively till 3rd April in hunting up bodies of rebels scattered through dense jungles, the men being frequently in the saddle from sunrise to sunset. On 2nd April, 'A' and 'H' troops were present at the attack of a village during some operations in the Gwalior district.

After the Battle of Gwalior on 19th June 1858, the headquarters of the Fourteenth had remained stationed in the Morar cantonments for nearly a year; 'C' and 'E' troops were sent for a time to Jhansi, but they returned, under Major Thompson, on 3rd August to Morar.

Most of the various troops of the Fourteenth had been kept employed in different expeditions, on field service, during these eventful times.

In recognition of their services Majors Scudamore and Gall were promoted Brevet Lieutenant-Colonels, and nominated Companions

---

156. It was the commandant of 'Meade's Horse,' Major Meade, who subsequently captured Tantia Topee.

of the Most Honourable Order of the Bath.

Captains Todd, Thompson, and Prettejohn became Brevet-Majors, and later on they received the brevet rank of Lieutenant-Colonel; and Captains McMahon and Need became Brevet-Majors.

Regimental Sergeant-Major Clark was awarded the medal 'for gallant conduct in the field.'

During the year 1858 the headquarters were at Kirkee in January.

On 1st February they were at Camp Rahala.

On 1st March	,,	,,	,,	Camp Jhilwand.
On 1st April	,,	,,	,,	Camp Goona.
On 1st May	,,	,,	,,	Camp Jhansi.
On 1st June	,,	,,	,,	Camp Calpee.
On 1st July	,,	,,	,,	Morar till the end of the year.

Brevet-Colonel Ainslie had been for a time at Jhansi in command of a brigade, which operated against the rebels and advanced towards Ranode in December of this year (1858).

DESCRIPTION OF LIEUTENANT-COLONEL GALL, C.B., 14TH LIGHT DRAGOONS.

(Extract from *Scraps from my Sabretache*, by G. Carter Sten T. W. H. Allen and Co., 1882.)

Colonel Gall deserves something more than a passing notice, and though I disliked him personally, I cannot refrain from expressing my admiration of him as a soldier and a daring officer.

He was a short, spare, sallow-visaged man; but in his little frame was an immense amount of courage and endurance. He, I believe, gloried in danger, and would face anything or everything—the devil himself. He had so much confidence in himself, and during the Sikh war was endeavouring to seize a standard, when he received a sabre-cut which rendered his right hand useless. He thought to get over that, however, by inventing a sword which could be fitted to his wrist; this, after a trial or two, he found did not answer, so he had to give it up and use his left hand. In leading a charge, either against the enemy or at a field day, he would turn round in his saddle and say, "Now, men, you are quite at liberty to gallop over me—if you can!" He was always so splendidly mounted that that was an impossibility.

In riding, his light frame seemed to grow out of the saddle; as the old soldier constantly remarked, "He sticks to the saddle like a sick monkey on the yard-arm!" He was reported never to undress, but always to sleep booted and belted, and dressed ready for a turn-out on the instant; and this would appear to be true, for at the first blast of the trumpet he would appear riding down the lines fully equipped, as if he had been waiting for the trumpet to sound. I am not his biographer, or I might write a volume concerning him; but I will conclude with observing that, though he was not very popular among his own men as a commanding officer, every man among us admired him for his daring as a soldier.

Sylvester, who lived in the same tent with him during the greater part of the campaign, says of Lieutenant-Colonel Gall:—

His energy wore him to a shadow; he was brave to a fault, but fussy to a degree. He often slept in his uniform, and when near the enemy would often get up in the night and ride round the picquets.

Since the 1st April 1858, a schoolmaster-sergeant had ceased to be borne on the strength of cavalry regiments.

During a portion of 1858, Captain J. Barrett had been in command of the headquarters, nearly all the other officers being with the various portions of the regiment engaged on service in the field some with the Nerbudda Field Force, some with the Central India Field Force, and some with the Gwalior Division. Five troops were present at the capture of Garrakota, 5 troops at the forcing of the Muddenpore Pass, and 3 troops at the capture of Chanderi.

Towards the close of the year 1858, the service-troops in India numbered 660 non-commissioned officers and men. The depot at Maidstone consisted of 134.

1859

From 1st January to end of April several of the troops were on field-service with the Gwalior Division, and some, as we have already related, were detached with flying columns through the provinces.

On 21st January the Fourteenth received permission to bear the word 'Persia' on their cap-plates and appointments in consideration of their services in that country in 1857.

On the 4th March, orders were received for the Fourteenth to go to Bombay, preparatory to giving up their horses and embarking for

England. There were 71 men who volunteered to remain in India, and they were transferred chiefly to the newly formed regiments, now the 19th and 20th Hussars, and the 21st (Empress of India's) Lancers, which were composed of volunteers from the old Bengal European Light Cavalry Regiments belonging to the late Honourable East India Company's service. On the 24th April the Fourteenth gave up their horses to the Commissariat Department

The headquarters remained at Morar (Gwalior) till 26th April, when they left by bullock-train *en route* to Bombay, the rest of the regiment having proceeded there in advance by same route.

On the 20th April, at Camp Serony, when the Fourteenth were about to proceed to Bombay, the following farewell order was issued by Brigadier-General Sir Robert Napier, K.C.B., commanding Gwalior Division:—

> I cannot part with the troops now leaving the Gwalior Division, after having been associated with them during a year's eventful service, without a few words to convey to them my admiration and regard for their excellent and soldier-like conduct. To Colonel Scudamore it is due that the State of Duttea and the central districts of Gwalior were protected from the rebels under the Rao Sahib, who were baffled by the movements of his small but undaunted column. The brilliant 14th Light Dragoons and their charges at Jowra-Alipore and Ranode will not easily be forgotten.

The brigadier's order was as follows:—

> Brigadier-General Stuart has to express his best thanks and acknowledgments to the officers, non-commissioned officers, and men of that part of the 14th Light Dragoons that served under his command with the Malwa and Central India Field Forces, for the gallantry and dash they have displayed on all occasions in which they were engaged with the enemy. Discipline and efficiency have been admirably maintained throughout under most trying circumstances. They have borne with great cheerfulness exposures and fatigues in all weather. In taking leave of this distinguished regiment, Brigadier Stuart feels that he is parting with tried friends and comrades, and most heartily wishes them all honour and happiness in their future career.'

By the 23rd May the regiment was assembled at Bombay preparatory to embarkation for England, but the order was countermanded, and it returned to Kirkee, where it arrived 26th May and remained for the rest of the year.

Being very short of horses, remounts were now quickly supplied to the regiment. On 6th June, 176 unbroken remounts joined, and by the 21st June, 14 days after these horses joined, 2 squadrons paraded in marching order for the inspection of Major-General Sir Hugh Rose, K.C.B., who complimented the commanding officer and all concerned at the promptitude with which the remounts had been trained.

On 22nd June a further batch of 88 remounts joined, and on 6th July 88 more. This completed the regiment up to 55 horses per troop. They mostly consisted of Arabs and Persians.

On 27th July a squadron of the regiment in review order escorted Major-General Sir Hugh Rose, K.C.B., on the occasion of his being invested with the order of G.C.B.

On 12th August, Captain T. Barrett died of hepatitis at Kirkee.

On the 22nd August the Fourteenth were present at a brigade field-day at Poona, and although only six weeks had elapsed since the last batch of remounts had been received, the whole of the regiment was now quite fit again for active service.

On 12th November an order was received for the regiment to prepare for immediate embarkation for England.

On 17th November, His Excellency General Sir H. Somerset inspected and was much pleased with the state of the regiment. He said that H.R.H. the Duke of Cambridge had repeatedly written to him expressing his admiration of the gallant conduct of the 14th Light Dragoons during the late campaign in Central India.

Volunteering was now opened, and 130 men volunteered to go to cavalry regiments serving in the Bombay and Madras Presidencies, and to the Bombay Horse Artillery.

Appendix A

Extracts from the *Illustrated London News* of 27th January 1849.
Extract from the letter of an officer of the Bengal Horse Artillery,
dated 1st December 1848:—

There has been a skirmish at a place called Ramnuggur, on the
River Chenab, about 40 miles north of Lahore. It was intended
for a reconnaissance, but circumstances turned it into a cavalry
fight, as I will endeavour to explain to you. Lord Gough, hearing that the enemy had drawn up in force on the opposite side
of the River Chenab, determined to reconnoitre them and two
fords across the river. For this purpose he detached two parties,
the first consisting of the:

3rd Light Dragoons,   8th Light Cavalry,

          Troop of Horse Artillery,

to examine one ford; the second party consisted of

14th (King's) Light Dragoons,   Irregular Cavalry,
5th Light Cavalry,   Troop of Horse Artillery,

to look at the other ford.

The force left camp about 3 a.m., 22nd November, and arrived
on the ground about 7 a.m.

One of the parties was going along steadily as directed, when
they came across the *nullah*, and seeing a large number of the
enemy's cavalry beyond, Colonel Havelock ordered a charge,
and, as the party were crossing the *nullah*, the enemy's guns on
the opposite side opened on them at about 300 yards' range.
The Sikhs had placed their guns in masked batteries, and, as

you may suppose, the sudden discharge took our people by surprise; nevertheless they went on, seeing a large number of the enemy beyond the *nullah*. The ground was very heavy and sandy; a large portion of our cavalry got into a quicksand, and the horses, being somewhat exhausted by the march over the heavy ground, were not able to extricate themselves as soon as they might have done. The enemy's infantry were, in the meantime, behind large sand hillocks, and steadily firing into our men, who were also being fired upon by the large Sikh guns on the other side of the river.

The Horse Artillery immediately unlimbered their guns and returned the fire as well as could be expected from six small guns. The retreat was then sounded, and in re-crossing the *nullah* one of our guns, as also two of our ammunition-wagons, stuck fast in the sand, the poles of the limber and the horses being shot; they had, however, previously spiked the gun so as to render it useless to the enemy. The commander-in-chief, hearing the firing, had ridden up to the spot. Meantime, Colonel Havelock was about to make another charge at the enemy with the 14th Light Dragoons, but the commander-in-chief sent an order by General Cureton, who commanded the cavalry division, to prevent the charge, and in conveying this order the general was shot through the heart.

Colonel Havelock had also fallen. Colonel Alexander, 5th Cavalry, was shot through the right arm, and has since had it taken out of the socket. Several officers of the 14th Light Dragoons were killed and wounded, also several officers of the 5th Light Cavalry, whose names we have not heard. The gun and ammunition-wagons were abandoned by order of Lord Gough, as the fire from the enemy's guns was very severe. The guns on the opposite side of the river, and the portion of the enemy's force drawn up behind a quicksand, has been a regular trap into which we have fallen most woefully.

Reported in the *Illustrated London News*

By intelligence from India, dated up to 28th November, from the army of the Punjaub, Shere Singh with his army was occupying a position on the right bank of the Ravee,[1] whilst Lord Gough's camp was situated about twelve miles from Ramnug-

---

1. This, evidently, should be Chenab—(Author).

138

gur, on the left bank. According as our troops advanced under Lord Gough the enemy were reported in force at several places, but always evacuated them before they were occupied by us; they were at length, however, ascertained to have determined on making a stand at Ramnuggur, and General Cureton was directed to halt until more troops came up. Brigadier-General Campbell joined his camp on the 12th November, taking command as senior officer and bringing up another brigade.

Considerable additions to the force of the camp were made during the five or six days following, and at length the commander-in-chief, having considered that the time had arrived for the commencement of operations, orders were issued late on the night of the aist November, in the camp of Brigadier-General Campbell at Saharun, for the troops to parade on the following morning at three o'clock in front of the centre of the camp without sound of bugle, trumpet, or drum; and a strong detachment marched under the personal command of the commander-in-chief (who had come up from the headquarters' camp to superintend the proceedings of the morning) at the appointed time, and reached the left bank of the Chenab near Ramnuggur at an early hour, in the hope of surprising the detachment of the enemy who were known to be on the same side. It would appear, however, that these had early intimation of the movement of the British troops, and had all retired across except a few stragglers and a picquet which fled, leaving their tents pitched. The object of the movement on our side was, however, mainly to ascertain the real strength and position of the enemy, and this was in some degree effected on clearing Ramnuggur towards the left bank of the river.

Then it became apparent that their camp was pitched along the right bank of the river, which was seen to be crowded by thousands of men, whose white and light-coloured garments strongly contrasted with the bodies of the British troops to which the eyes of our officers had been for some time past accustomed. In drawing out their fire to ascertain their real strength in guns, and pressing, perhaps, rather too zealously in pursuit of those of the fugitives who appeared to be within reach, while crossing at the ford with water to the waist, Lieutenant-Colonel Lane's troop of Horse Artillery (2nd of the 3rd Brigade) got into heavy sand before they were aware of it, and a leading horse having been shot, it was found when the order came to limber up and retire that one of the guns could not be moved.

The Sikhs were not slow at perceiving this most inopportune embarrassment, and directed so hot a fire upon the spot that it was found necessary to abandon the gun, although a light field battery was brought up to cover it. But the fire of the enemy from guns that were sheltered, while ours were exposed in an open plain, was so heavy that nothing could be done beyond scattering a few of the nearest groups of the enemy and then retiring. The cavalry were ordered to do the same and take shelter from the enemy's round-shot behind a tope of trees to the left, where they remained quietly for a time, the infantry being during that interim drawn up on the right. Some of the enemy being subsequently discovered on the left bank of the river further down to the left, a large number of our cavalry, among whom were the 3rd and 14th Light Dragoons, moved down by order to dislodge them.

The following letter from an officer, who was an eye-witness of the scene, graphically describes the interesting details of this brief but sanguinary combat which cost us so dearly:—

Camp Ramnuggur, November 25, 1848.
On the morning of the 22nd inst., at 2 a.m., the orderly-sergeant of the "E" troop came into my tent at Deeda Singh camp and showed me the order-book with the following command:—

The troops will parade in marching order at a quarter before 3 a.m., without sound of trumpet or bugle, and form up on their respective alarm-posts.

The morning was pitch dark when the order to move forward was given, and before we had advanced a mile, cavalry, camp followers, artillery, and infantry, were jumbled together. At length day broke, order was restored, and a report ran through the columns that Ramnuggur was in sight. Immediately after, our destination was confirmed, and the enemy was stated to be in position in our front. At 7 o'clock a.m. we reached Ramnuggur and saw the enemy and their camp in the distance. At half-past 7 o'clock the 3rd Light Dragoons, Holmes's Irregulars, and the Horse Artillery were pushed forward with Her Majesty's 61st Regiment in skirmishing order; and we, with the 5th Cavalry and some Native Infantry, were ordered to halt on the right of the city with the 2nd Europeans a little on the left rear.

A few minutes later the enemy opened their fire. This continued about an hour, during which time we stood inactively admiring their shot and shells as they flew through or burst in the air. By about half-past 8 a.m. our guns had got into position and began replying to the enemy, when the order came for us to advance, which we did, and were halted about three-quarters of a mile from where the enemy's picquet had been. Their picquet-tents were still standing on an entrenched piece of ground, but their picquet had retired across the river.

The round-shot now began to whistle near us, generally falling short, and the men began to get excited; when, about 9 o'clock a.m., the order came for us to move more to our left and get shelter from a *tope* of trees nearer to and more in front of the enemy's guns. Here we saw the 3rd Light Dragoons, who were more than a mile on our left, charging some Sikh cavalry, who, retiring before them, opened out and dispersed the moment they drew the Third within range of their batteries, which immediately opened on them.

One man was killed and three wounded by the fire, while several horses suffered. A staff officer sent by Lord Gough ordered them to retire immediately out of fire, as the guns were on the other side of the river. While doing so a 9-lb. shot struck Captain Ouvry's[2] horse, passing clean through him, but the rider fortunately escaped. In a few moments after the horse was stripped by the Sikh cavalry, who pressed on their rear, trying again to draw them under fire. During all this time the round-shot was flying over and through the 14th Light Dragoons, and, strange to say, doing no harm. A little after 11 o'clock a.m. the enemy's cavalry came across the *nullah* that protected part of their front, and formed upon the left bank, to the right front of the Fourteenth, in great force, when the 14th Light Dragoons and 5th Light Cavalry received orders to charge them.

Before saying anything of this charge, I must try to describe the Sikh position. The Sikhs to the number of 30,000 men occupied the right bank of the River Chenab, where they had

---

2. Afterwards Colonel H. A. Ouvry, C.B., 9th Lancers. *Cavalry Experiences and Leaves From My Journal*, by Henry Ouvry is also republished by Leonaur as *Cavalry Experiences* by Henry Aimé Ouvry.

a strong entrenched camp with several batteries erected. A little to the right front of Ramnuggur the river formed a bend; in it was an island containing a couple of acres of ground, and between that and the left bank the water was about 30 yards wide, with a precipitous fall from the left bank of from four to six feet before you got into its bed, which was in some parts four feet deep. This part is called the *nullah*, as the main branch of the river is on the right of the island.

It is as nearly as possible in front of the centre of the Sikh position; on it were about 4000 men and a battery of six guns, while the approach to it was swept by a cross-fire from two batteries on the mainland. Knowing nothing of this position, and deeming the *nullah* the river, the Fourteenth, when ordered to charge, galloped on to the enemy's cavalry, who retired through the *nullah* on to the island, while the enemy's batteries opened their fire, and their infantry on the island poured in their volleys.

Nothing daunted, Colonel Havelock cheering led on the first and second squadrons of the Fourteenth down to the bank, then into the *nullah*, crossed it at a gallop, sabred hundreds of the enemy under the most frightful shower of missiles from their guns and infantry. They then retired a short distance, formed up, were joined by the other squadrons, and the 5th Light Cavalry who had crossed a little higher up, and charged again. In this, the second charge, Colonel Havelock met his death, it was supposed, for he was not seen or heard of after General Cureton joined them with orders to retire, as, though the Fourteenth seemed so determined to destroy the enemy, they were utterly indifferent to their own loss.

The commander-in-chief having cleared the left bank of the enemy, did not wish for more. While General Cureton was giving the order to retire, a matchlock ball struck him in the throat, and another in the forehead, and thus fell this glorious man, the finest cavalry officer of the day, at the head of that regiment in which as a private soldier, under the assumed name of "Roberts," he had commenced his career, and out of which he received his first commission.

The 14th Light Dragoons then retired in order, formed up, and the roll was called, when 45 men were found missing and about 50 horses. Of the missing men, 14 were killed, and the remainder wounded. One of the killed, Sergeant Todd, had his head taken off by a round-shot. Colonel Havelock has not yet been found; the last seen of him was in the second charge, while he was crossing the *nullah*. His orderly states that both the Colonel and his horse fell wounded or killed, that he was hurried on, and he did not see him after. About twelve of the 5th Light Cavalry suffered, I am told, and one of the first round-shots fired at the charging regiments took off the arm of Colonel Alexander, who commanded the 5th Light Cavalry.

Nothing could exceed the accuracy of the enemy's fire: their range was beautifully taken for certain points, showing that they must have discovered them previous to our advance; and our artillery officers say they never saw anything finer than the way their horse artillery were brought up to the edge of the river and formed up. No nation could exceed them in the rapidity of their fire.

It is said that a Frenchman, late an officer in the Maharajah Runjeet Singh's service, and *aide-de-camp* to General Avitahile, named *L'Enfant*, commands them. No men could act more bravely than the Sikhs. They faced us the moment we came on them, firing all the time, and when we did come on them some opened out, and immediately after closed round us, while others threw themselves on their faces or turned their backs, protected by a shield from the stroke of the dragoon's sabre, and the moment that was given turned round, hamstrung the horse and shot the rider; while their individual acts of bravery were the admiration of all. Many stood before a charging squadron and singled out a man, after killing or wounding whom they themselves were cut down immediately; while many, before their blows could take effect, received the point of a sabre and fell in the act of making a cut.

Amongst our officers, Captain Gall's personal courage was most conspicuous. He took single-handed one of the enemy's standards, but before he could get assistance he was knocked over and his right hand nearly severed from his body; some of his men, however, rushed to his rescue and saved him from receiving a mortal wound, though they could not again recover the standard which he had so hardly fought and suffered for.

After Captain Gall was knocked over, a young cornet named D'Urban Blyth rode at the head of the troop, and while charging, saw Lieutenant McMahon fall wounded a little way off and a Sikh rushing forward to kill him. Cornet Blyth galloped forward, gave point, and sent his blade clean through the Sikh. On three different occasions afterwards he rushed out from his troop, and each time in single combat killed his man. Many private soldiers performed wonders. But I must not omit to mention that after Captain Fitzgerald fell, Captain Wilmer's troop was passing on their return, when they saw that he was alive. Captain Wilmer and four troopers dismounted and succeeded in bringing him in under the most frightful fire. All agree in one thing, however nobly the Fourteenth gained their laurels in the Peninsula, no charge they ever made could surpass this in gallantry, and yet no more than four or five of the officers and men had ever been under fire previously.

It is impossible to say what loss the enemy sustained; but had the Fourteenth not been broken by jumping into the *nullah*, more than half of the regiment must have been destroyed, so severe was the fire, as all the shot, had they charged in close order, would have taken effect. I have heretofore omitted saying anything of Colonel King, as he had little to do beyond assisting to keep the men together and obey orders, until Colonel Havelock was killed. From the moment, however, his loss was known, Colonel King took up the command and ably did he carry out the duties that were entrusted to him. . . . . To his watchful care the greater number of the wounded that were brought in owe their safety. Officers and men agree that his admirable conduct on that occasion proves him an able successor.

Lord Gough visited the wounded yesterday, and expressed himself to each in the kindest terms about his injuries, and with the strongest praise of his brave conduct.

As I conclude this we are erecting batteries and expecting to be joined by Brigadier General Wheeler's force, and two regiments of Eckford's brigade that remained behind at Lahore.

The enemy are about being reinforced by Chuttur Singh, who has 40,000 men and about 60 guns with him, and report says they will try to turn our rear; but we only wish that, as the men are all in high spirits and determined to show them no quarter. The enemy's guns never cease firing, we are continually having their round-shot bowling into us, but doing little damage.

144

Another writer observes:—

An attempt will doubtless be made to cast some blame upon the commander-in-chief for the result of these two affairs, but not justly. The facts are that General Cureton ordered in the first instance both movements, and if they had been carried out as he had wished, they would have been attended with the happiest results, but on both occasions mistakes in the execution, to a great degree unavoidable, marred the original plan. In both cases the ardour of our troops was too great. It was a rush who should get at the enemy first, but it must have been most gratifying to the commander-in-chief to witness the brilliant conduct of the regiments engaged and the intrepidity with which they were led by their officers.

Casualties at the Battle of Ramnuggur
Killed.

Brigadier-General Cureton, shot through the heart; Colonel Havelock, 14th Light Dragoons, missing, but subsequently found killed; Captain Fitzgerald, 14th Light Dragoons, killed.

Wounded

Lieutenant Hardinge, A.D.C., shot through the shoulder; Captain Scudamore, 14th Dragoons, sabred in the face; Captain Gall, 14th Dragoons, wounded in the hand; Lieutenant McMahon, 14th Dragoons, shot through the head; Lieutenant Chetwynd, spent ball in the side.

14th Dragoons, 3 privates killed, 9 missing, 23 wounded, 5 contused, 25 horses wounded, 34 horses missing.

3rd Light Dragoons, 5 privates wounded.

5th Light Cavalry, Quartermaster-Sergeant killed by a roundshot, which first took off the arm of Colonel Alexander and then contused the foot of Lieutenant Reilly. Twelve privates killed, 15 privates wounded. Forty horses killed and wounded.

8th Light Cavalry, Subadar-Major killed.

12th Irregular Cavalry, Captain Holmes wounded.

Horse Artillery, 1 private wounded, 2 *syces* killed, 4 horses killed.

Soon after this the Sikh army, which amounted to 30,000 with a park of heavy artillery, effected a retreat from their position and left the right bank of the Chenab on 3rd December under Shere Singh. They proceeded along the mountain chain in the

direction of the River Jhelum after remaining for nearly a fortnight in the presence of our army, which, during the greater
part of that period, was waiting the arrival of reinforcements. It
is computed that in the various affairs which took place on the
banks of the Chenab our killed and wounded have been about
400, while the loss of the enemy was 4000. By the latest advices
received, dated 18th December, from Bombay, it is stated that
Lord Gough had crossed the Chenab.

(End of Extracts from the *Illustrated London News* of 27th January
1849.)

General Lord Gough, G.C.B., Commander-in-Chief of the army
in India, writes as follows:—

Ramnuggur, November 23, 1848.
Deeming it necessary to drive the rebel forces at this side the
river across, and to capture any guns they might have had on
the left bank, I directed Brigadier-General Campbell, with an
infantry brigade, accompanied by the cavalry division, and three
troops of Horse Artillery under Brigadier-General Cureton, to
proceed during the night of the 21st from Saharun, four miles
in front of my camp at Nonbulla, to effect this object. I joined
the Brigadier at 3 a.m. to witness the operation.
I witnessed with intense anxiety, but equally intense admiration,
a charge made by Lieutenant-Colonel William Havelock at the
head of the 14th King's Light Dragoons, who, I fear, miscon-
ceived the orders he received from the officer commanding the
Cavalry Division, or, from the inequalities of the ground and
the fearful dust occasioned by such a rapid movement, mistook
the body he was instructed to charge, and moved upon and
overwhelmed another much closer to the river, which exposed
him to a cross-fire from the enemy's guns.
I never witnessed so brilliant a charge, but I regret to say the
loss was considerable, were it only in that of Brigadier-General
Cureton, than whom a better or braver soldier never fell in his
country's service. The brave leader of the 14th Light Dragoons,
Lieutenant-Colonel Havelock, is missing. He charged into a
gole of the enemy and has not since been seen, regretted by
every soldier who witnessed his noble daring. The enemy suffered severely; numbers were precipitated into the river and
drowned, and a standard was captured.

The Goorchurras were more daring than I have before seen them, but the brilliant charges both of the 3rd and 14th Light Dragoons will have taught them a lesson they will not readily forget. This was a cavalry affair alone.

Brigadier-General C. Campbell, C.B.,[3] Commanding 4th Division, writes—

Ramnuggur, November 27, 1848.

Captain Warner's and Lieutenant-Colonel Lane's troops of Horse Artillery were engaged. In withdrawing from the deep and heavy sand under the fire of the whole of the enemy's artillery, amounting to 28 guns posted on high ground overhanging the river on the opposite bank, I regret to say that one gun and two ammunition-wagons of Colonel Lane's troop got embedded in the heavy sand and could not be recovered. The enemy observing this immediately crossed with great confidence the whole of his cavalry at numbers between 3000 and 4000: they clung to the banks of the river and kept under cover of the fire of their artillery on the opposite bank.

This cavalry was charged on separate occasions by Her Majesty's 3rd and 14th Light Dragoons, and 5th and 8th regiments of Light Cavalry. His Lordship the Commander-in-Chief was an eye-witness of the brilliant conduct of these corps and of the intrepid manner in which they were led by their officers. The enemy were overthrown upon every occasion and fled for shelter to the riverside to be under the cover and protection of their artillery but I regret to say these several defeats of the enemy's cavalry were not effected without much loss. Brigadier-General Cureton, commanding the cavalry of the army, was killed while leading a squadron of the 14th Light Dragoons to the support of the 5th Light Cavalry. I regret also to have to report that Lieutenant-Colonel Havelock, commanding Her Majesty's 14th Light Dragoons, is reported to be missing. He was last seen charging the enemy at the head of his noble regiment, and has not since been heard of.

The following is an extract from the General Orders of the Commander-in-Chief in India, dated Camp Ramnuggur, 23rd November 1848:—

---

3. Afterwards Field-Marshal Lord Clyde, G.C.B., K. C.S.I.

The enemy were signally overthrown on every occasion, and only saved from utter annihilation by their flight to the cover of their guns on the opposite bank of the river. In the deaths of Brigadier-General C. R. Cureton, C.B., commanding Cavalry Division, and Lieutenant-Colonel Havelock, K.H., commanding 14th (King's) Light Dragoons, as well as Captain J. F. Fitzgerald of the same noble regiment, the service has sustained a loss which the commander-in-chief is sure the whole army will unite with him in lamenting.

The following statements were given, almost *verbatim*, to the author in answer to his questions by surviving officers of the 14th Light Dragoons who were present at Ramnuggur.

Captain R. P. Apthorp, who was Lieutenant and Adjutant of the Fourteenth at Ramnuggur, says:—

February 14, 1899.

I recollect the whole circumstances of the doings of the regiment at Ramnuggur, as if it were only yesterday it occurred. I have the whole scene in my mind's eye now. There were three charges.[4] We changed our front twice, as these Sikh *goles* scampered off before we could get to them, in different directions.

'It was in the second change of front that Herbert Gall rushed out from the troop he was commanding to seize a standard of the enemy, and very nearly had his right hand severed off. Some men of his troop rushed after him, but I, being near, stopped them, as it broke our line of advance. As it was, he never recovered the entire use of his hand again. It was a gallant act, but a very indiscreet one. It was Colonel Doherty who brought the regiment out of action. I never saw any artillery gun on our side of the *nullah*, and I do not think there were any. They played long bowls at us from the other side.

What made Lord Gough so impetuous was, that these large *goles* of Sikh horsemen, who persisted in remaining on our side of the *nullah*, although our artillery had been peppering at them for half an hour, would not disperse, and merely seemed to get out of the way of the shells. They took care to keep a long distance off. The 3rd Light Dragoons were sent by Lord Gough to disperse them (before we were ordered to charge), and they

---

4. Captain Apthorp refers to the first advance of Havelock before he changed front the first time, and he calls that advance a charge.

sent them across the *nullah*, but they were too wary to follow them over the *nullah*, and then the enemy returned to our side again, and this so nettled Lord Gough that he sent Colonel Cureton to ascertain the reason of the 3rd Dragoons retreating, and the former was told of the dreadful *nullah* which separated us from the main body of the Sikh army; and when Lord Gough was told this by Cureton he pooh-poohed it, and told him to order the Fourteenth to advance and go across the *nullah*, and of course it was there we lost Colonel Havelock and Fitzgerald and about fourteen of our men, besides several wounded.

On the other side of the *nullah* we came up to their guns and the whole force of the enemy we were entirely disorganised by the confusion caused by jumping into the *nullah* and out of it, and which was lined by sharpshooters under the taking-off bank. It was, of course, helter-skelter afterwards until we emerged to our side of the *nullah* again, and it was some little time before the officers could restore anything like order as the Sikh horsemen followed us again.

I, being well in the rear trying to halt our men, seeing these fellows coming on at us (the men generally knowing my voice well), I called out for skirmishers, and several men responded, and we covered our rear and kept the Sikh horsemen at bay, and then order was gradually restored. Colonel King was not in the charge at all. He was ordered to command the squadron which was left in support when we first advanced. He came up with this squadron as we were retreating, and it was a nucleus for us to form upon.

I recollect poor Colonel Havelock telling me that he was going to charge the enemy with three squadrons, and that he ordered one squadron to be in reserve to support them, and ordered me to go and find Colonel King and tell him to take charge of the supporting squadron and move up slowly after us. I did so. In the meantime Havelock had moved off to the front with the attacking squadrons, and I had to gallop after them to catch them up. It was just then that Havelock was changing his front to the left as the Sikhs had scampered off in that direction. When we got up to them, they, knowing they were in a line for the easiest part for crossing the *nullah*, made direct for it, and we saw them scamper down the banks; therefore, Havelock had to change his front again to follow them over the *nullah*, so there must have been three distinct charges.

There was no doubt that poor Havelock was killed at the *nullah*, as on recrossing, some of the men saw his charger (a grey horse) lying in the *nullah*, and one or two of the men were going to dismount and lead him back, but being near them, and on looking round I saw some of the Sikhs following us, I told the men there was no time to get hold of the colonel's charger, but to mount and get to the rear as fast as they could. With regard to Cornet Blyth, he had not long joined us, and I recollect that after his sabring four or five of the enemy, and saving McMahon's life, I dismissed him at once from any further sword-drill.

As to the question of whether there were two or three charges, Captain Apthorp says:—

I do not think it signifies much whether there were three charges or two. I considered Colonel Havelock's first advance was a charge, as he went direct for a large *gole* of the enemy's horsemen, but I was not with them, having been sent by Colonel Havelock to find Colonel King to direct him to take charge of the supporting squadron, and when I got up to the attacking squadrons Colonel Havelock was changing front to the left as the Sikh horsemen veered off in that direction. All I can recollect is that I saw the two charges, and we had to gallop a great pace to catch up the enemy, they having got well ahead of us while we were changing front.

It was in this charge that poor Fitzgerald and M—— got surrounded by some of the straggling enemy (as we came up to them) slipping through our squadron intervals, and their horses being blown, got into the rear. Poor Fitzgerald must have ridden eighteen to twenty stone with all his accoutrements on (he always rode Cape chargers), and M—— was at that time no lightweight. You may rest quite satisfied that there was *no* charge by Colonel King's supporting squadron, as they met us as we returned over the *nullah*, and we re-formed our straggling squadrons on them, got our usual strength of skirmishers out, and then made an orderly retreat. The Sikhs then stopped from following us.

With regard to the important point that Havelock had orders through Cureton to charge over the *nullah* I cannot corroborate it. What gave colour to it in my mind was, that Colonel Havelock (when he came up to me and directed me to find Colonel King, and give him directions to take charge of the supporting squadron) said, "I have just seen Cureton, and from what he says I expect to get immediate orders to charge to the front, as Lord Gough was displeased at the old 3rd Light Dragoons not pursuing the Sikhs further over the *nullah*."

We all thought that this *nullah* was the course of the Chenab, and that there was a ford over it, until Colonel White told Cureton it was a dry *nullah* with very steep banks, and he did not consider it expedient to cross it with his regiment, as the Sikhs were in great force on the other side and with a lot of guns. I have no doubt Colonel Havelock thought this almost tantamount to an order, as he (Colonel Havelock) said Cureton told him that Lord Gough said he did not understand a dry *nullah* stopping cavalry. There is no doubt Lord Gough thought better of this, as when poor Colonel Cureton was killed by a musket-shot he was galloping to stop us from going over the *nullah*, Lord Gough having noticed Havelock forming up the squadrons for a final attack over the *nullah*.

As for Sir Charles Gough, we know he was very biased in his statements about the affair as well as Chillianwallah. It has always appeared to me that it was Sir Charles Gough's aim all the way through to screen Lord Gough; for although all must admit that the latter was as brave an officer as ever drew sword, yet he was totally void of discretion as a commander. We have only to look at his tactics at Chillianwallah, where the 24th Regiment was decimated on account of his persisting that they should advance straight to their front, and attack and capture the Sikh guns, although he had been told that the Sikh gunners had the exact range for grapeshot, where they could pepper and annihilate the poor Twenty-fourth, and this was the result; but nothing could check Lord Gough's ardour when he had made up his mind, and all his reply to some of his cautious generals was: "Tell them to take the Sikh guns with the 'cold steel,'" of course meaning their bayonets.

Viscount Chetwynd, who, as Lieutenant the Honourable R. W. Chetwynd, was present with the Fourteenth at Ramnuggur, has given the following facts in reply to inquiries:—

The facts as to the squadrons of the Fourteenth at Ramnuggur are: Colonel Havelock went off with the 1st and 2nd squadrons in open column of troops, left in front, and made his first attack to his front, with the result that the 1st squadron, in which I was, got immediately into great confusion. The order for increasing the front I did not hear, and was afterwards told it was to form squadron on the move.

The 4th squadron, led by Captain Scudamore, received some order from a staff officer, the result of which was that Scudamore, after an independent charge of his own, joined Havelock's second charge. Scudamore's wound, mentioned in the newspaper, was received in guarding his face from a cut.

The 3rd squadron, led by Captain Wilmer, we met as we were retiring, a mob (we, not Wilmer's squadron). My recollection is that I saw Colonel King with the 3rd squadron, but would not state it without reserve. I have no recollection of ever hearing of this squadron charging, and do not believe they did. The story mentioned of Blyth having saved McMahon is exactly what I understood at the time. He also disposed of two or three more.

The story of the sergeant's head being taken off by a round-shot is exactly as Blyth, who saw it happen, described it to me, Havelock's body was not recovered till after we had crossed the Chenab in pursuit of the retreating Sikhs. Havelock certainly survived his first attack and led off the three squadrons (1st, 2nd, and 4th) for his second. I saw him in front of the line. Doherty was the senior officer in the three squadrons retiring from Havelock's second attack. I remember hearing him call out for Havelock. These squadrons were quite broken up.

The first attack (that of the two squadrons, 1st and 2nd) was, I imagine, pretty much a charge of the 2nd, the 1st following them in great confusion. I was afterwards told Havelock ordered increase of front from troop to squadron. I did not hear the order, and thought it was not repeated. It is possible Havelock did not give time for the increase of front, and that our left troop rushed ahead before we in the right troop could get into squadron. There was no interval between the first and second attack, which latter was made by the three squadrons, 1st, 2nd, and 4th, in line. The 1st, I think, outflanked the Sikh left.

As to the Sikh guns, they, I believe, were on the other side of the river; anyhow I saw nothing of them. They opened at once when Havelock moved off with the right wing. Their shot flew over our heads in the rear troop. I saw one round-shot take a rear-rank man in the rear troop very soon after moving off. This troop lost four killed. Another of the four I saw hit by a matchlock, the same volley that hit me, apparently from an ambuscade on our right.

As to the three charges Apthorp speaks of, there were three if you include Scudamore's with the 4th squadron on his way to join the right wing under Havelock. I do not see how Havelock could have charged twice to his front without the rear of the column getting up to him. When I emerged from the dust and confusion, the colonel was in front of the three squadrons forming line. I can distinctly tell who led the 1st and 2nd squadrons at Ramnuggur: Doherty led the 1st and Goddard the 2nd; Wilmer and Scudamore led the 3rd and 4th both at Ramnuggur and Chillianwallah, and, I fully believe, in the order here given. At Chillianwallah, Goddard led the 1st and Thompson the 2nd; Goddard's troop ("H") changed squadrons with the "D," Garratt's.

CHILLIANWALLAH

The mishap which occurred to Pope's Cavalry Brigade at the Battle of Chillianwallah has by some been attributed to panic, and to this the very best troops in the world are sometimes subject. On this occasion, however, there appears to have been another very potent cause for failure in the faulty tactics displayed by the Brigadier himself. He appears to have utterly disregarded all recognised rules of cavalry leading by deploying the whole of his nine squadrons of cavalry in one single line without any supports whatever. Cavalry in attack requires due supports to follow up an advantage or retrieve a check; it also requires a reserve or point to rally on. The jungly and obstructive nature of the ground was wholly unsuited for such an extended front as that of nine squadrons of cavalry in one line; and to add to the difficulty and confusion of advancing in presence of the enemy in such formation, under such circumstances, the fire of his own Horse Artillery guns was masked by the brigadier bringing his squadrons in front of them and overlapping them at a critical moment.

Such flagrant mismanagement courted disaster and is quite enough to account for the sequel. Thackwell's narrative of the second Sikh

War of 1848-49 gives many interesting particulars about the Fourteenth and the Battle of Chillianwallah. It completely vindicates the character of Lieutenant-Colonel King, and proves that the 14th Light Dragoons were by no means so much to blame as has generally been believed.

> The day after the action, a court of inquiry into the conduct of the regiment was held by Major-General Sir Joseph Thackwell, with closed doors, and from what transpired, the result was most satisfactory to that much-abused but brave body of men.[5]

Thackwell's *Narrative of the Second Sikh War* states that Brigadier Pope, who was a Lieutenant-Colonel of the Indian Native Cavalry, was quite unable to mount his horse without assistance at the time he was commanding a brigade of cavalry at the battle of Chillianwallah; also that it was asserted by some that the officer in command did give the order 'Threes About' for the purpose of placing the Horse Artillery in possession of a clear front, but if this was his object 'Threes Right' was the proper word of command, unless the Cavalry Brigade was parallel to the interval between Major-General Sir Walter Gilbert's Division and the Horse Artillery. The wound received by Brigadier Pope was a sword-cut on the head.

The following is the reference to the affair which appeared in Lord Gough's despatch, dated Camp Chillianwallah, 16th January 1849:—

> The brigade of cavalry under Brigadier Pope was not, I regret to say, so successful. Either by some order or misapprehension of an order they got into much confusion, hampered the fine brigade of Horse Artillery which, while getting into action against a body of the enemy's cavalry that was coming down upon them, had their horses separated from their guns by the false movements of our cavalry, and, notwithstanding the heroic conduct of the gunners, four of those guns were disabled to an extent which rendered their withdrawal at the moment impossible. The moment the artillery was extricated and the cavalry re-formed, a few rounds put to flight the enemy that had occasioned this confusion. With this exception the conduct of the troops generally was most exemplary.

The late General C. W. Thompson and Viscount Chetwynd have written an article in the *Journal* of the Royal United Service Institu-

---

5. Thackwell's *Narrative of the Second Sikh War of 1848-49* (1851).

tion, published in October 1895, which was a reply to an article in the same journal which was written by General Sir Charles Gough, V.C., G.C.B., and published in March 1895, and as the former article gives the true and authentic account of what happened at Chillianwallah, it is reproduced *verbatim* in these pages, so that all interested in the regiment may know exactly what these two officers saw with their own eyes on the occasion in question.

EXTRACT FROM THE *JOURNAL* OF THE ROYAL UNITED SERVICE INSTITUTION, OCTOBER 1895, VOL. XXXIX., No. 212.

By General C. W. Thompson, Colonel, 14th (King's) Hussars, and Viscount Chetwynd, late Lieutenant, 14th Light Dragoons.

Sir Charles Gough's account of the Battle of Chillianwallah, in the last March number of the R.U.S.I. *Journal*, has stirred the memories of some survivors of the 14th Light Dragoons, who are anxious that the whole truth should be known of the strange mishap which befell Pope's cavalry brigade on that occasion.

After standing dismounted for some time in column during the afternoon of the 13th January 1849, listening to the heavy firing on our left, but unmolested by the enemy, the brigade was ordered to mount and deploy, which it did deliberately, two squadrons of the 9th Lancers under Major (afterwards Sir) Hope Grant on the extreme right, then three squadrons of Native cavalry in the centre, with four squadrons of the 14th Light Dragoons on the extreme left of the brigade—nine squadrons in all—standing as above stated and not chequered by wings in the manner depicted in Sir Charles Gough's account.

As commanding the 2nd squadron of the Fourteenth (the 7th from the right of the general line of the brigade), I had a good view to front and flanks, and can attest that, to the best of my belief and recollection, the whole of the Native cavalry were on our right, forming the centre of the brigade line. The Fourteenth were on the left of the brigade from the first, and remained so throughout the day. Having previously drawn swords, the brigade was now ordered to advance at a trot, without a skirmisher or 'scout' in front, or a man in support or reserve in rear, through broken, jungly ground, where some of the enemy's horsemen were seen to loiter, watching our movements.

Brigadier Pope himself led the line in front of the Native cavalry, forming the centre by which we had been ordered to dress and regulate our pace, when insensibly its 'trot' dwindled to a 'walk,' and then came to a dead halt at the sight of a few Sikh horsemen peering over the bushes. Of course the flanks of the brigade had to do the same, being guided by the fluctuations of the centre which were not always clearly visible in the thick jungle, but were conformed to more by sound than by sight. I then saw Colonel King, commanding the 14th Light Dragoons, gallop to the brigadier in front, energetically pointing with his sword towards the enemy's position and evidently urging an attack, which the other seemed unable to make up his mind to order. The Sikhs seeing the hesitation, a handful of their horsemen, some forty or fifty in a lump, charged boldly into the thick of the Native cavalry, who instantly turned with the cry 'threes about,' and disappeared for the rest of the day at least I saw none of them.

This word of command, uttered authoritatively, was unfortunately repeated by the remaining squadrons in succession, but was no sooner found to be a mistake (as it might have been at a field-day), than the 'halt' and 'rally' were sounded amid redoubled shouts of 'halt!' from the officers, and the European lancers and dragoons were found in an open space like a ploughed field in the jungle facing to the front, where Lord Gough and staff shortly after rode by and were received with 'carried swords.' Why the order was not immediately given to advance and recover the two abandoned guns I never knew; but the brigadier had been badly wounded in the retreat (not in the advance, as stated by Sir Charles Gough), the men were naturally disappointed by the unexpected failure, and perhaps it was prudent not to attempt too much at the time.

Among the sights and sounds of the rallying troops, which have never faded from my recollection for the last forty-six years, I was much struck by the speech of a dragoon who, reining up his horse in line with the others, exclaimed: 'Ah, poor old Billy Havelock, if you had been here this would not have happened,' referring not to his immediate commanding officer who had done all that a good soldier could do under the circumstances but to the general handling of the brigade, which everyone could see was pitiable in the extreme. Those who remember *El chico blanco*, 'the fair boy' of Napier's *History of the Peninsular War*,[6] and witnessed the gallantry with which he 'rode into the jaws of death' at the head of his regiment at Ramnuggur a few weeks before, will appreciate the force of the dragoon's homely remark. Colonel William Havelock, K.H., was the elder brother of Sir Henry Havelock, the hero of Lucknow, whose statue stands in Trafalgar Square, and at the time of his death in November 1848, was much the more distinguished of the two.

Of the Honourable East India Company's (not Royal) Horse Artillery attached to the brigade I remember little, and do not think that they fired a shot during the advance. Following uselessly in rear, it was rumoured at the time that when the artillery officers complained to the brigadier that he was masking their guns in such a way as to prevent their opening fire, nothing was done to rectify this essentially false position—not even the simple expedient of dragging the guns into the squadron intervals, where they would have been comparatively safe, if unable to fire. In rear they were and in rear they remained until the line turned, when they turned with it, adding much to the confusion by blocking the way and some of them sticking fast and upsetting among the bushes, where they were captured by the enemy.

As illustrations of the scrambling nature of the *mêlée*, where so much was left to individual action and so little to superior command, I may mention that during one of our short rallies, followed by the enemy, Lieutenant Augustus John Cureton, a gallant youth of eighteen years of age, son of a gallant father, Brigadier-General Cureton, killed at Ramnuggur a few weeks previously, was seen to turn back and ride alone into the jungle, from which his horse shortly returned riderless; and I saw Cureton's body brought into camp a fortnight later, recognisable only by the sleeve of a regimental jacket on one arm.

In the course of the fight in the jungle several hand-to-hand encounters took place, not all to the advantage of the enemy. Major Steuart, of the Fourteenth, overtook a Sikh horseman belabouring an artillery officer (Captain Huish, I believe), and blew him out of the saddle *en passant* by a snap pistol-shot in the breast. Being immediately attacked by another Sikh, sword

6. Vol. v.

in hand, the major had not time to return his pistol (a long single-barrelled old-fashioned 'horse pistol'), but guarded with the barrel, from which the native's sabre glanced off, inflicting a slight cut inside the right arm, and Steuart came into camp bleeding profusely, but not seriously. His antagonist fortunately did not renew the attack, but rode away into the jungle.

One of our troop-sergeant-majors seeing a *ghorchurra* (Sikh horseman) conveniently in front gave him a prod in the back, where the point of the sword became so firmly fixed that the exertions of neither party, pulling different ways, could separate them until the dragoon's sword-knot broke and the Sikh rode off with the sword sticking in his back, apparently little the worse. Probably the presence of chain armour under a cotton-quilted jacket or *mirzai*, as generally worn by natives in cold weather, might account for this singular occurrence.

In his *Reflections* on Chillianwallah, Sir Charles Gough is mistaken in stating that 'the charge [of Pope's brigade] was badly delivered, and, instead of increasing the pace, the line was brought almost to a trot at the moment of collision. There was, in fact, no charge and no collision except the partial one above related, and on this point I can speak decidedly from my position as leader of the second squadron of the Fourteenth enabling me to take an uninterrupted view of the front as far as the centre, by which we were ordered to dress.

Had the 'charge' or even the 'gallop' been sounded all would have been well, for the men were in high spirits, and on drawing swords and trotting they fully expected the charge to follow (though there was hardly any enemy visible in front among the bushes of the broken jungle), when the gradual decrease of pace and sudden halt in the centre struck the first vague note of suspicion that something was wrong somewhere, though no one knew *what* it was nor *where*. And upon this the cry of 'threes about' arose from the Native cavalry, was passed down the line from squadron to squadron, and the catastrophe took place. The experience of the two squadrons of the 9th Lancers on the extreme right appears to have been much the same, as related by their commander, Major (afterwards Sir) Hope Grant, in his official report of the 15th of January, given in his *Life*, vol. i.

The 9th Lancers were dressing upon the 6th [Native] Light Cavalry, I think. . . . There were some few of the enemy now seen in our front, but nothing in the force to stop any body of Europeans. . . . The two squadrons were going along with the line steadily, and no hesitation was evinced; on the contrary, the flank-men were engaged with some of the enemy, and doing their duty, when the whole line checked and went about from the left, and my squadrons, certainly without a word from me, turned round too.'

It will be observed that Major Grant states above that 'the whole line checked and *went about from the left*,' i.e. his left, which doubtless was the case. My experience as second squadron leader of the Fourteenth when in line, was that the movement or 'wave' of retreat, together with the apparently authoritative words of command, came from the right, which would show that the disorder originated at some intermediate point between the two British regiments, *viz.* at or near the centre of the brigade line, held by the Native cavalry, as really was the case. Sir Charles Gough labours to disprove this by placing the Fourteenth at or near the centre (where they never were), and, speaking of the whole brigade as though the troops composing it were all of the same stamp, concealing the individuality of the Native cavalry under the generic title of 'British.'

'Now occurred what, happily, is a rare event in the annals of British cavalry,' he says—as if the Native cavalry of that day had any right to be considered British beyond the fact of being armed, mounted, and paid by the East India Company; or as if they were not on this occasion the authors of the mischief.

At that time, forty years ago, as Sir Charles will perhaps remember, there was no love lost between the Queen's and Company's services, and the mishap of Pope's brigade (himself a Company's officer) was hailed with something not unlike satisfaction by the local troops, as involving the reputation of two regiments of Peninsular fame, and cloaking the shortcomings of their own favourite Native cavalry.

In corroboration of the above account, I am happy to possess the following letter from the Serrefile of the 2nd squadron, the Hon. R. W. (now Viscount) Chetwynd, whose reminiscences in great measure confirm and supplement my own. With one witness in front and another in rear of the line, as he and I were then placed, at different points of view, yet at no great distance from each other, it is hardly possible to suppose that anything of importance could escape our observation. May the truth of our evidence tend to clear up the mystery of this 'inexplicable 'defeat and place the saddle of responsibility 'on the right horse'!

C. W. Thompson, General,
Colonel of the 14th (Kings) Hussars.

July 5, 1895.

My Dear Thompson, Having been the Serrefile of the squadron of the 14th Light Dragoons, which you led at Chillianwallah, I should like to state to you, as the present full colonel of the regiment, my impression of the account by Sir Charles Gough of Pope's brigade (including the Fourteenth), published in the March number of the *Journal* of the Royal United Service Institution.

Sir Charles begins by saying that the brigadier 'was to blame for his manner of handling his cavalry. Without consideration he ordered the nine squadrons under his immediate command to advance to the attack in one long line, without support or reserve, thereby preventing the guns from opening fire.' So far Sir Charles is, I believe, perfectly correct, but now begin his mistakes. The first I shall mention is, as to the wounding of the brigadier. I believe it occurred in the retreat, and that he was still leading the line in person when it turned; in which case the brigadier's being wounded would have no part in breaking down the advance, as Sir Charles suggests it had. I now come to another mistake, of greater importance. Sir Charles says: 'the charge was badly delivered, and instead of increasing the pace, the line was brought almost to a trot at the moment of collision,' clearly implying that the order to gallop had been given and acted on.

A complete misstatement from beginning to end, as regards the Fourteenth, for they received no order whatever to gallop, and consequently continued at the trot. As for delivering a charge, or any collision, I saw nothing of the kind. There was only one increase of pace in the Fourteenth from the walk to the trot. The reception of the order for that by your squadron was to me a fine and impressive sight.

As to the going about, Sir Charles speaks of some 'wholly inexplicable' cause. This 'inexplicable' cause was, in your squadron, exactly what the Duke of Wellington stated it to have been in the House of Lords: 'a word of command from some unauthorised person.' I heard the word and obeyed it, as did the men in front of me, and so we began trotting back again. Sir Charles further describes the going about as commencing in 'the centre regiment' and 'about the centre of the brigade,' having previously placed the Fourteenth between two wings of Native cavalry. He is, I believe, right in saying that the going about commenced in the centre, but wrong in placing the Fourteenth there, they being, I believe, on the left of the brigade. This has its importance, but not equal to that of what follows.

Proceeding to the retreat, Sir Charles refers to it twice, in one place speaking of a 'portion of the brigade,' in the other of the whole. He means, I think, the same thing in both places, *viz.* the nine squadrons forming the line led by the brigadier, a part of the brigade being detached to cover the flank. These troops Sir Charles describes as 'breaking into a reckless stampede, galloping to the rear, and riding right down upon the ten guns . . . upsetting and disabling them.' Now, anyone deriving his information from this description would certainly understand that these troops, including the Fourteenth, turned, went off at a gallop, and rode straight into the guns, upsetting and disabling them. Very different from what I saw in your squadron.

The squadron came about as already described, there being, as far as I could see just previously, only scattered horsemen in their front. Presently, as we were trotting to the rear, I heard a counter-order, which checked us, but was not obeyed; in my opinion, as I will explain, from the want of something to halt upon. I shortly saw ahead two of the ten guns Sir Charles describes as being ridden over and upset. The sight of them at once steadied us, because it supplied what was wanting—a common halting-point. There was every appearance of a halt upon the guns, when, as we were approaching with our attention fixed on them, off they started, with a fatal effect upon us. But this is not riding over guns and upsetting them; on the contrary, they upset us. As regards these two guns then, Sir Charles's description is, beyond a doubt, very unjust to the Fourteenth, even if—which is quite possible—they afterwards came to grief.

Further than that, it is, I think, not unreasonable to look upon what I saw in your squadron as some indication of the morale of the other three at the same time. They may or may not have had assistance, such as we had in the counter-order and seeing the guns in time. Some such assistance was wanted; as the Duke of Wellington pithily expressed it, 'a movement in retreat is not a movement in advance.'

In my opinion, founded on the incident of the guns, it was the fact of the Fourteenth being unsupported that made the going about fatal, and occasioned the loss of the guns and artillerymen. Supporting troops in the place of those guns would have stopped the mischief at once.

Those unsupported guns I take to have been in great danger, in any event, from the moment the unsupported cavalry advanced in front of them, and to have been the victims of bad generalship, as the Fourteenth themselves were.

I object then to this narrative of Sir Charles's, as unjust to the Fourteenth, from its misstatements of fact, both as to the advance and the retreat, and also from its general character a short dry statement that the brigade was badly commanded, without a word to connect the results with this cause. Positively, the word '*support*' only occurs once in Sir Charles's narrative; the matter of leadership is then put aside, and the alleged results are attributed to the cavalry alone, as though the guns and the leadership had no part in them.

Whether such an account from a general officer of Sir Charles Gough's services should remain uncorrected is a question I leave to you, as the full Colonel of the Fourteenth. If you determine to communicate with the Editor of the Journal on the subject, you are welcome to send him this letter if you think fit.—Yours sincerely,

Chetwynd,
Late Lieutenant, 14th Light Dragoons.

To General Thompson,
Colonel of the 14th Hussars.

Some two and a half years after these events took place the Officers of the 14th (King's) Light Dragoons caused a monument to be erected at Maidstone to perpetuate the memory of their fallen comrades. Maidstone was the place where the depot of the regiment had been stationed during the years the Fourteenth were in India, hence many of the officers and men were well known to the inhabitants of the town and its neighbourhood. Mr. R. Westmacott, junior, was the sculptor who designed and carried out the memorial. The monument stands eight feet high and four feet wide. It was placed in the All Saints' Collegiate Church at Maidstone in June 1851, and bears the following inscription:—

Sacred to the memory of
Lieutenant-Colonel William Havelock, K.H.
He served in Portugal, Spain, and France, at Quatre Bras, where he was wounded, and at Waterloo. He fell at the head of his regiment, charging the Sikhs, at Ramnuggur, on the Chenab, on the
22nd November 1848, aged 56 years.
Captain John Foster Fitzgerald.
He died on the 26th November 1848, of wounds received in action at Ramnuggur, aged 28 years.
Lieutenant Augustus John Cureton.
Killed at the battle of Chillianwallah on the 13th of January 1849, aged 18 years.
Lieutenant Ambrose Lloyd.
Killed at the Battle of Goojerat on the 21st of February 1849, aged 26 years.
Sergeant John Harwood,
Corporal William Parker Todd,
and Privates
John Alderton, William Alpine, Richard Bagg, William Brazeur, Charles Fox, John Hatton, Richard Hungerford, Benjamin Jennings, James Raines, Charles Tuttell, John Ward, George Williams, killed on the 22nd November 1848, and George Atkins, David Evans, George Tookey, killed on the 13th January 1849.

———

The Officers of the 14th (King's) Light Dragoons
erect this monument to
their Comrades
Who fell in the Campaign of the Punjaub.
Be thou faithful unto death.
Rev. n. 10.

Appendix B

Extracts from Despatches of Major-General Sir Hugh Rose, K.C.B., Brigadier-General Sir R. Napier, K.C.B., and other officers, relative to Jhansi, Koonch, Mundesor, Rathgur, Garrakota, Betwa, Lohari, Calpee, Gwalior, Morar, Jowra-Alipore, and Ranode.

JHANSI DESPATCHES

From Major-General Sir Hugh Rose, K.C.B., Commanding Central India Field Force, to the Chief of the Staff.

Camp Mote, April 30, 1858.

Sir, I have the honour to report for the information of His Excellency the commander-in-chief the operations of my force against the fortress and fortified city of Jhansi, on the 20th *ultimo*. The 2nd Brigade, under my command, arrived at Limra, one day's march from Jhansi. My 1st Brigade had not yet joined me from Chanderi. The same day I sent Brigadier C. Steuart, with the cavalry and artillery, as follows, to invest Jhansi, *viz*.

Six guns Horse Artillery.
14th Light Dragoons, 325 rank and file.
3rd Light Cavalry, 140   ,,   ,,   ,,
Hyderabad Contingent, 476 sabres.

I arrived the 21st *ultimo* with the remainder of my brigade before Jhansi. The picquets of the cavalry sent on the day before had sabred about 100 armed men, Bundeelas, endeavouring to enter Jhansi, having been summoned by the *ranee* to defend it I established seven flying camps of cavalry as an investing force round Jhansi, giving to Major Scudamore half a troop of Horse Artillery, and later to Major Gall two 9-pounders. These camps detached to the front outposts and vedettes, which watched

164

and prevented all issue from the city day and night. Each camp, on any attempt being made to force its line, was to call on the other for help. I gave directions also that the roads from the city should be obstructed by trenches and abattis.

I had made arrangements on the 30th March for storming, but the general action of the Betwa on 1st April with the so-called 'army of the Peishwa,' which advanced across the Betwa to relieve it, caused the assault to be deferred.

On the 2nd instant I issued a Division Order for the assault of the defences of the city wall, of which a copy with a plan of attack was furnished to the officers in command. I have the honour to enclose copies of reports from Brigadier Stuart, commanding my 1st Brigade, and Brigadier C. Steuart, commanding my 2nd Brigade, of the operations of their respective columns against Jhansi. Whilst engaged in the town I received a report from the officer commanding one of the Hyderabad Cavalry flying camps that a large body of the enemy, flying from the town, had tried to force his picquet; that a few had succeeded, but that the main body, from 350 to 500 strong, had been driven back, and had occupied a high and rocky hill to the west of the fort; that he had surrounded the hill with cavalry till reinforcements were sent. I immediately ordered out from the camps of the two brigades the available troops of all arms against the hill.

The enclosed report from Major Gall, 14th Light Dragoons, shows how satisfactorily these rebels were disposed of. Lieutenant Park was killed whilst gallantly leading on a party of the 24th Bombay Native Infantry along the ridge of the hill. The *ranee's* father, Mammo Sahib, was amongst the rebels. He was wounded on the hill and captured some days afterwards, and hanged at the Tokim Bagh. The next day Brigadier Stuart and myself occupied the rest of the city by a combined movement united by Major Gall, who spiritedly scaled the bastion iron gate from his flying camp and captured the gun that was there and threw it down the ramparts.

The following morning a wounded Mahratta *ectanca* of the *ranee* was sent into me from Captain Abbott's flying camp. He stated that the *ranee*, accompanied by 310 Velaitees and 25 *sowars*, fled that night from the fort; that after leaving it they had been headed back by one of the picquets, when the party and the *ra-*

nee separated, she herself taking to the right with a few *sowars* in the direction of the intended flight to Bandin. The observatory also telegraphed: 'Enemy escaping to the north-east.' I immediately sent off strong detachments of Her Majesty's 14th Light Dragoons, 3rd Light Cavalry, and Hyderabad Cavalry, to pursue, with guns to support them, as it was said Tantia Topee had sent a force to meet her. I also sent Brigadier Steuart with cavalry to watch the fords of the Betwa.

In sight of Bandin, 21 miles from Jhansi, the cavalry came in view of the irregular horse sent to meet the *ranee*, which separated, probably with a view to mislead her pursuers as to her real course. Lieutenant Dowker, Hyderabad Cavalry, was sent by Captain Forbes through the town of Bandin, whilst he, with the 3rd Light Cavalry and 14th Light Dragoons, passed it by the left. In the town, Lieutenant Dowker saw traces of the *ranee's* hasty flight, and her tent, in which was an unfinished breakfast. On the other side of the town he came up with and cut up 40 of the enemy, consisting of Rohillas and Bengalee irregular cavalry. Lieutenant Dowker was gaining fast on the *ranee*, who with four attendants was seen escaping on a grey horse, when he was dismounted by a severe wound and obliged to give up the pursuit.

The *ranee's* flight was the signal for a general retreat. Early in the morning I caused the outskirts of the city to be scoured with cavalry and infantry. It will give some idea of the destruction of insurgents which ensued when a party of the 14th Light Dragoons alone killed 200 in one patrol. The rebels, who were chiefly Velaitees and Pathans, generally sold their lives as dearly as they could, fighting to the last with their usual dexterity and firmness.

I beg leave to bring to the favourable notice of the commander-in-chief the conduct of the troops under my command in the siege, investment, and capture of Jhansi. They had to contend against an enemy more than double their numbers behind formidable fortifications, who defended themselves afterwards from house to house in a spacious city, often under the fire of the fort, then later in the suburbs, and in very difficult ground outside the walls. The investing cavalry force were, day and night, for seventeen days on arduous duty, the men not taking their clothes off, the horses saddled and bridled up at night.

The nature of the defence and the strictness of the investment gave rise to continual and fierce combats, for the rebels, having no hope, sought to sell their lives as dearly as possible. But the discipline and gallant spirit of the troops enabled them to overcome difficulties and opposition of every sort, to take the fortified city of Jhansi by storming, subduing the strongest fortress in Central India, and killing 5000 of its rebel garrison. According to the first reports which I received, 3000 rebels were killed, but those received since the withdrawal of the seven flying camps make the loss of the enemy amount to above 5000 killed.

Native accounts received by Brigadier Wheeler at Saugor make the loss of rebels to amount to more than 5000. I beg to recommend to His Excellency for gallant and good service in investing the fortress and city of Jhansi, Major Scudamore, 14th Light Dragoons, the senior officer in command of flying camps; Major Gall, H.M.'s 14th Light Dragoons; Major Forbes, C.B., commanding 3rd Cavalry; Captain Abbott and Lieutenant Dowker, Hyderabad Cavalry. I beg leave to state the obligations I am under to the following officers for the services which they have rendered me during the siege operations and capture of Jhansi:—

Brigadier Stuart, commanding 1st Brigade.
Brigadier C. Steuart, C.B., commanding 2nd Brigade.
Major Scudamore, commanding H.M.'s 14th Light Dragoons, &c.
Captain Todd, Major of Brigade, &C. [1]

> I have, &c.
> (Signed)   Hugh Rose, Major-General,
> Commanding Central India Field Force.

No. 236.

From Brigadier C. Steuart, C.B., 14th Light Dragoons, commanding 2nd Brigade C.I.F. Force, to the Assistant Adjutant-General, C.I.F. Force.

Sir, In obedience to orders received through you, the brigade under my command moved in two columns on the morning of the 3rd April to the assault of the town of Jhansi.

Captain Todd, Brigade-Major, and Captain Leckie, Deputy-As-

---

1. Other names, not connected with the Fourteenth, are omitted above.

sistant Quartermaster-General of the 2nd Brigade, on this as on every previous opportunity have afforded me every assistance, etc. etc. I have, etc.,

(Signed)   C. Steuart,
Commanding 2nd Brigade C.I.F. Force.

Total return of ordnance captured in the town of Jhansi on the 3rd April 1858 by the force under the command of Major-General Sir Hugh Rose, K.C.B.:—10 brass guns; 1 brass howitzer; 15 iron guns.
Captured in the fort of Jhansi on 5th April 1858:—8 iron guns; 1 brass gun.

(Signed)   Thos. S. Haggard, Lieutenant,
Commissary of Ordnance, C.I.F. Force.

KOONCH DESPATCHES

From Major-General Sir Hugh Rose, K.C.B., to General Sir William Mansfield, K.C.B., Chief of the Staff.

Camp Golowlee, May 24, 1858.

Sir, I have the honour to report to you for the information of His Extract from Excellency the Commander-in-Chief that the approach of Brigadier Smith's Brigade from Rajputana to Goona having secured Jhansi from attack by Kotah and Bundelcund rebels, I recalled Lieutenant-Colonel Lowth, commanding 86th Regiment, whom I had detached with a column to watch the road from Jhansi to Goona, and I marched with the 1st Brigade of my force from Jhansi on the 25th *ultimo* on Calpee. I left at Jhansi for its garrison the force detailed below, forming part of the 2nd Brigade, *viz.*:—

Headquarter wing, 3rd Bombay European Regiment.
Eight companies 24th Bombay Native Infantry.
Hyderabad Cavalry, 100 sabres.
Three guns Bhoopal Artillery.
Half company Sappers and Miners

I left there also Brigadier C. Steuart of the 14th Light Dragoons, with the remainder of his brigade, with orders to bring up to me the 71st Regiment and two troops of the 3rd Light Cavalry. I joined Major Gall's force at Pooch, 16 miles from Koonch, on 1st May. I had the honour to report on the 17th inst. the movements of this officer's movable column, as well as those of Major Orr's field force. I received information from Sir Robert Hamilton and Major Gall, whom I had detached along the road from Jhansi to Calpee with a flying column to watch the enemy and obtain information of their movements, that the *sepoy* garrison of Calpee of all arms, reinforced by 500 Velaitees under the Ranee of Jhansi, cavalry from Kotah, and guns and troops from disaffected *rajahs*—the whole under the command of Tantia Topee—had occupied Koonch, and thrown up entrenchments, which they had armed, to defend the roads leading to the town from Jhansi, and that they were determined to make a vigorous opposition at Koonch to my advance against Calpee.

All the accounts agreed that the rebels were strong in cavalry, consisting of mutineers from Bengal, regular and irregular regiments. Koonch is an open town, but is difficult to attack because it is surrounded by woods, gardens, and temples with high walls round them, every one of which is a defence.

My left, the 1st Brigade, was resting with its left flank on the village of Nagapoore; my centre, the 2nd Brigade, under Brigadier C. Steuart, was in the village of Choman; my right, Major Orr's force, in front of the village of Ormree.

I gave the orders that as soon as the three columns had taken up the position which I have mentioned they were to advance against the town and endeavour to effect a lodgement in it. When we came within sight of Koonch we perceived vedettes and strong picquets of the enemy's cavalry outside the wood. They conformed to our flank movement, and posted themselves nearly opposite to Nagapoore. A few rounds of shrapnel from Captain Lightfoot's guns emptied some of their saddles, and they disappeared into the wood.

The rebel infantry now showed in force behind a long wall to our front and in the wood to the left of it. I had marched the 1st Brigade a distance of 14 miles from Lohari that morning for the purpose of surprising the enemy by the flank movement, and not giving them time to alter their plan of attack. I ordered the men's dinners to be cooked for them, to rest and refresh them, and meantime battered the wall with the two 18-pounders and the 8-inch howitzer.

Lieutenant-Colonel Gall galloped gallantly into the wood to reconnoitre the enemy. Although he was within half musket range of them they did not fire at him, because the shelling from our Horse Artillery had caused confusion in their ranks. He ascertained that the infantry to the left had retreated further into the wood, having in their rear a large body of cavalry; that the siege-guns had driven the enemy from the cover of the wall, but that some way in rear of it was posted a large body of infantry with elephants. I determined to drive the enemy out of the wood, gardens, and temples surrounding Koonch, and then to storm the town and a dilapidated mud fort on a rising ground, a strong position which was opposite to the right of the 1st Brigade.

I effected the operation by throwing the left wing of Her Majesty's 86th Regiment, under Major Stuart, and the whole of the 25th Bengal Native Infantry, under Lieutenant-Colonel Robertson, into skirmishing order, their flanks supported by the half-troop Horse Artillery and a troop of Her Majesty's 14th Light Dragoons, and Captain Ommaney's battery and two troops of Her Majesty's 14th Light Dragoons. I left Captain Woolcombe's battery, one troop 14th Light Dragoons, and the right wing 86th Regiment in a second line in reserve, under command of Lieutenant-Colonel Lowth.

The rapidity and precision with which this formation was simultaneously made must have surprised the *sepoys*. The first line advanced, notwithstanding the artillery and musketry fire, through the whole north part of the town and took the fort. The troop 14th Light Dragoons made a circuit to their left, took all the obstacles to their front, and then brought their left shoulders forward. Just as the 86th Regiment and myself with the 25th were about to enter the town, Brigadier C. Steuart, 2nd Brigade, observed that a large number of the rebel infantry, strongly posted in cultivated ground, threatened the right of the line of attack of his brigade.

He moved up Captain Field's battery and Captains Thompson's and Gordon's troops of 14th Light Dragoons and one troop of 3rd Regiment Hyderabad Cavalry to dislodge them. The enemy held the position charge the obstinately, and it was not till a portion of the infantry of the 2nd Brigade moved down on them from another direction that they retreated, when Captain Gordon, whom I beg to recommend to His Excellency for his conduct on this occasion, with his troop and the cavalry above mentioned, charged and broke the mass, cutting up several of them, but *topes* of trees favoured the escape of the remainder. The 2nd Brigade, under Brigadier Steuart, owing to some misconception on his part, did not effect a lodgement in the town, but moving round to the south of it, his artillery and cavalry joined in the pursuit.

The cavalry of both brigades and Major Orr's force (except a party left to watch the Jaloun road and my rear), one troop of Horse Artillery, Captain Field's guns and the four guns No. 18 Light Field Battery, went in pursuit. in pursuit.

The pursuit was commenced by Captain William McMahon's squadron and Captain Blyth's troop 14th Light Dragoons charging, the first the right and the latter the left of the enemy's skirmishers. A piece of very heavy ploughed land caused a check in the pace, under a heavy fire, of Captain McMahon's squadron; but the heavy ground was not broad, the squadron got through it, Captain McMahon leading the way, and cut to pieces the enemy, who fought fiercely to the last. Captain McMahon received three sabre-wounds, but he continued the pursuit to the last. I beg to recommend him for his gallant conduct and unvarying zeal and attention to his duties. On the centre the Horse Artillery opened a hot fire, and the cavalry charged the skirmishers. The enemy now threw back the extreme right of their skirmishers so as to enfilade our line of pursuit.

I directed Captain Prettejohn to form line to the left, charge and cut off the enfilading skirmishers, which he did effectually. This officer, the horses of his own troop being knocked up, placed himself with well-timed zeal at the head of a troop with fresh horses which was without an officer, and continued the pursuit with them to the end. I beg to submit his name to the favourable consideration of His Excellency, as well as the names of Captain Blyth, 14th Light Dragoons, and Captain Abbott, commanding 3rd Cavalry Hyderabad Contingent, who each very gallantly charged and captured a gun from the retreating enemy under a heavy fire. In the course of the pursuit (up to seven miles from Koonch) more guns and ammunition were captured by the cavalry.

The sun, fatigue, and scarcity of water told on my artillery and cavalry, a great part of whom were Europeans, and had been marching and engaged for 16 hours, so I marched them back at sunset to Koonch.

The enemy must have lost about 500 or 600 men in this action and pursuit. Nine guns and quantities of good English ammunition and stores furnished to the Gwalior Contingent were captured. Tantia Topee had disappeared at Koonch as rapidly as he had done at the Betwa, leaving to its fate at the most critical moment the force which he had called into existence under the pompous title of 'The Army of the Peishwa.'

Brigadier C. Steuart, C.B., commanding 2nd Brigade, mentions that his staff, Captain Todd, Major of Brigade, and Captain Leckie, Deputy-Assistant Quartermaster-General, afforded him every assistance. Enclosed are returns of killed and wounded, and of the guns and ordnance stores captured in the action.—I have, etc.

(Signed)   Hugh Rose, Major-General,
Commanding C. I. Field Force.

Abstract of Casualties (14th Light Dragoons).

Left wing.—5 men wounded.

Right wing.—4 men killed; 1 man died of his wounds.

Wounded.

Captain William McMahon, wounded severely (sword-cut in right hand and leg); 12 men wounded.

Horses of right wing.—3 killed; 6 wounded; 4 missing.

Captain Need, Lieutenant Travers, and 16 men, struck down by the sun, of whom 2 men died.

Mundesor Despatch

No. 10.

———

No. 47 of 1858.

London Gazette, 11th March 1858.

The Right Honourable the Governor in Council has very great satisfaction in publishing for the information of the army the following report made to His Excellency the Commander-in-Chief, by Brigadier Stuart, commanding the Malwa Field Force (now 1st Brigade Nerbudda Field Force), of his successful operations against the insurgents assembled near Mundesor during four days, from the 21st to the 24th November last:—

No. 11.

———

No. 201 of 1857.

Extracts from the report of Brigadier Stuart, commanding the Malwa Field Force, and published in the *London Gazette*, dated 11th March 1858.

The rebel enemy at Mundesor, hearing of our approach, had posted picquets entirely covering the country over which we were advancing, and observing our picquets thrown out, they mustered in some force outside the walls of the town, and appeared inclined to attack. I, however, contented myself with reinforcing the picquets, and leaving the whole charge of the front to Major Robertson, 25th Regiment Bombay Native Infantry. The field officer of the day returned to camp about 3 o'clock p.m. I received intimation from him that the enemy were advancing in force, and threatened both our flanks and centre at the same time. I accordingly moved out to meet them. They advanced steadily, with banners flying, and appeared in great numbers.

On approaching our right front they were most gallantly charged by Lieutenant Dew, Her Majesty's 14th Light Dragoons, who with some of his men occupied that ground as a picquet. Captain Orr, commanding 3rd Regiment Cavalry Dragoons, Hyderabad Contingent, supported Lieutenant Dew, and the enemy were driven charges with back with great loss, and before our guns, which had quickly moved up, could open upon them. The attack on our centre was repulsed by a few rounds of our artillery, whilst that on our left was successfully met by the Field Force under Major Orr.

The enemy having been thus driven back at all points, were pursued for some distance—in fact until they nearly reached the walls of the town. Just previous to the camp being marked out intelligence came that Heera Sing's baggage had just left the village of Goraria, on the Neemuch road, and a party of cavalry, about 300, were observed in a north-westerly direction; so Her Majesty's 14th Light Dragoons, left wing, under Major Gall, and the 1st and 4th Regiments Cavalry Hyderabad Contingent, galloped off in pursuit, the 3rd Cavalry Hyderabad Contingent remaining as a reserve. They caught up the enemy about two miles south of Peeplia, and after cutting up about

200 of them, returned to camp.

On the 23rd November my line advanced, covered by skirmishers. The enemy's infantry, with banners flying (many of them green), moved down to meet us through the intermediate fields of high *jowarree*, and their guns opened fire. I immediately halted my line and replied to the fire with Captains Hungerford and Woolcombe's batteries, at a range of about 900 yards. After a few rounds I again advanced the line and permitted Captain Hungerford to move his half-battery to a position on our right front, from which he could enfilade the enemy. After an advance of about 300 yards our line was again halted, and firing resumed, that from both batteries being very effective.

A most gallant charge was then made on the enemy's guns by the escort of Her Majesty's 14th Light Dragoons attached to Captain Hungerford, led by Lieutenant Martin, who found, however, that the position was still very strongly held by the enemy's infantry, and was compelled to retire, he himself being very severely wounded. Captain Hungerford's half-battery was again advanced to within 100 yards, and after a round or two of grape, the guns were at once charged and captured, the enemy flying in great numbers into the village to the right.

I learned that during the afternoon, when we were hotly engaged in the front, a strong body of the enemy from Mundesor attacked our rear, and endeavoured to carry off the siege-train, baggage, etc. They were, however, most gallantly repulsed on every occasion. In one of these attacks I regret to say that Lieutenant Redmayne, Her Majesty's 14th Light Dragoons, was killed while most gallantly leading his men against the enemy. Notwithstanding the many attempts made by the enemy to press upon and harass our rear, it gives me great satisfaction to be able to state that not a particle of baggage was lost nor a follower injured.

On this occasion Lieutenant Leith, commanding a squadron 14th Light Dragoons, appears to have done good service. A perusal of the report made by Captain Gall, commanding left wing Her Majesty's 14th Light Dragoons, will convey to His Excellency the Commander-in-Chief some idea of the good service performed by all under his command. I most fully concur in Captain Gall's report,[2] and beg to recommend to the

---

2. This Report is not available. See Despatches.

consideration of His Excellency all the officers and men mentioned by him. Of Captain Gall himself I must in justice add, that a more able, zealous, and hard-working officer I never met with, nor one more worthy of distinction.

No. 12.

Nominal roll of officers and men of the 14th Light Dragoons killed and wounded in the engagements with the insurgents before and in the vicinity of Mundesor from 21st to 24th November 1857.

Killed.—Lieutenant Redmayne.
Wounded.—Lieutenant James Leith.
Lieutenant L. Gowan.
Lieutenant C. Martin.
Regimental Sergeant-Major T. Clark.
Troop Sergeant-Major S. Whittaker.
Privates Cooper, Harris, O'Neill, Remmington, and Buchanan.

RATHGUR DESPATCH

Extract from the reports of Major-General Sir Hugh Rose, K.C.B., commanding Central India Field Force, and published in the *London Gazette*, dated 11th May 1858, relating to Rathgur.

No. 2.

I moved in the order of march which I always adopted when near the rebels, as a precaution against their system of surprises, that is, a line of flankers of H.M.'s 14th Light Dragoons on each side of the road 50 yards in front of the leading file of the advance-guards, which, with a file of irregulars, has charge of the guide; another line of irregular cavalry, 150 yards in echelon, in front of the outward flanks of the Fourteenth, and, should thick jungle border the road, a company of infantry, in extended order on each side of it, to support the flanks of the men of the 14th Light Dragoons and the advance-guard. By this means all dangerous ground is searched, surprises are almost impossible, and spies lying concealed at a great distance from the road are frequently seized.

I followed with four guns of the Horse Artillery and a troop of H.M.'s 14th Light Dragoons in support under Lieutenant-Colonel Turnbull, ordering the rest of my force to follow, with the exception of Captain Hare's infantry and guns, which remained at the ford to prevent the rear being cut off. I was not at all sure that my camps with the siege artillery and numerous stores, left with a small force at Rathgur under Brigadier Steuart, might not be attacked during my absence, as they had been before.

I therefore halted in the village only for a short time in order to rest the troops, who had been on duty for at least five days, and marched back the same night to Rathgur, as they had been marching or engaged 15 hours. The enemy's loss was severe they themselves state it to be from 400 to 500, which is not surprising, as they were exposed to a well-directed fire for a length of time. Amant Sing, their ablest military leader, as well as a nephew of Fazil Mahomed Khan, were killed, and the Rajah of Banpore was wounded. The 14th Light Dragoons had one horse killed.

Garrakota Despatches (Extracts)

No. 6.

Camp Koomeeri, March 9, 1858.

. . . However, I ought to add that even if the Paunch Ghat had been occupied, it would have been quite impossible to have invested completely Garrakota with a force of my numbers, which, strictly speaking, was only sufficiently strong to guard its camp and work the field and siege artillery. My force was more than usually weak, as, in order to protect Saugor, in my absence I had left there a troop of H.M.'s 14th Light Dragoons and two companies of the 24th Regiment Bombay Native Infantry. I had also sent the 3151 and 42nd Bengal Native Infantry to Koray to guard Saugor from the possibility of an attack from the north. I have observed that nothing alarms the rebels more than a move to cut off their retreat.

I sent off immediately Captain Hare with a half-troop of Horse Artillery, a troop of H.M.'s 14th Light Dragoons (under Captain Need), and a troop of the Hyderabad Contingent Cavalry in pursuit of the rebels, by a route which, from information I had received, I thought would enable them to cut into their line of retreat. They had, as I supposed, made a round to the south, and then turned northwards towards Shaghur.

Captain Hare came up with the rear of the rebels as they had just crossed the River Beas, at the village of Beas.[3] The river was

3. Or Bias (Malleson).

not practicable for guns. Captain Hare therefore sent the troop of H.M.'s 14th Light Dragoons, under Captain Need, and the Hyderabad Cavalry across the river after the enemy. They cut up 70 or 100 of them, of whom the greater part were mutineers of the 52nd and other native regiments. They had all abundance of ammunition and copper caps. Captain Hare speaks very highly of the conduct on this occasion of Captain Need and his troop. He describes Captain Need as a 'good and dashing officer,' and adds, 'he killed with his own hands five of the rebels, of whom three were *sepoys*, and pursued the rebels with his gallant troop till dark.' I beg to recommend Captain Need to your Excellency, as well as Captain Hare for his intelligence and activity in pursuing and coming up with the enemy.

Extracts from the *London Gazette*, published 31st May 1858.

No. 23.

The Adjutant-General of the Army to the Secretary to Government Secret Department, Bombay.

> Adjutant-General's Office,
> Headquarters, Mahableshwar,
> 10th April 1858.

No. 140.

Sir, In continuation of the letter from this department (No. 2701) under date of the 20th *ultimo*, transmitting a despatch from Major-General Sir Hugh Rose, K.C.B., commanding Central India Field Force, dated Koomeeri, 9th *idem*, I am desired by the commander-in-chief to request you will bring to the notice of the Right Honourable the Governor in Council the favourable mention made by the major-general of the under-mentioned officers in the affair with the insurgents, which resulted in the evacuation of the strong fortress of Garrakota:—
Lieutenant-Colonel Liddell, commanding 3rd European Regiment; Captain Lightfoot, commanding No. 18 Light Field Battery; Captain Hare, Hyderabad Contingent; Captain Need, H.M.'s 14th Light Dragoons, etc. etc.

His Lordship in Council will doubtless observe that Major-General Sir Hugh Rose, K.C.B., has particularly noted the conduct of Captains Hare and Need and Lieutenant Sturt, and His Excellency therefore solicits that the Right Honourable the Governor in Council will accord to them, as also to the other officers, the approbation they have so well deserved. I have, etc.

(Signed)   Edward Green, Colonel,
                                   Adjutant-General of the Army.

Betwa Despatch

(Published in the *London Gazette*, 10th August 1858.) despatch.

No. 1.

Major-General Sir Hugh Rose, K.C.B., commanding Central India Field Force, to the Adjutant-General, Bombay Army.

Camp Pooch, April 30, 1858.

Sir, I have the honour to report to you, for the information of His Excellency the Commander-in-Chief in India, that on the 1st April the forces under my orders fought a general action with the so-called army of the Peishwa, which attempted to relieve Jhansi while I was besieging it, and gained a complete victory over it, pursuing two miles beyond the River Betwa, taking 18 guns, of which one was an 18-pounder, one an 8-inch mortar, two 12-pounders, and two English 9-pounders, and killing upwards of 1500 rebels. For some time past Sir Robert Hamilton had given me information that Tantia Topee, a relative and the agent of Nana Sahib, had been collecting and organising a large body of troops in the neighbourhood of Mhow and Nowgong, in Bundelcund,[4] which was called 'the Army of the Peishwa,' and had displayed the standard of that abolished authority.

After the fall of Chanderi[5] this army was reinforced by the numerous rebel troops, *sepoys* from Calpee and Bundeelas, who had besieged and taken it. Towards the end of last month I received constantly reports that the force, estimated at 20,000 or 25,000 men, with 20 or 30 guns, was advancing against me. On the 30th *ultimo*, Sir Robert Hamilton informed me that its main body had arrived at Burra Saugor, about three miles from the Betwa, would cross that river during the night and attack me next morning. The enemy crossed the Rajpore, the upper ford, in great numbers on the 30th March, preceded by an advance-guard of Velaitees, and took up after sunset a position

---

4. 'Bandalkand' (Malleson).
5. 'Chandairee' in original despatch.

in order of battle opposite the rear of my 2nd Brigade.

The details below show how weak I was compared with the enemy:—

Artillery—3 siege guns; 16 light field guns.

14th Light Dragoons, 243 rank and file.

Hyderabad Cavalry, 207 sabres.

86th Regiment, 208 rank and file.

3rd Bombay European Regiment, 226 rank and file.

24th Bombay Native Infantry, 298   ,,   ,,

25th Bombay Native Infantry, 400   ,,   ,,

I sent Major Orr with a party of his cavalry along the road to the Betwa to watch the enemy's movements.

I drew up my force across the road from the Betwa, half a mile from my camp. On the right flank of my first line, the 2nd Brigade, I placed Lieutenant Clark's Hyderabad Horse, a troop 14th Light Dragoons, and four guns Horse Artillery; in the centre, detachments of the 24th Bombay Native Infantry and 3rd Europeans, three heavy guns and detachments Hyderabad Infantry; on the left flank, Captain Lightfoot's battery and two troops 14th Light Dragoons.

The second line, my 1st Brigade, was in contiguous columns at quarter distance, consisting of a weak troop 14th Light Dragoons on the right, and Hyderabad Cavalry on the left flank, in the centre Her Majesty's 86th Regiment, Captain Woolcombe's battery of 6-pounders, and Captain Ommaney's battery of 9-pounders, with detachments of the 2 5th Bombay Native Infantry.

I threw out picquets and lines of vedettes of the 14th Light Dragoons and Hyderabad Cavalry well to my front and flanks. The Velaitees' outposts called out during the night that they were very numerous, that we were very few, that in the morning they would finish us off! My force was not in position till long after dark. Both ourselves and the enemy slept on our arms opposite each other.

Hearing that the enemy were crossing in large numbers at the lower, the Kolwar ford, with the object of turning my left flank and forcing their way along the Burragong road, through Major Scudamore's flying camp into Jhansi, I detached Brigadier Stuart, in the middle of the night, with the 1st Brigade along the Burragong road, about eight miles to the village of Burragong, close to the River Betwa, where he could oppose and outflank the enemy, who had crossed by the ford above the village. The departure of the 1st Brigade left me without a second line. I was therefore obliged to withdraw the detachments of the 24th Native Infantry from the first line, and make a second line of them.

The enemy, before daybreak, covered by a cloud of skirmishers, advanced against me. My outposts retired steadily, closing to each flank. Shortly after the enemy opened a very heavy artillery, musket, and matchlock fire on my line from the whole of his front, to which my batteries answered steadily. The enemy were in rear of a rising ground. I ordered my first line of infantry to lie down, the troop of Horse Artillery to take ground diagonally to the right and enfilade the enemy's left flank. In this movement a round-shot broke the wheel of a Horse Artillery gun. Captain Lightfoot took up an advanced position to his left front, which made the fire of his battery much more efficacious.

Whilst the enemy were suffering from the fire of the troop and battery I directed Captain Prettejohn, 14th Light Dragoons, to charge with his troop, supported by Captain McMahon, 14th Light Dragoons, with his troop, on the enemy's right flank, and I charged myself on their left with Captain Need's troop, 14th Light Dragoons, supported by a strong troop of Hyderabad Cavalry. Both attacks succeeded, throwing the whole of the enemy's first line into confusion and forcing them to retire

I beg to do justice to Captain Need's troop: they charged with steady gallantry on the enemy's left, which was composed of the best rebel troops, the Velaitees and *sepoys*, who, throwing themselves back on the right and resting the flanks of their new line four or five deep on the rocky knolls, received the charge with a heavy fire of musketry. We broke through the dense line, which flung itself amongst the rocks, and bringing our right shoulders forward took the front line in reverse and routed it. I believe I may say that what Captain Need's troop did on this occasion was equal to breaking a square of infantry, and the result was most successful, because the charge turned the enemy's position and decided in a great measure the fate of the day.

I have the honour to recommend to His Excellency's favourable consideration Captain Need and his devoted troop, and Lieutenant Leith, who saved Captain Need's life, for which I have ventured to recommend him for the 'Victoria Cross.'

The enemy's right gave way before the squadron of the 14th Light Dragoons, under Captain Prettejohn, reached them; he pursued and cut up several of them. I moved forward the whole of the artillery and cavalry in pursuit. Severe combats occurred between the pursuing cavalry and the fugitives, who fought with desperation.

I ordered two troops of the 14th Light Dragoons and the Hyderabad Cavalry across the Betwa. The enemy kept up a heavy fire on us as we crossed the ford and ascended the steep road leading up the opposite bank. The 14th Light Dragoons and Hyderabad Cavalry gallantly surmounted all opposition and sabred the rebels who still held their ground.

About a mile and a half from the Betwa the 12-pounder, being the eighteenth and last gun of the rebel army, was captured. Two standards also were captured.

Horses and men being completely exhausted by incessant marching and fighting during the last forty-eight hours, and being now nine miles from Jhansi, I marched the troops back to camp.

I beg leave to bring to the favourable notice of the commander-in-chief the conduct of the force under my command, which, without relaxing in the least the arduous siege and investment of a very strong fort and fortified city, garrisoned by 10,000 desperate men, fought, with the few numbers left in camp, a grand action with a relieving army, beat and pursued them nine miles, killing 1500 of them, and taking from them artillery, stores, and ammunition. The officers whom circumstances called prominently into action, and who, profiting by the opportunity, did valuable service, were Brigadier Stuart and the officers whom he mentions—Lieutenant-Colonel Turnbull, Bombay Horse Artillery; Captain Lightfoot, Bombay Artillery; Captain Need, 14th Light Dragoons; Lieutenant Leith, 14th Light Dragoons, etc. etc.

Sergeant Gardiner, 14th Light Dragoons, attacked and killed a cavalry soldier as well as two armed men on foot. His gallant conduct at Dhar had been previously honourably mentioned. The conduct of the men of the 14th Light Dragoons was so uniformly good that their commanding officer finds it difficult to bring any particular case of good conduct to notice. I am much indebted to the following officers for their zeal and assistance to me during the action, to Major Orr, commanding Hyderabad Contingent Field Force; Captain Prettejohn, commanding 14th Light Dragoons; Captain Hare, commanding Regiment Hyderabad Force, and Lieutenant Haggard, Commissary of Ordnance in command of the siege-train; as also to my Staff—Captain Macdonald, Assistant Quartermaster-General; Captain Wood, Assistant Adjutant-General; Captain Rose, Rifle Brigade, my *aide-de camp*, and Lieutenant Lyster, 72nd Bengal Native Infantry, my interpreter.—I have, etc.

(Signed)   Hugh Rose, Major-General,
Commanding Central India Field Force.

Extracts from Return of Killed and Wounded of the Central India Field Force during the engagement with the enemy on the 1st April 1858 on the Betwa.

HER MAJESTY'S 14TH LIGHT DRAGOONS.

Killed—5 men; 11 horses.

Wounded—24 men; 16 horses.

Names of the killed and wounded:—

Regimental Sergeant-Major Thomas Clark,	slightly wounded.
Sergeant John Myers,	,, ,,
Private Thomas Ransom,	killed,
,, Walter Roberts,	severely wounded.
,, Cornelius Gray,	killed,
,, Leonard,	slightly wounded
Lance-Sergeant William Roxby,	killed,
Private R. Barker,	,,
,, J. Leigh,	,,
,, W. Watkin,	,,
Sergeant Thomas Bowen and 9 privates,	slightly wounded
,, Wm. Parkins and 5 privates,	severely wounded
Private J. Waite,	dangerously wounded.
,, J. Byott,	,, ,,
,, Richard Baker,	,, ,,

Total casualties of the force engaged—15 killed; 66 wounded.

Return of Horses killed and wounded of the Central India
Field Force on 1st April 1858.

1st troop Horse Artillery,	2 killed.
Her Majesty's 14th Light Dragoons,	11 killed; 16 wounded.
	————
Total of the forces engaged,	13 killed; 16 wounded.

(Signed)   A. H. Wood, Captain,
Assistant Adjutant-General Central India Field Force.

LOHARI DESPATCHES

Extracts from the *London Gazette*, 31st August 1858.

No. 1.

General Orders by the Governor-General of India, Military Department.

No. 198 of 1858.

Allahabad, June 5, 1858.

The Right Honourable the Governor-General is pleased to direct the publication of the following despatch from the Deputy
Adjutant-General of the Army, No. 373A, dated 31st May 1858,
forwarding one from Major-General Sir Hugh Rose, K.C.B.,
enclosing a report from Major R. H. Gall[6] of Her Majesty's
14th Light Dragoons, of his capture of the fort of Lohari on
the 2nd May.

The Governor-General desires to express the entire approval
of the gallant conduct of the officers and men engaged under
Major Gall in this affair, and his cordial appreciation of the
merits of Major Gall himself, both in the present affair and on
all occasions on which he has been employed.

No. 2.

The Deputy Adjutant-General of the Army, to the Secretary to the
Government of India.

No. 373A.

Headquarters Camp, Futtehgurh,
May 31, 1858.

Sir, —By desire of the Commander-in-Chief, I have the honour
to transmit for the information of the Right Honourable the
Governor-General a copy of a despatch [7] from Major-General

6. Report not available. See Despatches.
7. Published in *London Gazette*, July 28, 1858.

183

Sir Hugh Rose, K.C.B., dated 17th instant, enclosing a report from Major R. H. Gall of H.M.'s 14th Light Dragoons, of his capture of the fort of Lohari on the 2nd *idem.*

His Excellency heartily concurs in the praise bestowed by the Major-General upon Major Gall and the officers and men engaged in this gallant affair. I have, etc.

(Signed)   H. W. Norman, Major,

Deputy Adjutant-General of the Army.

BETWA DESPATCH (ADDITIONAL)

Extract from the *London Gazette*, published 24th December 1858.

Victoria Cross.

14th Light Dragoons, now of Lieutenant, now Brevet-Major,
  the 6th Dragoons.   James Leith.

For conspicuous bravery at Betwa on the 1st April 1858, in having charged alone and rescued Captain Need of the same regiment when surrounded by a large number of rebel infantry.

Date of Act of Bravery, 1st April 1858.

Despatch from Major-General Sir Hugh Henry Rose, G.C.B., dated 28th April 1858.

Extracts from Calpee despatches, dated Gwalior, 22nd June 1858. Difficulties to which the troops were exposed on march from Jhnnsi to Calpee, May 1858.

CALPEE DESPATCHES

From Major-General Sir Hugh Rose, K.C.B., Commanding F.D.A. and Field Forces, to Major-General Sir William Mansfield, K.C.B., Chief of the Staff of the Army in India.

Gwalior, 22nd June 1858.

Sir,—In reporting to you for the information of the Commander-in-Chief in India my operations against Calpee, it is my duty, in justice to the unvarying devotion and discipline of the troops under my command, to state the new and very serious difficulties which beset them after leaving Jhansi. They had to contend not only against the rebel army, fighting as usual with all the advantages on their side of very superior numbers and knowledge of the ground, but they had to encounter also a new antagonist, a Bengal sun at its maximum of heat. This formidable ally of the rebel cause was more dangerous than the rebels themselves: its summer blaze made havoc amongst troops, especially Europeans, who, already exhausted by months of over fatigue, and want of sleep by continued night watchings and night marches, were often exposed to its rays, manoeuvring or fighting, as at Koonch, from sunrise to sunset. At Koonch the thermometer was 115°; before Calpee, 118° in the shade; and on the march to Gwalior it burst in an officer's tent at 130°.

Whilst my force suffered so much from sunstroke, they were deprived in a great measure of its antidote water. Between Jhansi and Calpee we found no streams; all was well-water. The wells, which are neither numerous nor abundant, being of extraordinary depth as we approached the Jumna, which increased the difficulties of obtaining water. Forage also was very scarce. The information which I had collected on the road, and a reconnaissance made by Lieutenant-Colonel Gall, H.M.'s 14th Light Dragoons, with his usual skill, confirmed all I had the honour to state in my report of the action at Koonch as to the enemy's elaborate lines of defences for the protection of Calpee, on the main road from Koonch to that fortress. Calpee.

The Jumna is fordable at Golowlee, which stands in the *nullahs* running down to the Jumna just outside the dangerous labyrinth of ravines which surround Calpee.

On the 14th May I marched with the 1st Brigade and Major Orr's force for Golowlee, which I reached with no other opposition than an attack on the baggage by the rebel cavalry concealed in a ravine. They were put to flight by a troop of the 14th Light Dragoons, which, in anticipation of an ambuscade, I had sent to reinforce the rearguard. In this march we crossed the high road from Jubbulpore to Calpee. On my arrival at Golowlee I sent two of the Hyderabad Cavalry across the Jumna to Lieutenant-Colonel Maxwell, commanding a column of the Bengal army, who -was on the left bank, and from whom I was to receive a supply of ammunition for the siege of Calpee, to make good the large amount which my force had expended in the sieges of Chandhairee (or Chanderi) and Jhansi.

My force had now marched from Bombay to the Jumna, and had effected a union with the Bengal Army, the immediate result of which was a combined operation of Bengal and Bombay troops against Calpee. Having heard at Golowlee that Major Forbes, commanding rearguard of the 2nd Brigade, leaving Etawa [8] was hard pressed, and hearing a heavy cannonade in his direction, I marched with the following troops to his assistance:—

Half troop Bombay Horse Artillery.
One troop 14th Light Dragoons.
One troop Hyderabad Cavalry.
Three guns No. 4 Light Field Battery.
38th and 25th Regiments Bombay Native Infantry.

The enemy were pressing forwards. I immediately gave orders to the troops who were retiring from the village of Muttra, to reoccupy and hold it at any price; ordering up in their support, at a trot, the half-troop Horse Artillery, half of No. 4 Light Field Battery, a troop of the 14th Light Dragoons, and the 3rd Hyderabad Cavalry, with some Native Infantry. Brigadier Stuart, commanding the 1st Brigade, at Golowlee, and Captain Hare, commanding at Tehree, met the attack on Golowlee with vigour. Out of 36 men of the 14th Light Dragoons forming part of our forage escort, 17 were brought back to camp in *dhoolies* after only two hours' exposure to sun.

When I speak of the of springing to their arms, I ought to make special mention of H.M.'s 14th Light Dragoons, for the admirable order and celerity with which their in-lying and out-lying picquets mounted on the frequent occasions when I turned them out, on alarms or sudden attacks of the enemy. Their vedettes and patrols also were always watchful and intelligent.

My first and most important instructions were to take Calpee. On the morning of the 22nd May (1858) I made the following disposition of my troops to resist the expected attack: The picquets on right front of the 86th Regiment were reinforced by the remainder of the 86th Regiment in skirmishing order.

In support were three guns of No. 4 Light Field Battery, one troop 3rd Bombay Light Cavalry, and four companies of 25th Bombay Native Infantry, the whole under command of Brigadier Stuart; my left centre facing the plain, and the village of Tehree, was guarded by No. 1 troop Bombay Horse Artillery, supported by two troops H.M.'s 14th Light Dragoons. I reinforced the picquets on the left, in the first instance, with a squadron of the 14th Light Dragoons under Lieutenant-Colonel Gall,

---

8. Otherwise Etora.

and the 3rd Hyderabad Cavalry under Captain Abbott, and afterwards directed the troops to retire slowly before the enemy, obliquely across my front, in order to conceal my heavy guns and draw the rebel cavalry into their fire.

On the 23rd I marched long before break of day against Calpee.

Once clear of the ravines, I instantly directed Lieutenant-Colonel, then Major, Gall, H.M.'s 14th Light Dragoons, to pursue the enemy as closely and as far as he could, with horse artillery and cavalry, and for this officer's very successful pursuit of the enemy I beg to mention him specially. His column took the whole of the guns with which their main body retreated from Calpee, and six caparisoned elephants. The Hyderabad Cavalry and scouts brought in more guns, which detached parties of the rebel army had abandoned in their wild flight; so that every piece of field artillery which the enemy had was taken. The pursuing cavalry made great havoc of the rebel *sepoys*, the Sind Velaitees, and the mercenaries of the Nawab of Banda, till neither horse nor man could go further. The rebels, broken completely by Lieutenant-Colonel Gall's column, fled in the utmost disorder, in twos and threes across-country, throwing away their arms and accoutrements, and even their clothes, to enable them to run faster.

From information furnished by Lieutenant-Colonel Gall, it was clear that the principal part of the rebels had retreated by the Jaloun road, and Sir Robert Hamilton was of opinion that they would make to the north for the Sheer Ghat, a ford across the Jumna, or another ford higher up the river. Colonel Riddell was guarding the former ford with a movable column. I detached without delay Lieutenant-Colonel Robertson with a pursuing column as follows, along the Jaloun road:—

One troop 14th Light Dragoons.
One squadron 3rd Bombay Light Cavalry.
No. 18 Light Field Battery.
160 Hyderabad Cavalry.
25th Regiment Bombay Native Infantry.

To overtake the enemy was hopeless, for European cavalry riding eighteen stone could not catch Indian cavalry riding ten or at most eleven stone. The operations of the pursuing column will be detailed in my report of the operations against Gwalior.

I am much indebted for his goodwill and assistance to Major Rickards, Political Agent for Bhopal, who was wounded when spiritedly accompanying the charge of Captain Need of H.M.'s 14th Light Dragoons at the Betwa.—I have, etc.

(Signed)   Hugh Rose, Major-General,
Commanding F.D.A. and Field Force.

From Major Forbes, C.B., Commanding Rearguard, to Captain Todd, Brigade Major, 2nd Brigade, Central India Field Force.

Camp, near Deopore, 16th May 1858.
Sir,—I have the honour to report, for the information of the brigadier commanding the 2nd Brigade, the arrival in camp of the rearguard, having been closely followed up from within a mile of our last encampment at Etawa[9] by 4000 to 5000 of the rebel army, of which 1000 to 1200 were cavalry. I withdrew first the guns and infantry to a position on this side of a ravine, then the troop of H.M.'s 14th Light Dragoons, and lastly, the remainder of the cavalry, at a walk, until concealed from the enemy by the nature of the ground, then at a gallop. This retrograde movement, as I expected, brought the enemy on us. For the first three miles of the remainder of our march we were almost surrounded by the rebel cavalry, and fired into by their artillery; but alternately halting and retiring, we succeeded in preventing any of the baggage from falling into their hands.—I have, etc.

(Signed)   J. Forbes, Major,
3rd Bombay Light Cavalry,
Commanding Rearguard.

From Lieutenant-Colonel Campbell, Commanding 2nd Brigade C. I. Field Force (Brigadier C. Steuart being on the sick-list), to the Chief of the Staff, Central India Field Force.

Camp Deopore, 18th May 1858.
Sir,—I have the honour to report, for the information of the Major-General, that a large body of upwards of 1200 of the enemy's cavalry, with three guns, moved suddenly out yesterday at 2 p.m. from the rear of a large village on our left flank, advancing with an evident intention of attacking our camp. The

---

9. Or Etora.

small village of Muttra on our left was then occupied by two companies of 71st Highland Light Infantry, and two guns of Bombay Light Battery No. 18, with some of the 24th Bombay Native Infantry in support. I immediately reinforced this post with the whole of the 71st Highland Light Infantry and two guns of the Bombay Light Battery No. 18, giving orders for the 14th Light Dragoons and two guns of the Royal Artillery to follow, proceeding at once to meet the enemy, taking with me the 3rd Light Cavalry and the half battery whom I met on the way to Muttra.

The 14th Light Dragoons under Major Scudamore, and the two guns of the Royal Artillery, took up a position connecting our line with Muttra. A heavy fire commenced on both sides, but the superior fire of our artillery effectually stopped all further advance on the part of the enemy.—(*True Extract.*)

(Signed)   G. E. Rose, *A.D.C.*

From Major Gall, Commanding Left Wing, 14th Light Dragoons, to the Chief of the Staff, Central India Field Force, Calpee.

Camp Calpee, 25th May 1858.

Sir,—I have the honour to report, for the information of the Major-General Commanding the Central India Field Force, that on the 23rd instant, when directed by your order to pursue the enemy, supposed to be retiring from Calpee by the Gwalior or Taloun road, with the following troops:—

14th Light Dragoons, 4 troops, 153 sabres;

Six guns Horse Artillery;

3rd Regiment Hyderabad Contingent Cavalry, subsequently increased by one troop 14th Light Dragoons (48 sabres);

50 sabres 1st Regiment Hyderabad Contingent Cavalry;

I immediately proceeded to assemble the force placed under my command on the road indicated to me, which proved to be the high road from Calpee to Jhansi. This, however, diverges to Jaloun about three miles, as near as I can recollect, from Calpee. Here I left Captain Need, who had accompanied me thus far with his squadron, to bring up the Horse Artillery I had sent back for. Lieutenant Dowker, 1st Regiment Hyderabad Contingent, I detached a little to my right; and accompanied by Captains Abbott and Barrett at the head of their detachments, I charged through the enemy's retiring line and dispersed it.

The rebels were cut up in all directions, with the loss of two guns, which they abandoned to Lieutenant Dowker on the right. The dragoons in the centre sabred a great many of the fugitive *sepoys* who, firing wildly and completely panic-stricken by the suddenness and rapidity of our advance, fell an easy prey to their pursuers, in some instances casting away their arms, in others suffering themselves to be followed into ravines where they were slain. Four elephants were soon after captured as the pursuit continued. Between 200 and 300 of the rebels had been sabred, without any casualties on our side guns and 4 beyond the following:—2 men wounded; 1 horse killed; 1 horse lost; 1 horse wounded.

On my left the sound of Captain Lightfoot's guns had been heard as we approached by the Jhansi road, preceded by Captain Need, who, extending to the right and left of the road, charged the rear of an infantry column, of whom he cut down nearly 200, while Captain Lightfoot plied them with shot and shell. Captains Need and Lightfoot captured three pieces of ordnance during this advance, continued by the former to the eighth milestone on the Jhansi road.

After watering, I joined the Horse Artillery on the Jhansi road, and proposed advancing, but the exhausted state of the Horse Artillery horses, and indeed of our men generally, would not admit of this, and I gave orders for the return of the force to camp at Calpee, which we reached after having been upwards of 13 hours in the saddle. The very weak squadron of dragoons that I had with me was ably led by Captain Barrett, whose good conduct whilst serving under my immediate command I have already had occasion to bring to the notice of the Brigadier Commanding 1st Brigade Central India Field Force, for favourable recommendation to the Major-General.

Captain Barrett's men did great execution amongst the rebels, and the *sowars* of the 1st Cavalry Hyderabad Contingent, led by Lieutenant Dowker, emulated them. Surgeon Stewart, 14th Light Dragoons, I have to thank for his attention to those who fell sick during the pursuit, carried on through the hottest part of the day. My thanks are also due to Assistant-Surgeons Lofthouse and Lumsdaine. Lieutenant and Adjutant Giles, left wing, 14th Light Dragoons, as on many previous occasions, distinguished himself in several personal encounters with armed *se-*

poys.

I specially recommend Captains Abbott, Barrett, and Need, and Lieutenant Dowker, to the notice of the Major-General. Acting Regimental Sergeant-Major Clark and Private Winton, 'B' troop, 14th Light Dragoons, behaved with great gallantry. The captures were as follows:—

5 guns.	6 elephants.
1 gingall on wheels.	8 camels.
3 hackeries.	1 native tumbril.
1 spring cart.	20 boxes of ammunition.
2 artillery wagons filled with ammunition	42 bullock draughts.

I have, etc.   R. H. Gall, Major; Left Wing,

14th Light Dragoons.

(True Copy.)   (Signed)   G. E. Rose, *A.D.C.*

GWALIOR DESPATCH

From Major-General Sir Hugh Rose, K.C.B., Commanding Field Forces South of the Nerbudda, to Major-General Sir William Mansfield, K.C.B., Chief of the Staff of the Army in India.

Poona, Bombay, 13th October 1858.

Sir,—I have the honour to report, for the information of the Commander-in-Chief in India, the operations against Gwalior of the Central India Field Force, and other troops placed under my command by His Excellency. After the capture of Calpee (17th to 23rd May), a short rest having enabled my European troops to recover a little, I reinforced Lieutenant-Colonel Robertson (commanding column of pursuit) with the following troops:—1 wing H.M.'s 86th Regiment; 2 squadrons H.M.'s 14th Light Dragoons.

Lieutenant-Colonel Robertson reported to me in two expresses that the Calpee rebels had certainly taken the road to Gwalior. Not many hours after the arrival of Lieutenant-Colonel Robertson's last express, Sir Robert Hamilton received similar intelligence; when I instantly ordered off Brigadier Stuart with the following force to reinforce Lieutenant-Colonel Robertson and march after the rebels, *viz.*—

No. 4 Light Field Battery.

Four companies 25th Bombay Native Infantry.

Two troops Her Majesty's 14th Light Dragoons.
Half company Bombay Sappers and Miners.
One wing Her Majesty's 71st Regiment.
One wing Her Majesty's 86th Regiment.
Two 18-pounders.
One 8-inch Howitzer.

An express letter received a few days later from Scindiah's agent at Gwalior removed apprehensions for his safety and that of his Government. Subsequently news came that the rebel army had attacked Scindiah at Bahadurpore, nine miles from Gwalior. His troops of all arms, with the exception of a few of his bodyguard, had treacherously gone over, the artillery in mass, to the enemy. His Highness had been obliged to fly to Agra, accompanied only by one or two attendants. The rebels had entered Gwalior, taken Scindiah's treasury and jewels—the latter said to be of fabulous value; the garrison of the fort of Gwalior had opened its gates to the rebels, and finally from 50 to 60 fine guns had fallen, as well as an arsenal, with abundance of warlike stores, into the hands of the enemy. To render this state of things still more embarrassing, Gwalior fell into rebel hands at the most unfavourable time of the year for military operations, on the eve of the great rains, and when the heat of summer was at its maximum.

It was of vital importance that troops should reach Gwalior before the rains set in. I therefore, leaving by order Captain Ommaney's Royal Artillery Battery of four 9-pounders belonging to the 2nd Brigade Central India Field Force, as part of the permanent garrison of Calpee, with one troop Bombay Light Cavalry, one company Royal Engineers, a wing of the 3rd Bombay Europeans, and 400 men of the 24th Bombay Native Infantry, to garrison Calpee until relieved by Bengal troops, marched with the following force from Calpee on 6th June, following Brigadier Stuart's column by forced marches on the road to Gwalior by Jaloun, marching by night to avoid the sun, *viz.*:—One troop Bombay Horse Artillery; one squadron 14th Light Dragoons; one squadron 3rd Bombay Light Cavalry; Madras Sappers and Miners.

One day the heat in the shade rose to 130°. The officer commanding the outlying picquet of Her Majesty's 14th Light Dragoons having reported to me, on the night of the third day, that his men had fallen from their saddles from exhaustion, I had the picquet relieved by a party of Hyderabad Cavalry. My plan of attack on Gwalior was as follows: to invest it as much as its great extent would allow, and then to attack it by its weakest side, the investing troops cutting off the escape of the rebels. I directed Brigadier Smith with the Rajputana Field Force to move to a point (Kota-ke-Serai) seven miles to the east of Gwalior. I myself with Brigadier Stuart's column and the small one I had brought from Calpee marched against the Morar cantonments, which are about five miles from Gwalior on the River Morar. Once in possession of the Morar cantonments I could establish there my hospital, parks, etc., and then, joining Brigadier Smith, I intended to attack Gwalior with his force and my own.

I sent Colonel Riddell to the Residency, about seven miles to the north of Gwalior, to extend his force from thence down the west side of Gwalior, and thus to invest it from that side as far as possible. On 16th June I formed my force in two lines:— First line, 1st Brigade, under Brigadier Stuart; second line, under Brigadier-General Napier, in support of the first, consisting of only a small part of the 2nd Brigade, as the rest of it was left at Calpee.

Both lines advanced, artillery in the centre, 86th Regiment on their right, 25th Bombay Native Infantry on their left, the 14th Light Dragoons on each flank. The *nullahs* and broken ground prevented the advance of Captain Abbott's cavalry and of the 14th Light Dragoons under Captain Thompson on the right, who reinforced my left. The success of the day was completed by the destruction of the rebels in the *nullahs*, and a most successful pursuit of them by Captain Thompson, with a wing of the 14th Light Dragoons. These rebels had been turned by Captain Abbott's advance from the ford of the river, across which and the bridge the main body had retreated, but Captain Thompson caught them in the plains before they could reach the hills, and made a great slaughter of them. I beg to mention specially Captain Thompson, 14th Light Dragoons, for the very good service which he did on this occasion.

Brigadier Smith at Kota-ke-Serai having asked for reinforcements, I directed Lieutenant-Colonel Robertson with three troops 14th Light Dragoons, four guns, and 25th Bombay Native Infantry, to join him. The arrival of the troops from Calpee on 18th Tune enabled me to march from Morar that afternoon, leaving for its protection Brigadier-General Napier with the following force:—

One troop Bombay Horse Artillery.	Royal Engineers
Three troops 14th Light Dragoons.	Bombay Europeans.
Hyderabad Cavalry.	Bombay Native Infantry.
Meades Horse.	Three guns Hyderabad Artillery.

And taking with me to Kota-ke-Serai:—

Two troops 14th Light Dragoons.	86th Regiment.
Light Field Battery.	Hyderabad Infantry.
Wing 71st Highland L. Infantry.	Madras Sappers and Miners.
Two 18-pounders and one 8-inch Howitzer.	

On the 19th June, at the attack on Gwalior, I directed Brigadier Smith with No. 3 troop Bombay Horse Artillery and a squadron of 14th Light Dragoons to be ready to attack the enemy's positions at the Phool Bagh and beyond it; and I had some time before ordered up No. 4 Light Field Battery with two troops of the 14th Light Dragoons to the heights to cover my advanced line, and to answer the enemy's batteries in position in front of Gwalior. The hilly and difficult ground prevented their arrival. The attack on Phool Bagh by the No. 3 troop of Bombay Horse Artillery and a squadron of Her Majesty's 14th Light Dragoons protected the right of the troops attacking the grand parade, and also turned the enemy's left.

Two troops of the 14th Light Dragoons were held in support on the lower slopes. Brigadier Smith speaks very highly of the steadiness with which the Dragoons. 14th Light Dragoons, escorting 3rd troop Bombay Horse Artillery, stood the enemy's artillery fire, shot and shell, and of the ardour with which they afterwards fell on the guns and the retreating enemy.

The morning after the capture of Gwalior, His Highness the Prince of Gwalior arrived there with Sir Robert Hamilton, agent to the Governor-General for Central India, and his retinue. I received Scindiah with every possible mark of respect, and, accompanied by all the superior officers of the forces and all my personal and divisional staff, had the honour of escorting His Highness to his palace in 'the Lushkar' with a squadron of Her Majesty's 8th Hussars, and another of Her Majesty's 14th Light Dragoons, most honourable representatives of my force.

Our road lay through the long and handsome street which leads from the grand parade to the palace, which was lined by crowds of inhabitants who greeted Scindiah with enthusiastic acclamations.

I venture to recommend all the troops engaged in the 'Gwalior' operations, the Central India Field Force and Brigadier Smith's brigade of the Rajputana Field Force, to his Lordship's most favourable consideration.

I marched on the 6th June from Calpee for Gwalior, and on the 19th of the same month the Gwalior States were restored to the prince.—I have, etc.

(Signed)   Hugh Rose, Major-General,
Commanding Field Forces of the Nerbudda.

Morar Despatch

Extracts from despatch of Brigadier-General Napier, C.B., Commanding 2nd Brigade Central India Field Force, to the Adjutant-General, Central India Field Force.

Camp Morar, 18th June 1858.

Sir,—On the 16th inst. the 2nd Brigade, composed as follows:—

> 1st troop Horse Artillery, No. 18 Light Field Battery;
> 14th Light Dragoons (10 officers, 259 men);
> 3rd Light Cavalry, Madras Sappers and Miners;
> 71st Highlanders, Hyderabad Cavalry, Infantry,
>   and Artillery;
> Towana Horse;

when in sight of the cantonments of Morar, was ordered by the Major-General commanding the Central India Field Force to advance in echelon from the right, in support of the left of the 1st Brigade.

The force was disposed as follows:—No. 18 Light Field Battery on the right, supported by Johnstone's Hyderabad Horse; in the centre, Madras Sapper and Miners, and wing of Her Majesty's 71st Highland Light Infantry; while on the left was a wing of Her Majesty's 14th Light Dragoons.

On approaching the right of the cantonment the enemy opened upon us from six guns, and I directed Lieutenant Harcourt, commanding No. 18 Light Field Battery, to engage them, an order which he had barely received when he was summoned to join the 1st Brigade.

My brigade being then reduced to the wing of Her Majesty's 71st Highland Light Infantry, the right wing of Her Majesty's 14th Light Dragoons, Madras Sappers and Miners, and 100 horse of the Hyderabad Contingent, continued to advance on the enemy, who were retreating in large numbers towards their right rear. The ground in front was completely intersected with ravines, lined with the enemy's infantry. I therefore directed Colonel Campbell, commanding the wing of the 71st Regiment, to throw it forward in skirmishing order, supported by the 14th Light Dragoons, which was executed with great spirit by Major Rich on the right, who cleared the ravines on his front, leaving them filled with the enemy's dead, and relieving the Horse Artillery from much annoyance by their musketry.

I regret to say that this service was not performed without the loss of a very promising young officer of Her Majesty's 7 1st Highland Light Infantry, Lieutenant Neave, who was shot whilst gallantly leading his men to the ravines. Colonel Campbell took two companies of the Seventy-first under Lieutenant Scott and cleared some ravines on his left and front, killing every man of the enemy that held them; after which he was directed to clear the top of a hill, where a party of rebels held a temple and some strong ground. This duty was thoroughly effected, and thirty of the enemy left dead on the hill.

Whilst this was going on a troop of Her Majesty's 14th Light Dragoons passed round the base of the hill and cut up all the enemy who attempted to escape from it. The protection of the left of the force and the rear being placed under my especial charge by the major-general, I moved the remainder of the 14th Light Dragoons and Johnstone's Hyderabad Horse towards the left to cover the rear, and to intercept the enemy's cavalry, who showed some disposition to move in that direction; but on observing our cavalry they rapidly disappeared through the hills to the south of Gwalior.

The front being now clear of the enemy I withdrew my brigade to the shelter of the cantonments. The conduct of the whole of the troops under my command was excellent. Their perfect steadiness while under the fire of the enemy's batteries, and the gallantry with which they advanced to clear the ravines, were deserving of the major-general's warm commendation.

The Seventy-first dashed into the ravines and encountered the enemy hand to hand. I beg particularly to recommend to the Major-General's notice Colonel Campbell, commanding Her Majesty's 71st Regiment; also Major Rich, Seventy-first, and Lieutenant Scott, Seventy-first; also Major Scudamore, commanding the right wing of Her Majesty's 14th Light Dragoons, which was skilfully handled and ready for every call for its services. His skirmishers attacked and destroyed many of the enemy in the ravines. Lieutenant Gowan, with his troop, most efficiently cut off the enemy's retreat from the hill and destroyed many of them.—I have, etc.

(Signed)   R. Napier, Brigadier-General,
                    Commanding 2nd Brigade C.I.F. Force.

JOWRA-ALIPORE DESPATCH

Extracts of despatch from Brigadier-General R. Napier, C.B., commanding 2nd Brigade Central India Field Force, to the Assistant Adjutant-General, Central India Field Force.

Camp Jowra-Alipore, 21st June 1858.

Sir,—I have to report that I received at 5.15 a.m. on the 20th June orders to pursue the enemy, with the details shown in the margin, which marched within an hour and a half after receipt of order.[10] The fort, which had been reported 'in our possession,' opened upon us as we came within range, and obliged us to make a detour to reach the Residency. We arrived late in the evening at Sumowlee, having marched about 25 miles. The enemy were reported to have 12,000 men and 22 guns, and to have marched from Sumowlee to Jowra-Alipore in the forenoon.

We were too tired to go beyond Sumowlee, the heat of the sun having been terrific; so we rested until 4 o'clock a.m. on the 22nd, then advanced on Jowra-Alipore, where we found the enemy strongly posted, with their right resting on Alipore, guns and infantry in the centre, and cavalry on both flanks. I directed Captain Lightfoot to take up a position about 600 yards from the enemy's left flank, and enfilade their line; and to act afterwards as circumstances might dictate. Our column of march was the most convenient formation for attack: Abbott's

---

10. Lightfoot's battery Horse Artillery, Prettejohn's troop 14th Light Dragoons (60 sabres), Abbott's Hyderabad Cavalry, 3rd Light Cavalry (2 troops), Meade's Horse.

Hyderabad Cavalry in advance; Lightfoot's troop of Horse Artillery, supported by Captain Prettejohn's troop of 14th Light Dragoons, and two troops 3rd Light Cavalry, under Lieutenant Dick, with a detachment of Meade's Horse under Lieutenant Burlton in reserve.

When the troops came into view of the enemy after turning the shoulder of the rising ground (which hid our approach), the whole were advanced at a gallop, and as soon as the artillery had reached the flank of the enemy's position, the line was formed to the left, and the guns opened on the enemy at a distance of 600 yards. After a few rounds the enemy's guns were silenced, and a rapid thinning and wavering of their ranks took place. Captain Lightfoot limbered up, and advanced at a gallop; and Captain Abbott with his Hyderabad Cavalry charged at the same moment, followed by the rest of the cavalry, who swept through the enemy's batteries and camp into the open plain, driving before them and cutting down the rebels for several miles. We advanced about six miles from our first point of attack. The enemy were dispersed in every direction, throwing away their arms. Twenty-five guns had been captured, and were lying broadcast over the plain; men and horses were exhausted, and it was necessary to retrace our steps.

Besides the guns, a considerable quantity of ammunition and elephants, tents, carts, and baggage fell into our hands. Never was the route of an army more complete. I believe between 300 and 400 of the enemy were killed. The good discipline of the troops of all arms under my command has only been equalled by the courage with which they charged such a superior force. Many occasions arose when it was necessary for detached parties to act against the enemy's infantry, and they were invariably met with the promptest gallantry. Private Novell of Her Majesty's 14th Light Dragoons charged alone into the village and killed one of the enemy under a very heavy fire, for which act of gallantry I beg to recommend him for the 'Victoria Cross.' Those experienced officers, Captain Prettejohn, Her Majesty's 14th Light Dragoons, and Lieutenant Dick, 3rd Light Cavalry, were charged with the duty of supporting the guns, which they performed to my entire satisfaction.

To Surgeon Stewart of Her Majesty's 14th Light Dragoons, and the medical officers of the force, I am much indebted for their attention to the sick and wounded.—I have, etc.

(Signed)   R. Napier, Brigadier-General,
Commanding 2nd Brigade Central India Field Force.

RANODE DESPATCHES

Extract from the London Gazette, 18th April 1859.

No. 12.

From Brigadier-General Sir Robert Napier, K.C.B., commanding Gwalior Division, to the Chief of the Staff.

Camp Ranode, December 21, 1858.

Sir,—I have the honour to report, for the information of the Right Honourable the Commander-in-Chief, that I received, on the morning of the 12th instant, intimation from Captain McMahon, Her Majesty's 14th Light Dragoons, commanding a small force near the confluence of the Jumna, Chambal, and Sind Rivers, that the rebels had passed into the Lohar Purgunnah of Kuchwazhur.[11] Believing that their course would be up the jungles of the Sind

river, I marched from Gwalior with a force, as below, on the 12th instant, intending to proceed to Dubbia,[12] on the Jhansi road, and then according to information I might receive, to intercept the enemy:—

No. 4 Light Field Battery, two guns.

14th Light Dragoons, 150 non-commissioned officers, rank and file.

2nd Gwalior Mahratta Horse, 100 sabres.

71st Highlanders, 117 non-commissioned officers, rank and file.

25th Bombay Native Infantry, 50 non-commissioned officers, rank and file.

Camel Corps, 40 camels.

At Antri, where the force rested during part of the night, I received at 2 a.m. on the 13th, when on the point of proceeding to Dubbia, an express from the political agent of Gwalior to the effect that his information led him to believe that the rebels would pass by Gohad, to the north of Gwalior. This caused me to halt until I should receive by the morning post precise

---

11. Or Kuchwagar.
12. Or Dutheah.

information from Captain McMahon. At 10.30 a.m. the Tussildar of Antri informed me he had just ridden in from Dubbia, the very place of my destination, and had seen the smoke of the staging bungalow which the rebels were then burning, and that they were proceeding in a south-westerly direction. I immediately marched south in pursuit, and at Beettiwar,[13] where I arrived at 1.30 a.m. on the 14th, I was informed that the enemy were three *kos* (in this country eight or nine miles) distant. The force had been on the move for thirteen and a half hours, and required a rest.

Owing to a delay in getting grass and disposing of a rear party of the enemy's infantry, in which some of the Mahratta Horse, under fire for the first time, greatly distinguished themselves, I did not get away until 10 a.m. I continued the pursuit through Nurwar, where I left behind the greater portion of the detachment of the Seventy-First and the artillery, which could not keep up with me, and took on merely the cavalry and 38 men of the 71st Highlanders on camels, and 25 of the Balandshar Horse, that were halted at Narwar on their way to Kerara,[14] owing to the news of the enemy's approach, and after a very exciting though fatiguing chase we overtook the rebels on the morning of the 17th at Ranode.

Their course had been south of Nurwar and through the Amola Pass, and their direction appeared to be along the right bank of the Sind. Twice we were encamped within a few miles of them, but owing to the darkness and our ignorance of the country, and to its hilly and jungly character, we could not take advantage of it. They chose the most difficult and unfrequented paths, evidently guided by some one well acquainted with them.

Once or twice we were close on their traces and cut off stragglers or took their horses, the riders throwing themselves off and darting into the dense thickets which almost close up the paths. At one moment I believed they were driven into the hands of Colonel Scudamore, Her Majesty's 14th Light Dragoons, who, according to the instructions and information I had sent him, had posted his detachments on the right bank of the Sind below Kolarus to intercept them.

I expected every moment to hear his guns open fire, when I

---

13. Or Bhitarwar.
14. Or Karehra.

found on getting into a more open country that the enemy had turned away from the river and were going towards Ranode. They took a circuitous and difficult road through the jungles, whilst we marched by a more easy and direct one, where the country was open. I found the people of Ranode in great excitement, and was informed that the enemy was close at hand and in full march to attack them, guided by Pyroo Sing of Tehrea, a rebel *zemindar*, whose fort a few miles off had been recently destroyed by Scindiah.

The enemy advanced in an irregular mass, extending on a front of nearly a mile. Their numbers must have been increased since they crossed the Jumna. We had barely time to form up the 14th Light Dragoons when the enemy were within a few hundred yards. The Mahratta Horse were impeded in crossing a deep ravine by the riding camels, and were thus a little behind. Our force actually engaged consisted of—

133 of Her Majesty's 14th Light Dragoons, commanded by Captain Prettejohn.

60 of the Mahratta Horse, under Captain F. H. Smith.

38 of the 71st Highlanders, under Captain Smith, mounted on camels, and guided by Captain Templer, commanding Camel Corps.

It was a complete surprise. The 14th Light Dragoons, excellently led by Captain Prettejohn, dashed at once into the centre of the enemy, who never attempted to stand as a body, though individuals died fighting desperately. Captain Prettejohn having received a severe wound, the command devolved on Captain Need, who, with much energy and judgment, continued the pursuit for nearly eight miles, cutting up great numbers, particularly at the end, where the fugitives were stopped by a ravine, those who could not cross it taking refuge in the jungle, impracticable for cavalry.

One hundred and fifty dead bodies of the enemy have been counted immediately at Ranode, and a much larger number must have fallen during the pursuit. Captain Need estimates these last at 300. Many of these were 12th Irregulars, the murderers of Major Holmes and his family. I fear Ferozshah has escaped for the present. Six elephants were taken, and numbers of horses, ponies, arms, etc.

It is with much pride and satisfaction that I beg permission to bring to the notice of the Right Honourable the Commander-in-Chief the admirable charge made by the 14th Light Dragoons, and the soldier-like and exemplary cheerfulness with which the troops of all arms bore the fatigue and privations inseparable from such service. With such men and officers, the general's task is easy. It was a cause of very great regret to me, and equally to themselves, that the remainder of the Seventy-first, under Major Rich, and Captain Brown's guns were necessarily left behind.

I beg to recommend most particularly Captain Prettejohn, Her Majesty's 14th Light Dragoons, commanding the cavalry, for the very gallant manner in which he led his men until severely wounded; also Captain Need, 14th Light Dragoons, who succeeded to the command and most ably exercised it. Lieutenant Giles of the 14th Light Dragoons, and Lieutenant Gough of the Mahratta Horse, are very favourably mentioned by their commanding officers.

I am greatly indebted to Dr. Cruickshank for his prompt and extreme attention to the wounded. Mr. Apothecary Waite, an old and excellent servant of the government, who has been present with the 14th Light Dragoons in every engagement, was in the field and performed valuable service. I am under great obligations to Captain Todd, 14th Light Dragoons, Assistant Adjutant-General, for his invaluable aid at all hours during the pursuit and in the action. Captain Need mentions very favourably the forward conduct of Regimental Sergeant-Major Thomas Clark, 14th Light Dragoons, and Corporal George Best of 'H' troop, 14th Light Dragoons.

I subjoin a list of casualties. The wounded are doing well. I have, on a former occasion, the honour to report the good service performed by two of the officers above mentioned, Captains Todd and Prettejohn, of Her Majesty's 14th Light Dragoons, for their distinguished conduct in the action with Tantia Topee at Jowra-Alipore; but I fear from some accident that my report has not reached the Right Honourable the Commander-in-Chief. I therefore beg permission to submit a copy of it, and most earnestly solicit the favour and protection of the Right Honourable the Commander-in-Chief and the Government for the officers and soldiers therein mentioned, as well as for those named in this report.—I have, etc.

(Signed)   R. Napier, Brigadier-General,
Commanding Gwalior Division.

No. 13.

From Captain Need, 14th (King's) Light Dragoons, to the Assistant Adjutant-General, Gwalior Division.

Camp Ranode, December 17, 1858.

Sir,—I have the honour to report, for the information of the general commanding, that, on Captain Prettejohn becoming disabled this morning from a severe wound, I assumed command of the squadron 14th Light Dragoons, strength 133 sabres, in pursuit of the rebels, following them for about seven miles, cutting up great numbers, and capturing several elephants, horses, etc. I beg to bring to the general's notice the good services rendered by Lieutenant Giles and all under my command, as well as Captain Lumsden, Assistant Quartermaster-General, and Lieutenant Gough of the Mahratta Horse who accompanied the squadron.

The gallant conduct of Corporal Best, 14th Light Dragoons, came particularly under my notice; but when every man of the squadron behaved so well, and did such good service, it is almost unjust for me to recommend any man in particular. The pursuit was principally through low jungles, very bad ground, and full of holes, which will account for the great number of missing horses in my casualty report which accompanies this report.—I have, etc.

Arthur Need, Captain, 14th Dragoons.

CASUALTIES TO 14TH LIGHT DRAGOONS AT RANODE,
17TH DECEMBER 1858.

Wounded.—Brevet-Major R. B. Prettejohn, severe sabre-cut on the outside and back of left thigh, three inches above the knee; one sergeant; one corporal, eleven men.

One officer's charger wounded; one missing; three troop-horses killed; five troop-horses wounded; thirteen troop-horses missing.

LEONAUR

ALSO FROM LEONAUR

AVAILABLE IN SOFTCOVER OR HARDCOVER WITH DUST JACKET

ZULU:1879 *by D.C.F. Moodie & the Leonaur Editors*—The Anglo-Zulu War of 1879 from contemporary sources: First Hand Accounts, Interviews, Dispatches, Official Documents & Newspaper Reports.

THE RED DRAGOON *by W.J. Adams*—With the 7th Dragoon Guards in the Cape of Good Hope against the Boers & the Kaffir tribes during the 'war of the axe' 1843-48'.

THE RECOLLECTIONS OF SKINNER OF SKINNER'S HORSE *by James Skinner*—James Skinner and his 'Yellow Boys' Irregular cavalry in the wars of India between the British, Mahratta, Rajput, Mogul, Sikh & Pindarree Forces.

A CAVALRY OFFICER DURING THE SEPOY REVOLT *by A. R. D. Mackenzie*—Experiences with the 3rd Bengal Light Cavalry, the Guides and Sikh Irregular Cavalry from the outbreak to Delhi and Lucknow.

A NORFOLK SOLDIER IN THE FIRST SIKH WAR *by J W Baldwin*—Experiences of a private of H.M. 9th Regiment of Foot in the battles for the Punjab, India 1845-6.

TOMMY ATKINS' WAR STORIES: 14 FIRST HAND ACCOUNTS—Fourteen first hand accounts from the ranks of the British Army during Queen Victoria's Empire.

THE WATERLOO LETTERS *by H. T. Siborne*—Accounts of the Battle by British Officers for its Foremost Historian.

NEY: GENERAL OF CAVALRY VOLUME 1—1769-1799 *by Antoine Bulos*—The Early Career of a Marshal of the First Empire.

NEY: MARSHAL OF FRANCE VOLUME 2—1799-1805 *by Antoine Bulos*—The Early Career of a Marshal of the First Empire.

AIDE-DE-CAMP TO NAPOLEON *by Philippe-Paul de Ségur*—For anyone interested in the Napoleonic Wars this book, written by one who was intimate with the strategies and machinations of the Emperor, will be essential reading.

TWILIGHT OF EMPIRE *by Sir Thomas Ussher & Sir George Cockburn*—Two accounts of Napoleon's Journeys in Exile to Elba and St. Helena: Narrative of Events by Sir Thomas Ussher & Napoleon's Last Voyage: Extract of a diary by Sir George Cockburn.

PRIVATE WHEELER *by William Wheeler*—The letters of a soldier of the 51st Light Infantry during the Peninsular War & at Waterloo.

www.ingramcontent.com/pod-product-compliance
Lightning Source LLC
Chambersburg PA
CBHW032058080426
42733CB00006B/320